COUNTRY HOUSE SOCIETY

About the Author

Dr Pamela Horn lectured on social history for over twenty years at Oxford Brookes University. Her books include *High Society: The English Social Elite 1880–1914*, *Ladies of the Manor*, *Rise and Fall of the Victorian Servant*, *The Victorian Country Child*, *Flunkeys and Scullions* and *Behind the Counter*.

COUNTRY HOUSE SOCIETY

The private lives of England's upper class after the First World War

PAMELA HORN

AMBERLEY

First published 2013
This edition first published 2015

Amberley Publishing
The Hill, Stroud
Gloucestershire, GL5 4EP

www.amberley-books.com

British Library Cataloguing in Publication Data.
A catalogue record for this book is available from the British Library.

ISBN 978 1 4456 4477 6 (paperback)
ISBN 978 1 4456 3538 5 (ebook)

Typeset in 10pt on 12pt Sabon.
Typesetting and Origination by Amberley Publishing.
Printed in the UK.

Contents

Contents

Foreword and Acknowledgements

In recent years television period dramas have depicted the ups and downs of life in an imaginary aristocratic household before and after the First World War. *Country House Society* seeks to examine the realities of the daily round and the joys and sorrows experienced by families who were actually living through the often turbulent years between 1914 and 1930. In collecting material for the book I must thank the staff in the libraries and archives where I have worked for their expert help and ready co-operation.

In particular, my thanks are due to staff at the Bodleian Library, Oxford, and especially to those in Special Collections; the British Library; the British Library Newspaper Library at Colindale; the Liddell Hart Centre for Military Archives, King's College Archives, London; Market Harborough Museum, Leicestershire; the Museum of English Rural Life, University of Reading, whose members of staff have so readily provided material from the Astor collection; the Rhodes House Library, Oxford; Shugborough Hall Oral History Transcripts, Staffordshire County Council; St. Barbe Museum and Art Gallery, Lymington, and especially Sarah Newman; and the Wiltshire and Swindon History Centre, Chippenham.

Pamela Horn, August 2012.

1

The Impact of War: 1914–1918

The First World War brought grievous sacrifices to the whole nation, and it perhaps brought greater losses to the landed families, with their long military traditions, than to any other class. It would be impossible to measure how much the quality and vitality of landed society in the post-war years suffered from the absence of the sons killed in France, or from the natural hedonism of the survivors of the holocaust.

F. M. L. Thompson, *English Landed Society in the Nineteenth Century* (London, 1963), p. 327.

The Pre-War World

In the early weeks of the summer of 1914, when temperatures soared to 90 degrees Fahrenheit, there were few indications that Britain was about to be engulfed in a devastating war, which would lead to the deaths of almost three-quarters of a million Britons.[1] The social elite were to be particularly hard hit, with about one in five of the British and Irish peers and their sons who served in the war being killed. Many titled families lost the direct heirs to their titles and estates, though usually there were younger sons or other male relatives to inherit both the title and the land. It seems only three titles out of the 558 which had been linked to estates of at least 3,000 acres at the beginning of the 1880s were extinguished by the First World War.[2]

In political and social circles, however, in the late spring of 1914 it was the threat of civil war in Ireland over the issue of Home Rule, and labour unrest on the mainland, including the possibility of a general strike, that were the prime causes of concern. Little attention was paid to the assassination by a Serbian nationalist of the Archduke Franz Ferdinand, heir to the Austrian imperial throne, and his wife in Sarajevo on 26 June. Conflicts in the turbulent Balkans appeared to offer little immediate threat to Britain itself.

Meanwhile, for members of High Society the London social season was following its traditional course. There were the usual presentations at Court of debutantes, the regular round of dinner parties, balls, visits to the theatre and opera, and attendance at important sporting events, as well as a multitude of Saturday to Monday house parties. For the widowed Lady Airlie, one of Queen Mary's ladies-in-waiting, the 1914 Season proved particularly strenuous since not only had she to chaperone her youngest daughter, Mabell, to balls almost every night but she had to carry out the duties of Mistress of the Robes to the queen at the Courts, to replace the Duchess of Devonshire, who was ill.[3] Chaperonage remained extremely important for young unmarried girls, so while they could play golf, ride or go on the river with young male friends in the country, when they were in London they were supposed never to 'cross the street alone, go shopping, travel in a taxi or take a journey' without a responsible older married woman or a maid accompanying them.[4]

More daring girls, like Lady Diana Manners, the beautiful daughter of the Duke and Duchess of Rutland and the centre of a group of friends calling themselves the 'Corrupt Coterie', flouted these restrictions when they could. After a visit to Venice in 1913, Lady Diana recalled the carefree gaiety she had enjoyed: 'dancing and extravagance and lashings of wine, and charades and moonlit balconies and kisses'.[5] Dancing was a major preoccupation, with the syncopated rhythms of ragtime and jazz beginning to penetrate British society, although their true conquest of the elite social scene was to come more than half a decade later.[6] There was, however, a darker side to these exuberant activities, with drug-taking (particularly chloroform) and gambling part of the wider background. Of Alfred Duff Cooper, who married Lady Diana Manners in 1919, it has been said that on a single evening in 1914 playing *chemin de fer*, one of his favourite gambling games, he lost £1,645 to a Captain Taylor. That was nearly four times his salary as a Foreign Office diplomat.[7]

Nancy Cunard, the rebellious eighteen-year-old daughter of Sir Bache and Lady Cunard, was another girl determined to go her own way as far as possible. In part her feelings of alienation arose from her dislike of her mother, whom she referred to mockingly as 'Her Ladyship', and from her resentment at Lady Cunard's life as a prominent society hostess and devoted admirer of the leading conductor, Thomas Beecham. Maud Cunard was estranged from Sir Bache, and on one occasion when Nancy and Lady Diana Manners were discussing maternal attitudes and restrictions, Nancy declared defiantly: 'My mother's having an affair with Thomas Beecham; I can do as I like.'[8] She was presented at

Court in 1914, 'wearing a pink dress with a train of tulle
and rose petals', and with the obligatory display of ostrich
feathers on her head. It was a London Season she little
enjoyed and it was to be her

> first and last, I swore to myself, as one ball succeeded
> another until there were three or four a week and the faces
> of the revolving guardsmen seemed as silly as their vapid
> conversation among the hydrangeas at supper.[9]

More to her liking were the clandestine excursions undertaken
with her friend, Iris Tree, who was a year her junior. As Iris
remembered years later, she and Nancy would visit the Eiffel
Tower restaurant, kept by Austrian-born Rudolf Stulik. It was
a popular venue for artistic and literary figures, as well as for
members of the Bohemian avant garde and the fashionable
elite. According to Iris, the two girls also patronised other
'fugitive' haunts, unbeknown to their parents:

> We were bandits, escaping environment by tunnelling
> deceptions to emerge in forbidden artifice, chalk-white
> face powder, scarlet lip rouge, cigarette smoke, among
> roisterers of our own choosing ... and the 'coterie'
> crowned by Diana Manners, which included the most
> brilliant and exuberant spirits united at the various Inns
> and outings; Cavendish Hotel, Cheshire Cheese, pubs in
> Limehouse, river barges, cab shelters and a secret studio
> which Nancy and I shared for secret meetings with the
> favourites ... Nancy and I loved dressing up for the
> Chelsea Arts balls, given at Albert Hall, designing our
> own costumes ...
>   On one occasion we were arrested for swimming in the
> Serpentine, and emerged in dripping feathers and velvets

to receive a summons, returning scared to our solemn doors and stealthy, clockticking stairways. After this, though latch keys were confiscated and curfew imposed, we somehow tricked the watch.[10]

Even their lavish use of make-up was controversial, at a time when this was thought appropriate only for actresses – and prostitutes. Nancy and Iris rented a room in Fitzroy Place, which they called their studio, and where they could escape to meet their friends unchaperoned, or write and paint, and design their costumes. To Lady Diana Manners, though, the premises seemed to be 'always in chaos', and she found it unacceptably 'squalid'.[11]

But for most members of High Society the hedonism of these years took a less hectic and more respectable form, involving balls, visits to friends, and attendance at such events as Ascot or the Eton and Harrow cricket match at Lords, where those who aspired to belong to the social elite contrived to be seen.

In these circumstances, therefore, the society magazine *The Bystander*, in its 'holiday issue' of 8 July 1914, referred to the 'whole of the English year being now a holiday season':

We make holiday, it is true, in July; but so we do in all the other months. We have summer holidays durating ... from June to October inclusive; then we run an autumn holiday season (shooting, hunting etc.) up to round about Christmas. Then our Winter holidays (ski-ing, skating, etc.) until February, or thereabouts, followed by the 'Spring in the Sunny South' Season, which gives place in turn to that furiously active spell known as the London Season ...

July, despite Henley and the call of the river, Sandown,
Goodwood, a Court, a few dances, a garden party or two,
and the last gasps of the opera, is a holiday month.

Three weeks later it noted that the London Season had
finally ended: 'From now till May we shall all behave like
sensible "grown-ups" and neither receive nor accept more
invitations than we have leisure to enjoy. One well-known
lady habitually bids her friends "goodbye" at the beginning
of each season, for she says "We shan't see each other again
till the rush is over." Leisured classes, indeed! Why for
months they don't exist, in London at any rate', so frantic
had the demands of pleasure-seeking and the social round
become.[12]

Leading hostesses nonetheless continued to hold their
Saturday to Monday house parties. At Highclere Castle,
home of the Earl and Countess of Carnarvon, 18 July marked
the start of the last big house party of the 1914 Season, with
twenty-six guests, plus their servants, in residence.[13] At
Taplow Court in Buckinghamshire Lady Desborough, too,
organised weekend hospitality, including water parties on
the Thames.

There was so little concern about the international
situation that Margot Asquith, the second wife of the
Prime Minister, Herbert Henry Asquith, allowed her only
daughter to leave on a visit to friends in Holland on 25
July, although she did recall her a few days later, thereby
enabling her to reach England on 1 August. Yet, according
to Margot, the apprehensions she had already begun to feel
were shared by few others in London society. On 29 July,
when she was hosting a luncheon party at Downing Street,
attended by the Archbishop of Canterbury among others,
she remembered her guests expressing surprise when she

told them she had stopped her sister visiting France on a painting holiday, 'and had telegraphed for Elizabeth to return from Holland'.[14]

Similarly Lord Crawford departed on 23 July to attend the Wagner festival at Bayreuth and, apparently unaware of the imminence of war, complained to his wife four days later that the Austro-Serbian crisis was 'wrecking Bayreuth!' He was able to hear the Niebelunglied and then had to hurry away 'owing to the Dublin disturbances'. Ironically before he got 'halfway to London mobilisation had begun and my journey was adventurous'.[15]

Lord Carnarvon's sister, Winifred, and her husband, Herbert, Lord Burghclere, had travelled to Europe, too, in June. Only belatedly did they become aware of the growing tensions and decide to return early from the Vichy spa where they had intended to spend some weeks. They arrived back in London on 25 July.[16] Interestingly, however, Lady Carnarvon, who was the illegitimate daughter of the wealthy banker Alfred de Rothschild, had become anxious about the European situation several months earlier, doubtless benefiting from her father's extensive foreign contacts. She had already been given permission to turn Highclere Castle into a hospital for wounded officers, should the need arise.[17]

In late July, events in central Europe gathered ominous momentum. Within Britain, it has been said that until 24 July, it was the danger of civil war in Ireland that seemed to the Cabinet 'a much nearer and graver risk than war in Europe'.[18] Two days before this *The Bystander* expressed alarm about the European situation and it reproached the national press for ignoring this in favour of its usual parochial preoccupations, at a time when some leading Continental countries were 'armed to the teeth and in a state of preparedness at any moment for war'.[19] Yet, despite these comments, its own columns still concentrated on the social events that marked the end of the London Season.

On 28 July Austria-Hungary finally declared war on Serbia. Two days later Serbia's ally, Russia, began to mobilise its forces, while the following day Germany and France ordered the mobilisation of their armies, and Germany declared war on Russia and France. Events were speeding up as pre-war alliances and animosities came to the fore. Britain initially had hoped to avoid conflict but when on 3 August Germany issued an ultimatum to neutral Belgium, it was clear that efforts at mediation were at an end. The following day, 4 August, as Germany invaded Belgium, Britain declared war on Germany. Given this rapid international transformation it is difficult to disagree with the conclusion of the *Annual Register* for 1914 when it commented drily, 'The war had come suddenly upon Great Britain.'[20]

The Onset of War

Almost at once, war fever gripped the nation, and there were optimistic predictions that if determined opposition were shown to the German aggressors, hostilities would be over by Christmas. The landed classes, with their long-established military commitments, were at the forefront of the drive for mobilisation. Not only were they linked to the county yeomanry regiments but the officers of the regular Army were largely recruited from their ranks. Lord Crawford, observing the rising enthusiasm for war, noted gloomily in his diary, 'We are ringing our bells today, tomorrow we shall be wringing our hands. The insouciance and lack of foresight in the patriotic crowds fills me with consternation.'[21] The Marquis of Tavistock, the pacifist son and heir of the Duke of Bedford, was still more appalled. To add to his personal aversion 'to re-entering what was to me the slavery of Army life ... it would be definitely wrong for me, after my known and proved incapacity to do the right thing in a sudden emergency, to take a commission and then, by some blunder on the battlefield, perhaps sacrifice the lives of my men uselessly'. When he informed his father he would not serve, the duke disinherited him, although 'legal difficulties ultimately prevented him from being deprived of an income. He spent the war working in a centre for troops in Portsmouth, cleaning and washing dishes.'[22] He and his father remained estranged until the duke's death in 1940.

It was not merely the unthinking mass of the population which greeted the outbreak of war with enthusiasm. Landowners and their sons sought to get to the front as speedily as they could, and encouraged the workers on their estates to join the colours, too. Those landowners who were themselves too old to volunteer nevertheless encouraged their sons and employees to do so. Lord Derby, for example, according to his biographer, devoted all his time and energy to Army recruiting during the first year of the war, particularly in Lancashire, where he enjoyed a position of dominance. In a typical speech given at Rainford, he noted that he had two sons, one of whom was at the front and the other was in the artillery and when fully trained would go to the front, too, stating, 'If I had twenty sons I should be ashamed if every one of them did not go to the front when his turn came.' Then, in a covert threat to his tenants and workers, he added,

When the war is over I intend, as far as I possibly can, to employ nobody except men who have taken their duty at the front. I go further than that, and say that, all things being equal, if two men come to me for a farm and one has been at the front there is no doubt which is going to get the farm.[23]

Lord Willoughby de Broke, who served with the Warwickshire Yeomanry in England, and was chairman of the Imperial Maritime League, was another enthusiastic recruiter. He claimed that his organisation had held a thousand meetings in country villages during the first half of 1915. Lectures were given with lantern slides, and according to him, 'Few meetings failed to produce one to a dozen recruits in small villages.'[24]

Sometimes a more direct pressure was exerted. G. L. Courthope, who was MP for the Rye Division of Sussex, not only joined up himself but took fifteen of his estate workers with him. 'While Mr. Courthope's employees are on service,' reported the *Sussex Express*, 'their families will not be worried about rent or food.'[25] In Gloucestershire, the 11th Earl of Wemyss in late August 1914 issued an 'abrupt ultimatum to all his employees, servants etc. – to join the Army or leave his service'. He then went off to London leaving his wife to 'cope with the situation'. According to Violet Asquith, who was staying with Lady Wemyss, he had not consulted her before making the statement and it was 'too cruel as the people here have hardly heard of the war'. In the end the ultimatum was withdrawn, but efforts were made to persuade the men to join up.[26] On the Duke of Bedford's estate a rather milder approach was adopted, with employees who volunteered promised that half their weekly wages would be paid to their dependants at home while they were away. At that time, few envisaged that the struggle would last for so many years, but it seems that the promise was kept since the families of some Bedford estate workers were still receiving payments in 1918.[27]

Exhortations were also issued in journals like *Country Life* and *The Bystander*. On 15 August 1914, a correspondent to *Country Life* appealed to all hunting men and polo players to 'join either the Army or the Territorial Forces. We ought to behave as far as possible as if there were conscription … I am in favour of every sportsman doing his duty and more.' A fortnight later it returned to the theme, declaring there was 'no excuse for idleness, and it would be criminal on the part of the population to permit it. Every able-bodied man of the required age should join the ranks of the regular or the Territorial regiments.'[28] *The Bystander* considered that the outbreak of hostilities would have a salutary moral effect on the male population, too;

> Whatever the issue of this war – victory, defeat, or stale-mate – it is going to make a new man of the Englishman. After years of fat prosperity and lazy frivolity, it brings him up against the brute realities. It calls him to a service of his country, which is also the service of himself: to prepare to die that Britain may live.[29]

Within the ranks of the military there were officers like Julian Grenfell who also welcomed the new situation. He was the eldest son of Lord and Lady Desborough and was stationed in South Africa when hostilities broke out. He was soon to return to Britain and by the autumn of 1914 had been sent to Flanders. In a letter to his mother, written two days after the expiry of the British ultimatum to Germany, he declared that it 'must be wonderful in England now … it reinforces one's failing belief in the Old Flag, and the Mother Country and the … Thin Red Line and the Imperial Idea'.[30]

He arrived at Taplow Court on 25 September for two days' leave, before departing on 4 October with his regiment for Flanders. There within a very few months he was to win the DSO for his courageous actions against the enemy.

Julian's enthusiasm to become involved in the hostilities was shared by other military men, such as the Hon. Lionel Tennyson, who was an officer in the Rifle Brigade based at Colchester in the summer of 1914. He was able to spend occasional weekends away at a London hotel, until in the middle of the night on 3 August he received a message that he must return to duty at once. He leapt out of bed; 'I remember dressing and packing with the night porter's help in fevered haste, so anxious was I not to run any chance of missing the war, and a very few moments later saw me speeding through sleeping London on my sixty-mile taxi drive back to Colchester.'[31]

Oswald Mosley, the son of a Staffordshire landowning family, was also keen to join up quickly so as not to miss any of the action. 'Our one great fear,' Mosley wrote of his generation, 'was that the war would be over before we got there.' Events were to show his concern was needless as the war dragged on for almost four and a half years.[32] Mosley himself was eventually invalided out with a badly injured leg before he was twenty, after service in the air and in the trenches.

At the leading public schools, too, youngsters who had reached the end of their school career opted to join up rather than go to university, as they would normally have done, while young men from Oxford and Cambridge also flocked to the cause. Of 13,403 members of Oxford University and 13,126 from Cambridge who served in the war, 19.2 per cent and 18 per cent respectively were to be killed.[33] Among the schoolboys who joined up from Eton was the Hon. Yvo Charteris, who, according to his sister, Lady Cynthia Asquith, was in a fever of impatience to get into the Army after achieving his goal of a few days in the sixth form. After a period of training, he departed for France in September 1915. On 5 October 1915 he had his nineteenth birthday and a few days later, having spent just three weeks at the front, he was killed instantly while leading his men in an effort to capture a German trench position at Loos. When his sister received the news she was in despair, 'Oh how it hurts and how little one ever faced the possibility for an instant! ... How can one believe it, that it should be the object to kill Yvo? That such a joy-dispenser should have been put out of the world on purpose. For the first time I felt the full mad horror of the war.'[34] The following year she was to lose her eldest brother, Lord Elcho, heir to the Earl of Wemyss. Many other friends were killed, and as early as 11 November 1915 she wrote plaintively in her diary,

> Oh why was I born for this time? Before one is thirty to know more dead than living people? Stanway, Clouds, Gosford – all the settings of one's life – given up to ghosts. Really, one hardly knows who is alive and who is dead.[35]

Yet, paradoxically, she continued to lead an active social life, even when her husband was away on military duties, and also to engage in harmless flirtations. She became particularly addicted to the game of poker and regularly lost money that she could ill afford. Her friend, Mary Herbert, even warned her about her unhealthy enthusiasm for the game.

However, following the outbreak of hostilities many country-house wives and daughters, like their menfolk, became infected with war fever and were involved in Army recruitment drives. Lady Tullibardine, for example, arranged a series of concerts in Scotland to support her husband's recruiting campaign in Perthshire. Another supporter of the cause was the Hon. Mrs Gell. She recalled holding a recruitment meeting in a tent at her Derbyshire home, and 'when the speeches were over, one after the other of the boys we had known from childhood shyly stepped forward and offered themselves, and ... after they were enrolled, it was hard to congratulate them with a steady voice'.[36]

A number of women, like the Countess of Carnarvon, offered their homes as hospitals for the wounded and the convalescent. At Highclere Castle, Lady Carnarvon made accommodation available for twenty wounded officers in a well-equipped hospital, with trained nurses and domestic servants to wait upon the patients. According to her biographer, she treated the men as guests, in much the same way as she would have treated her friends at Saturday to Monday house parties before the war.[37] Later, as the demand for places increased, Lady Carnarvon transferred her hospital to a large house in London, where she was able to take up to forty patients in comfortable accommodation, and with modern equipment that included her pride and joy – an X-ray machine.

So great was the patriotic seal of estate owners that as soon as 21 August, the *Hexham Weekly News* claimed that the authorities had been 'literally inundated' with offers of houses for use by the wounded. At Woburn Abbey, the riding school and indoor tennis court were converted into a 100-bed hospital, and although there were trained nurses employed, such tasks as those of orderly and stretcher bearer were carried out by domestic servants, gardeners, chauffeurs and grooms on the estate who were unfit for military service.

The duchess herself, who had become a trained nurse, took an active part in the running of the hospital, often spending sixteen hours a day on duty. During the time it was open 'she never left the hospital for a single night and in the final three years she was responsible not only for all the operating theatre sister's work but the whole of the official correspondence, book-keeping and returns associated with its running'.[38]

Some of the wealthiest or most determined ladies established hospitals in France, or, in the case of the younger women, themselves volunteered as VADs, or Voluntary Aid Detachment Nurses. Lady Desborough's elder daughter, Monica, sharing her brother's enthusiasm to take part in the war effort, on 19 August 1914 volunteered to become a nurse and went with her mother to the London Hospital in Whitechapel, where her friend Angie Manners had been trained. Monica underwent a three-month course before being despatched to a private hospital set up by Lady Norman, the wife of an MP, at Wimereux in what was described as 'the semi-squalid Hotel Bellevue'.[39] It was one of several such initiatives by members of the social elite in the early days of the war, and their efforts earned the criticism of the Prime Minister, Herbert Asquith, and of Lord Crawford. Asquith called the Wimereux and Boulogne hospitals 'overstaffed annexes of London Society'.[40] Lord Crawford was still more scathing, noting in his diary a conversation he had had concerning 'the grand ladies who are running hospitals in France':

> On the whole, Millicent, Duchess of Sutherland, seems to have given most trouble. She got into debt and seemed to expect the Red Cross to extricate her. Her chief crime is body-snatching. All these ladies are known as

'body-snatchers', for they seize an invalid whenever they can catch him, and carry him off willy-nilly to their private hospital ... [The] Duchess of Westminster is herself most tiresome, but has an excellent staff. Lady Sarah Wilson [sixth daughter of the 7th Duke of Marlborough] has been giving a good deal of trouble. Lady Diana Manners is trying to get permission to have a hospital of her own; let us hope the Red Cross which can now control the permissions granted to these adventuresses, will be sufficient proof against the influence of society, to veto any more expeditions of this character.[41]

Ironically, however, as early as 8 August 1914, Lady Crawford herself had begun adapting the laundry at Haigh, their country house, as a hospital, and her husband noted it would 'make an excellent one'. By December it was accommodating wounded Belgian officers, who were able to join in the family's Christmas celebrations at Haigh.[42] In 1915 Crawford himself joined the Royal Army Medical Corps (RAMC) as a private, at the age of forty-three, and by the following June was in charge of the operating theatre in a makeshift casualty clearing station in Flanders, near the front. There he spent the next twelve months. However, he became extremely critical of the 'lady nurses, employed at the front more because it pleased sentiment at home than for any practical reason,' and who treated the RAMC orderlies with scant consideration; 'Each woman seems authorised to give as many orders as she pleases to any man she selects.'[43]

Those comments were harsh but, to some extent, these female initiatives were also being criticised by Lord Rothschild, chairman of the council of the Red Cross Society, when he noted in August 1914 that the speed with which private houses were being converted into hospitals and convalescent homes was leading to confusion and duplication. The aim should be to weld 'all miscellaneous efforts into one general and far-reaching system'.[44]

It was doubtless on these grounds that the offer of the Duchess of Rutland and Lady Diana Manners to open a hospital in France was rejected. Nothing daunted, the duchess determined to turn her Arlington Street home in London into a hospital for wounded officers, and this time the venture went ahead. Meanwhile Lady Diana herself had undergone a period of training as a nurse at Guy's Hospital. There she had been subject to a strict disciplinary regime for a few months, but it had enabled her to escape the vigilant eye of the duchess for a time. As a VAD, Diana could not claim professional status, but she was pleased to find 'that she was soon treated as a not particularly expert but still capable member of the nursing staff. She recorded proudly that she was allowed to give injections, intravenous and saline, to prepare for operations and cut abscesses.'[45] She also used her expertise at giving injections to a less desirable end, administering morphia to herself and some of her friends, when the pressures and sorrows of the war became intolerable. Her friend, Katharine Asquith, was 'a staunch champion of this drug', too, and in December 1915, Diana informed her friend, Raymond Asquith, who was Katharine's husband, that the only pleasure

she had found in the last month had arisen when she and Katharine had lain 'in ecstatic stillness through too short a night, drugged in very deed by my hand with morphia … It was a grand night, and strange to feel so utterly self-sufficient – more like a Chinaman, or God before he made the world.[46]

The habit never became regular enough for her to become addicted, but three weeks after her letter to Raymond, she and Katharine had another session and as a result she had to spend the next day in bed 'with an alarmingly violent hangover'. 'I hope she won't become a *morphineuse*', commented her future husband, Duff Cooper. 'It would spoil her looks'. One of his own sisters had already become addicted to morphia as a result of losing her lover in the war. Alcohol proved equally attractive, with champagne, vodka and absinthe the drinks of choice. Champagne was apparently the most popular in Lady Diana's circle, but it was so much associated in her mind with the 'hysteria of war' that in later life she 'viewed it with distaste'.[47]

While she was at Guy's Hospital her social life was limited to her evenings off, when between 8 p.m. and 10 p.m. she was allowed to be away from the premises. As she commented in her autobiography, at eight o'clock

> I would fly out of the ward, across the court into my room, noting as ran the taxi waiting outside the great iron gates ... The nearest restaurant was called De Keyser's. A quarter of an hour to get there, a quarter of an hour to get back – two crowded hours of glorious life ... The big party evenings were thrown at the Cheshire Cheese. This was a bit farther away, but the atmosphere was alluring ... I would have to leave the candlelight and merriment and like Cinderella tear back to my brooms.[48]

As she later wrote, on looking back 'on these nightmare years of tragic hysteria, it is frightening to live them again in memory ... The young were dancing a tarantella frenziedly to combat any pause that could let death conquer their morale.'[49]

Diana left Guy's Hospital after six months when her mother made plans to open her own hospital. The Arlington Street premises were duly converted to receive wounded officers, with the duchess's own bedroom equipped as an operating theatre. Three trained nurses were recruited, and Diana worked there, together with her sister, Letty, the wife and later the widow of Lord Elcho, and another friend. In these new surroundings, discipline was far more lax. Friends arrived with cream cakes and sherry for their elevenses, and there were plenty of bolt-holes should they be in an escaping mood. Even when Diana used her nursing skills to help at an operation, she might rush off afterwards to dine at a friend's house or to attend a ball. On one occasion she had to leave a dinner at the Cheshire Cheese to help in an operation, and then rejoined the party three hours later when it had moved on to a private house.[50] Should work be slack at Arlington Street she and Katharine Asquith might go down to the East End to provide an evening meal in a canteen for workers from the munitions factories. Or she might take part in charity concerts and similar entertainments.

During the war the strict rules of chaperonage were allowed to slip, but the Duchess of Rutland was anxious that her daughter's reputation should not be compromised. So she never shut her bedroom door when she was staying at Arlington Street, and insisted that Lady Diana looked in before she went to her bedroom; no matter how late it was. This meant Diana must always 'sober up before returning', and she would claim that a female friend had escorted her home when in fact she had been driving round and round Regent's Park in a taxi with a man. She also visited Duff Cooper, who was a noted womaniser, in his rooms clandestinely. Yet although she had several passionate affairs and was in love with the married Raymond Asquith until his death in 1916, she successfully protected her virginity.

That was not true of all her female friends, and especially of Nancy Cunard. According to Iris Tree, she and Nancy would entertain young officers on leave in their London studio, or at the country house in Kent that Iris's mother had rented. As early as 1915, when Nancy had learnt of the deaths of some of her friends, she responded to the horrors of the war by turning to casual sex in order to comfort young soldiers who were soon to face possible death or injury at the front. Although, for her, such encounters appear to have been followed by a strong sense of remorse, despair and loneliness. There were also wild drink parties in the Café Royal Brasserie 'with tipsy poets and "chaps" on leave, [and] poker playing'. All the time, though, there was 'the dread, more and more justified, that every young man one liked' was going to be killed at the front. 'Many of the soldiers left Nancy's bed for the bottomless mud of Flanders Field', writes Lois Gordon. Alongside this, there was her work in canteens and her involvement in charity concerts and other shows.[51] Despite the bombs which pounded London during the war years, there were many people, like Nancy, who continued to patronise the theatres and restaurants that remained open. At the Savoy, among other venues, the *thé dansant* was started and was soon taken up by a wide range of other hotels, restaurants and clubs. The management of the Savoy remained anxious to bring 'some cheer to guests anxious to forget the horrors and carnage':

Saxophones sobbed defiance and even silly ragtime lyrics breathed a poignant significance for the officers who danced, drank and flirted on the too-short nights before their trains left Victoria. In the men's cloakroom nailbrushes were tactfully fixed over the wash basins so that 'soldiers who have lost an arm or hand can scrub the other hand quite easily' ... In the huge, half-empty kitchen with a skeleton staff of clumsy boys and tired old men, the maître-chef ... tried somehow to camouflage his rissoles.[52]

Night-clubs, too, became established during these years, and it was into this world of wartime gaiety mixed with anxiety and sorrow that Nancy Cunard stepped, while the military losses continued to mount. It was during these years, too, that she met and married Sydney Fairbairn, a young officer who had been injured at Gallipoli, and who while recovering from his wounds in England met his future wife in 1916. Her friends were astonished at her sudden decision to marry, and her mother opposed the match, since although Sydney came from a socially respectable family, culturally and intellectually he had little in common with his vibrant future wife. It is not easy to decide why she married him. Some have suggested that it was to get away from her mother and to give herself more personal freedom away from maternal surveillance. In any event, Nancy and Sydney were married on 15 November 1916, at the Grenadier Guards' Chapel, with the bride wearing a long gold dress, a turban-shaped toque of orange blossom, and a veil that was as long as the dress and enveloped her shoulders.[53]

The couple departed for a honeymoon in Devon and Cornwall, and when they returned they moved into a house on Montague Street, which Lady Cunard had provided as a wedding present. Almost immediately, Nancy found the new relationship unbearable. As Lois Gordon, one of her biographers, points out drily, 'It was one thing to spend an evening with a wounded soldier; another to marry him.' Later Nancy described the twenty months she spent with

Sydney before he again departed for the front as one of the most miserable periods of her life. Although he survived the war and for some time during it Nancy continued to write to him, they never lived together again, and separated in 1919. They finally divorced in 1925.[54] The brevity of their courtship may have contributed to the marriage failure, and in this connection it is significant that after the war there was a general upsurge in the divorce rate, as couples who had married in haste found that in peacetime they had little in common.

Meanwhile, on a purely domestic front, even affluent households found increasing difficulty in recruiting servants. At the Duke of Richmond's Goodwood, where there had been an indoor staff of over twenty before the war, numbers dropped to twelve in 1917, of whom only three were male.[55] Similarly, when Rosina Harrison was appointed a lady's maid to the two daughters of Lady Ierne Tufton in London during that year, she discovered that only the chauffeur was a man. All the rest of the staff were female, with Major Tufton's valeting being carried out by the second parlourmaid.[56] Even women servants were becoming scarce, as more attractive wartime employment became available. Lady Cynthia Asquith noted the despair of her sister-in-law, Katharine, in April 1916 as a result of her fruitless efforts to recruit a new parlourmaid. As Lady Cynthia commented, 'They are almost as extinct as the dodo.'[57] These changes were the result of male military conscription as well as the appearance of alternative employment outlets in factories and in other war work. Household expenditure, too, was reduced as a result of war-time restrictions, even in larger households and despite the general sharp rise in prices. At Goodwood it fell from £8,922 in 1913 to £3,248.[58] Given the inflation of the war years, with retail prices on average more than doubling between 1914 and 1918, the reduction in real terms was very considerable.

Country Life would have approved of the changes. On 15 August 1914, it declared sternly that 'the rich ought to live more sparingly, so that they may not consume food that might otherwise be available for the poor. Let it be fully understood that indulgence in luxury is not only a foolishness but a crime.' Early in the following year it sought to shame grandees into ensuring that they did not employ any male servant who was fit enough to fight: 'Have you a Butler, Groom, Chauffeur, Gardener or Gamekeeper serving *you* who, at this moment should be serving your King and Country? Will you sacrifice your personal convenience for your Country's need? Ask your men to enlist TO-DAY.'[59] However, not all its readers welcomed this hectoring tone. On 5 September 1915, 'Country Invalid' wrote angrily to the editor to deplore the way in which the 'patriotic wave which has now swamped England' had brought

> in its train some ugly followers, an unchristian disposition to judge others and a total inability to calculate another's circumstances ... Great folk, dwelling in palaces, may well dispense with three-fourths of their retainers without feeling any pinch of inconvenience, and dwellers in towns with shops and taxis handy, may think a chauffeur unnecessary; but does that give them any right to abuse a dweller in the wilds of the country, perchance an invalid who retains one or two menservants ineligible for the Army.[60]

Some of the heat was taken out of the debate in 1916 when conscription was introduced for men of military age.

The scarcity of domestic labour was matched by the

growing shortages of food and fuel. Members of High Society were often better able to cope with disruptions to food supplies than was the population at large, as they were able to grow vegetables and fruit, and raise poultry and livestock, on their country estates. Fuel was more problematic, despite the availability of timber for felling on most estates, and there were, of course, difficulties with imported consumer goods like sugar; not until 1917 was a rudimentary system of rationing introduced, initially to cover sugar.[61] On 6 February 1917, Lady Cynthia Asquith, who was staying with a sister-in-law in London, noted in her diary that there was a 'great domestic crisis – poor Frances! Cellar quite empty and no coal to be procured for love or money. The phenomenal cold still worse than ever and now we can't even "keep the home fires burning". We all shivered ... but we got through the evening very well with the help of silly round games.' The next morning she breakfasted in her fur coat. 'At last we are beginning to feel the pinch of war in material things ... [These] last days each hostess's brow has been furrowed by mentally weighing meat, bread, and sugar. Frances says the allowance of sugar is larger than what she consumes, on the other hand the meat allowance could mean a reduction by one half.'[62]

But those with great wealth and influence could circumvent some of the shortages. Lady Cynthia wrote enviously of the wealthy American Consuelo Duchess of Marlborough, now living apart from her husband. She had invited a friend to dinner and had provided a six-course meal, much as she might have done pre-war. And when a relative arrived to stay with her at Brighton, where she was currently living, the duchess offered her a choice of six bedrooms, in each of which a fire had been lit 'in case it should be chosen!'

'Enjoyed being shocked over this impious extravagance', added Lady Cynthia acidly.[63]

Some grandees responded to the scarcity of food by converting their pleasure grounds and gardens to more utilitarian purposes in order to boost food production. At Blenheim Palace in 1915 the Duke of Marlborough substituted 'sheep for mowers in the gardens' and planted cabbages in the flower beds. 'The national food problem,' declared *The Times* wryly, 'may not have been greatly lessened by these practices', but it was a patriotic gesture.[64] On a more ambitious scale, the widowed Countess of Airlie, despite her formidable range of duties in connection with VAD recruitment nursing training and hospital provision, as well as her role as a lady-in-waiting to Queen Mary, managed the family's Cortachy estate. Her sons were away at the war and her elderly factor had retired. Consequently, much of her time at Cortachy was occupied 'in teaching such workers as she could get the rudiments of farming and gardening necessitated by the national drive for food production. "My entire horizon was bounded by potatoes," she wrote. "Every vine house was stuffed full of them; even the little hut at the back of the gardens was stacked with potato boxes from the floor to the roof."'[65]

Furthermore, despite the determination of members of the social elite to follow at least some of their pre-war pleasures, including the holding of house parties, the copious consumption of alcohol, dancing, gambling and flirtations, plus, in a limited fashion, the field sports of hunting and shooting, they were also under serious financial pressure. The cost of goods and services was rising inexorably and yet landowners could not benefit from the increased agricultural prices by raising rentals, because of war-time restrictions. Taxes, too, were becoming increasingly burdensome, thereby further eroding living standards. On the Earl of Pembroke's Wilton estate, income tax, which had 'taken barely 4 per cent of gross rents ... before 1914, was taking over a quarter by 1919'.[66] A similar situation existed at Savernake, and overall on these estates the burden of direct taxation, including land tax, rates and income tax, had risen from 9 to 30 per cent of income. In those circumstances, some landowners began to sell outlying parts of their estates in order to raise capital, despite the difficult wartime conditions. Lord Pembroke disposed of a detached estate he owned in North Wiltshire in 1917. He followed this by the sale of 8,400 acres of outlying portions of the Wilton estate itself in 1918, with many tenant farmers taking the opportunity to buy their holdings.[67] Likewise, Sir Francis Ashley-Corbett, whose seat and main estate were in Lincolnshire, sold his entire 4,500-acre Everleigh Manor property in Wiltshire, while at the end of 1918 the sale of outlying portions of the Marker estates in Devon and Somerset realised over £70,000. In these circumstances *Country Life* claimed that the record of land sales in 1918 would 'take a lot of beating'.[68] In the event, they were to be comfortably exceeded between 1919 and 1921. Among the purchasers were tenant farmers and businessmen who had profited from the war and were anxious to acquire the social status attached to land ownership.

Other hard-pressed estate owners, like the Earl of Carnarvon, who were concerned about their rising tax bills, adopted a different solution. In May 1918 Lord Carnarvon sold some of the furniture from one of his subsidiary houses at Bretby in Derbyshire.[69]

In the meantime many wives and daughters wanted to support the war effort in other ways than through nursing and hospital provision. The future Lady Curzon, for example, ran a night canteen at Waterloo station and

Lady Victoria Bentinck, daughter of the Duke of Portland, worked in a munitions factory. Others, like the Hon. Mrs Gell and Lady Horner, arranged village sewing and knitting parties to provide 'comforts' for the troops and set up Red Cross branches where participants could roll bandages and make swabs. At Mells in Somerset, Lady Horner organised a large work party in the loggia of her home where the women could meet to make shirts and socks and gossip to one another. Lady Horner read aloud to them while they sewed. But, most important in her view, was the opportunity it gave them to meet and to feel they were 'working for their men, and hearing all the latest news I could get for them'.[70]

At Glamis Castle, which was quickly converted for hospital use to receive wounded or sick soldiers sent to convalesce after treatment at Dundee Infirmary, the young Lady Elizabeth Bowes Lyon, the future Queen Elizabeth, remembered that during the first few months of the war 'we were so busy knitting, knitting, knitting and making shirts for the local battalion – the 5th Black Watch.' Parcels were despatched containing thick shirts, socks, mufflers, belts and sheepskins, the latter to be made into coats and painted with a waterproofing varnish. The Earl and Countess of Strathmore, Lady Elizabeth's parents, apparently intended to provide every man in the thousand-strong local Black Watch battalion with a sheepskin. 'Socks were packed with presents of cigarettes, tobacco, pipes or peppermints in the toe.' Lady Elizabeth remembered that one of her tasks was 'crumpling up tissue paper until it was so soft that it no longer crackled, to put into the lining of sleeping bags'. And when the soldier patients arrived, she helped to entertain them, visiting their ward for a 'lively game of whist before supper'. There were sing-songs in the ward, too, with Elizabeth's older sister playing the piano, and trips to the village shop to purchase cigarettes and tobacco for the men.[71] Her sister eventually departed to train as a nurse in London but as the younger girl was not old enough to take a nursing course, her principal responsibility was 'to make the soldiers feel at home', something she, with her bright personality, was well-fitted to do.

Even Queen Mary and her ladies-in-waiting joined in the war effort. At Sandringham in early October 1917, Bertha Dawkins wrote to Lady Airlie to tell her that among her other activities they had been 'very busy ... picking up chestnuts for making acetone, & we have already got over a ton. I am very well ... which is lucky, as chestnut picking is extremely hard work when done for 4½ hours every day!'[72] In February 1918, when the Royal Family had returned to Buckingham Palace, she also told Lady Airlie of the nightly air raids they were then enduring: 'Three of my windows were blown out on Saturday evening by that very big bomb in Chelsea.'[73]

Edith Castlereagh, or the Marchioness of Londonderry as she became in 1915 on the death of her father-in-law, had far more ambitious plans. At an early stage in the war she was invited to become Colonel-in-Chief of the Women's Volunteer Reserve, which she saw as a means of enabling women of all classes to replace the men who were now joining the armed forces. This meant taking on work in a variety of different spheres. However, she quickly became dissatisfied with the militaristic spirit that underlay the Reserve and left to form a breakaway organisation of her own, called the Women's Legion. The new body grew rapidly under Edith's dynamic and determined leadership, and soon had women available to work on the land. A special section was then set up to equip women to take on military cooking. After a few months' trial working in convalescent homes, comments Lady Londonderry's biographer, 'their work was so appreciated that by July 1915' it was agreed 'to allow the Legion to provide cooks for … convalescent hospitals … at £26 a year, with free rations and accommodation'. The scheme proved very successful and within a few months this section of the Women's Legion was taken over by the War Office and put under the control of the Inspector of Army Catering. The next section to be set up in 1916 was that for Army Service Corps drivers, who drove anything from generals' cars to heavy lorries. 'They wore General Service buttons and the ASC badge in addition to their Women's Legion badges, had the same hours and did the same work as men but … were paid less. They were quickly followed by women dispatch riders and mechanics.'[74]

It is often claimed that by contributing to the war effort in these ways and through their employment in munitions factories and the transport system generally, women helped along the cause of female suffrage. For despite the determined and sometimes violent pressure exerted by suffragettes and suffragists before 1914, they had in practice achieved little. Female suffrage was, incidentally, a cause to which Lady Londonderry was committed, not because she saw the vote as an end in itself but because she regarded it as a means of raising the status of women. Before the war, among the most determined opponents of the female vote had been the Liberal Prime Minister Herbert Asquith, and most of his Cabinet. However, in December 1916 he was replaced as head of the coalition government by a fellow Liberal, the energetic David Lloyd George, who was not so ideologically hostile to the issue of women's suffrage. As a consequence, in February 1918 an Act was passed giving the vote to women householders and the wives of householders who were aged thirty or over. In contrast, all men aged twenty-one or over were enfranchised, whether they were householders or not. In the first post-war election, held on 14 December 1918, 6 million women were entered on the electoral register for the first time.[75] At the general election the Asquithian wing of the Liberal Party fared very badly, Asquith himself losing his seat, to his wife Margot's bitter disappointment. Her one consolation was that, as a strong opponent of female suffrage, none of the women candidates who stood for election in Britain itself succeeded. The solitary female victor in 1918 was a Sinn Fein candidate in Ireland, Countess Constance Markievicz, who had been imprisoned for her part in the Dublin Easter Rising and had contested the election from Holloway prison. Like other members of her party she refused to take her seat in Parliament. In a diary entry for 28 December 1918, the day the polls were declared, Margot noted with some satisfaction that '*all* the women were beaten. This ... gave me the only Pleasure to be got out of the most *cruel* wicked election ever concocted by Foolish men.'[76]

Edith Londonderry, by contrast, was dissatisfied with the limited electoral concession extended to women. She wanted full equality, and in 1919, still determined to increase both the franchise and women's place in public life, she wrote a pamphlet which stated that what she and other like-minded women sought to achieve was a removal of 'the sex disability and to extend the franchise to all duly qualified [females] on the same basis as that possessed by men at the present day'.[77] Not until 1928 were women granted an equal franchise, in the way she desired, with the introduction of the so-called 'Flapper' vote.

Lady Londonderry, however, did not confine her wartime activities to the Women's Legion and the cause of female political emancipation. She also embarked on a round of entertaining at Londonderry House. Each Wednesday from early 1915 a group of friends, labelled 'The Ark', met for a late dinner on the top floor of the house, since the greater part of it had been converted into a hospital. The aim was to give Edith's friends the opportunity to relax in a congenial atmosphere of fun, gossip, jokes and 'silly games'. But what made The Ark unique was that each member was given the name of a real or mythological beast, with an appropriate fictional address, with the name matching the first letter of the Christian name of the respective members.[78] Edith herself, as the central figure, called herself Circe, the legendary Greek sorceress. Lady Cynthia Asquith regarded the whole idea as 'ridiculous', but Edith broke new ground by inviting an eclectic mixture of society figures, politicians, artists and writers. The Ark was established on more formal lines after 1918, and it continued to flourish into the post-war period.[79] So while many hostesses were confining their invitations to fellow members of High Society, Lady Londonderry was 'fascinated by artists and writers no less than by politicians long before it became the fashion to lion-hunt', by searching out celebrities.

The Human Cost of the War

Overshadowing these developments on the home front, there was the tragedy of the war itself, as the deaths and injuries of young soldiers, particularly young officers, mounted from the early days of the hostilities. C. F. G. Masterman later wrote emotionally that in the retreat from Mons and the First Battle of Ypres, during 1914 to 1915, 'the flower of the British aristocracy' had perished. At some stages of the war the average life expectancy of an infantry subaltern on the Western Front was put at only about three months. As Masterman commented despairingly, 'In the useless slaughter of the Guards on the Somme, or of the Rifle Brigade in Hooge Wood, half the great families of England, heirs of large estates and wealth, perished without a cry. These boys, who had been brought up with the prospect before them of every good material thing that life can give, died without complaint, often through the bungling of Generals.'[80]

Particularly vulnerable were the youngest and most inexperienced. According to J. M. Winter, of those aged under twenty in 1914 who came from Oxford and Cambridge Universities and who served as army officers during the war, 23.7 per cent from Oxford and 26.7 per cent from Cambridge were killed. Among those aged twenty to twenty-four in 1914, 27.2 per cent and 21.8 per cent, respectively, were killed. In 1917 H. A. L. Fisher, President of the Board of Education, 'spoke with some justification when he said: "The chapels of Oxford and Cambridge display long lists of the fallen and no institutions have suffered greater or more irreparable losses than these ancient shrines of learning and piety."'[81]

Of course, not all the young officers killed were university men. One of the earliest victims, killed on 1 September 1914, was George Cecil, grandson of the Victorian Prime Minister Lord Salisbury. He had already embarked on a military career before the war broke out, and had passed his examination for a French interpretership. When war came, like other youngsters, he was anxious to take part, despite the fact that he was still only eighteen. As Lady Cecil, his mother, subsequently recorded, it was on an extremely hot day, 12 August 1914, that he and his friend, the Hon. John Manners, with other members of the Grenadier Guards departed for the front. His mother and sister went to the station to see the men set off, Lady Cecil taking a basket of fruit each for her son and his friend to sustain them on what was bound to be a hot and uncomfortable journey. The night before he left, George had written his will and left it in the care of his banker, to be sent to his mother only if he were killed. In it he bequeathed his shares and cash to his teenage sister, Helen, his sword to his mother, as 'it is an emblem of sorts. I want Papa to have my watch. Otherwise distribute my few goods as you think fit.'[82]

Following his arrival on the Continent, on 21 August, he wrote a cheerful letter to his mother, assuring her that up to then 'we have had the greatest fun in the world. We have now all recovered from the effects of inoculation.' However, six days later the picture had considerably darkened, after they had been involved in a 'violent artillery duel between us & the enemy'. They were now retreating 'by strenuous stages, hardly any sleep & very early start, until one day, very tired, we billeted out at a certain town, as we thought at least 20 kilometres from the enemy. This evening, just as we were sitting down to dinner, the alarm was given that hostile cavalry had been seen quite close to the town ... Soon, sounds of very heavy firing were heard. I then had to go to brigade headquarters to carry messages.' Shells continued to rain down and he 'had the greatest luck. I was stepping [into] the gateway when a shrapnel burst about 50 yards to my left and all the ground was cut up by this shrapnel ... We cleared out and started on a ten mile walk. The men were so footsore & tired that we took nearly seven hours.'[83] Five days later, when taking part in the Battle of Lanrecies, he was shot through the head and chest. His body was never recovered, and for months thereafter his distraught mother pursued the military authorities in an attempt to get details of what had happened.[84] For a time she had the vain hope that he might have been taken a prisoner-of-war. His close friend, the Hon. John Manners, was killed the following day. According to the young Helen Cecil, her 'mother's period of mourning lasted the length of the conflict'.[85]

Another victim of the war in its early months was Julian Grenfell. Confident as ever, on 21 November 1914, he had written to his friend and near neighbour in Buckinghamshire, Nancy Astor, the vivacious American-born wife of Waldorf Astor. They lived at Cliveden near Taplow. In the letter he declared they had given 'these Huns a great walloping, when they apparently outnumbered us (at one time) by about 5–1. I have enjoyed it all tremendously every minute of it: but it has been damnably cold. The worst trenches are the ones under heavy shell fire – most of them are. Then you simply crouch in the wet clay for 48 hours and wait for the shells coming. You can hear them coming, and bet on whether they are going to land in the trench or outside it. The noise is the worst thing – it makes your head simply buss by the end of the day ... I wish I could get some cavalry work, and get in at the brutes with our swords and horses.'[86] Less than six months later, on 13 May 1915, Julian received a head wound when fighting near Ypres. Shrapnel penetrated his brain and although he was taken to a Boulogne hospital, his condition quickly deteriorated. On 16 May, as Julian's younger brother, Billy, was about to depart for France, Lord and Lady Desborough received a telegram informing them of their son's condition. They were able to get permission to go to him and remained in the hospital with him until he died, after suffering great agony, on 26 May.[87] Billy, who had arrived in Boulogne with his battalion, was also able to visit Julian briefly before he was himself despatched to the front. Julian was buried in a war cemetery near Boulogne.

The death of this dynamic young officer shocked members of the elite social circle in which he and his family moved, and particularly those who were personal friends of Ettie Desborough, his mother. As Lady Cynthia Asquith noted in her diary, 'One is haunted by the thought of Ettie seeing her glorious son die by inches. How can such things be endured by women?'[88] She also wrote to Billy Grenfell, who was undergoing his own baptism of fire. On 12 June he replied and already he seemed to have become reconciled not only to his brother's death but perhaps to his own. 'Death selects our bravest and best,' he wrote, 'but the barrier between two worlds is so gallantly and light-heartedly crossed here by many every day, that one can hardly feel it as a separation or even an interruption of their gallant and beautiful lives. Death is swallowed up in victory.'[89]

Billy also wrote in a similar fashion to his close friend Nancy Astor, with whom he was more than a little in love, despite the fact that she was married and was the mother of young children. She was his 'Darling Nance' and as he declared,

> How could a man end this life better than in the full tide of strength & glory – Julian has outsoared our night, & passed on to a wider life ... We are just off to the trenches, looking like Iron Pirates, so no more now except all my love.[90]

About a fortnight later he wrote in a more flippant tone during a period of respite from the trenches that

> such a Chamber of Horrors we have past [*sic*] through, shells thicker than flies, & flies thicker than air, & our nearest & dearest neighbours 37 English & 22 German

corpses of varying age & savour … There is fine Bosch stalking & shooting for them as likes [it].

It is v. boring behind the lines; I s'd like a week in Paris …

This is written between the overs of the boringest cricket match I have ever played in. But for cricket we should have been a finer nation.[91]

Billy, a noted sportsman, preferred the more vigorous recreations of boxing and tennis, at which he was a noted expert. In another undated letter he noted drily that the war was 'so gigantic that apparently only a very small number can take part in it at the same time. The rest are kept in reserve for 1920. One is … tempted to doubt whether it is wholly an advantage that the Army should be run by the stupidest of the stupid.'[92] His last letter to Nancy was written on 28 July, two days before he was killed at the Battle of Hooge. His body was never recovered.

Billy's death, following so quickly that of his brother, devastated his parents, not least when they discovered that the attack in which he died had been a mistake, 'one of the worst of the many blunders of the war'.[93] Despite the overall heavy death toll in these years, within London society the loss of the two brothers in such quick succession was profoundly shocking. Significantly Queen Mary herself visited Ettie in early August to offer sympathy. To Duff Cooper, who had been at Oxford with Billy and had already learnt of the deaths of many of his friends, the news came as a terrible blow; 'When I think of Oxford now I see nothing but ghosts.'[94]

Ettie herself was determined to show a brave face to the world and to carry on as usual. Lady Cynthia Asquith noted admiringly the amazing way in which she appeared, on the surface, to be 'absolutely normal in company. The same old extraordinary zest unimpaired, and the exaggerated interest in everyone and everything.' But directly the two women were alone, she showed a different side: 'Tears pour down her cheeks, and she talks on and on about the boys, and yet preserving such wonderful sympathy for others ... She told me she found the complete, sudden disappearance of Billy harder to bear than the long, loving farewell to Julian.'[95]

Other mothers, too, displayed the same steely determination not to let grief dominate their lives. The Hon. John Manners' mother, whose son was killed less than a month after the declaration of war, proudly declared that if she had six such sons 'she would give them all'. While a mere four days after a memorial service had been held at Stanway for the teenage Yvo Charteris, his mother, Lady Wemyss, took out three convalescent soldiers from Winchcombe hospital for a drive through the Cotswolds, followed by tea. The next day she again gave them tea, this time at Stanway, her home. In the weeks and months ahead she carried out a range of war work, seeking to numb her pain by constant activity.[96]

For Lady Diana Manners, who had lost so many members of her close personal circle, the solution, according to her future husband, Duff Cooper, was to treat sorrow 'like an illness which must be got over as soon as possible, doing all she can to be cheerful, laughing and talking till tears come like a sudden seizure and she has to give way. She tells me that when she cannot stop crying she reminds herself that in a comparatively few days she will cease to wish to.'[97]

Some of these grief-stricken families turned to spiritualism in an attempt to contact the dead. This was true of Lady Wemyss, Cynthia Asquith's mother, who had lost two sons.[98] Lady Cynthia herself also contacted a palmist in an effort to discover the fate of a close friend, Lord Basil Blackwood, who was initially thought to be missing. In fact he had been killed and the palmist herself held out no hope to her of his survival. Even Duff Cooper in January 1917 decided to have a séance with a spiritualist. 'I had never done such a thing before. I was most disappointed ... I came away very sceptical of the whole business.'[99] But others among his friends had a different view. The previous December he had attended a dinner party where a fellow guest was Clare Tennant, whose brother, Edward, had been killed in the summer of 1916 in the Battle of the Somme. She claimed to have taken part in a number of séances and to have had 'many messages' from her brother and also from young Yvo Charteris, who, according to her, was apparently much discontented with the afterlife.[100]

So far, Duff Cooper himself, as a Foreign Office clerk, had been granted exemption from conscription to the armed forces. However, in May 1917, with the government seeking ever more men for the Army, it was decided to release some civil servants. Duff Cooper welcomed the move, which one uncharitable acquaintance described as combing out 'the scrimshankers'.[101] Duff passed his medical examination successfully and on 18 June noted in his diary that to his 'delight ... I am to be allowed to join the army'. He was accepted into the Grenadier Guards and by 5 July was on his way to begin training at Bushey in Hertfordshire.[102] After his previously pampered existence he found the transition to military life rather uncomfortable at first, but he soon settled down and on 22 November 1917, was gazetted as an officer in the Grenadiers. For some time he continued to remain in England and to enjoy an active social life in his free time, meeting Lady Diana and also more disreputable friends.

Thus on 27 February 1918 he went to a 'small party in Teddie Gerard's flat'. She was an Argentinian-born actress and singer, and Duff found it all 'most amusing – everybody there being slightly drunk but not too much, everybody also being rather amorous to one another quite promiscuously and nobody being jealous ... Ivor Novello played the piano ... There was plenty of champagne.'[103] Nor did he give up his gambling habits and on 1 March noted that he had been sent for by his commanding officer, who told him 'he had heard I was one of a set of officers who had been gambling very high – that I had lost a large sum of money and I had paid up like a gentleman of which he was glad'. Nonetheless, he 'warned me that gambling was against King's Regulations and generally gave me a short lecture on the subject'.[104]

Even this did not bring about Duff's reformation and when he was in reserve, away from the front line in France, during June 1918 he noted that he and some fellow officers had 'played that absurd game Marmora. I like a fool lost £220 ... We got rather drunk.'[105]

Duff Cooper had arrived in France on the 28 April 1918 and was pleased to discover when he reached the front line that he was 'no more frightened than other people'.

> We had a good deal of excitement at night and were often severely shelled ... Later when we were in reserve we had an unpleasant moment when they started sending over gas shells in the early morning ... I had some difficulty in finding my gas mask which I had imprudently taken off to sleep. We had a sergeant killed that morning.[106]

Despite the dangers he faced, he avoided injury and behaved with considerable bravery when he single-handedly captured a number of German soldiers. For this he was awarded the Distinguished Service Order, 'a rare achievement for a subaltern in the Guards', comments Philip Ziegler.[107] Lady Diana Manners, needless to say, was immensely proud of his achievement.

By then the war was drawing to an end, and on 31 October Duff was granted leave to return to England. Unlike almost all his pre-war friends and university contemporaries, he had emerged from the conflict unscathed, as well as with a good military record. But for many men and their families the situation was very different, not merely as a result of personal loss and injury but on economic grounds, too. Although special war-time legislation had reduced the burden of death duties levied on landed estates in respect of those who had died as a result of the war, for the largest properties these could still represent a crippling burden. That was especially true when an owner's death was quickly followed by that of his heir, killed at the front. This was true of the Wyndham family of Clouds, with George Wyndham dying suddenly in 1913 and his son and heir, Percy, killed in France on 14 September 1914. In some cases it was necessary to sell the whole or part of an estate in order to meet the duties. In 1915 the Amesbury Abbey estate in Wiltshire was put on the market after the death of its owner, Sir Edmund Antrobus, was followed by that of his only son in battle. In this instance the farms were purchased by their tenants, but the abbey itself remained unsold. Again, at Hawarden in Flint, when the young squire was killed, the duties paid at his death were six times the old-style succession duties levied on his predecessor's estate in 1891. In the immediate aftermath of the war outlying parts of the estate were sold for the then substantial sum of £112,000.[108]

So it was that when the Armistice was finally signed on 11 November 1918 and the war came to an end, many found difficulty in believing it was over. To Mrs C. S. Peel, it seemed 'almost as if one heard a dead silence and then ... the whole nation gave a sigh of relief. A few moments later the people had gone mad.'[109] To *Country Life* it was 'Britain's Proudest Moment'. 'Before the war,' it declared,

> it was frequently asserted by evil prophets ... that the British race had fallen into the sere and yellow leaf. Decay was assumed to have set in ... It will be proudly related as long as the race exists how resolutely the unmartial English nation set about remedying its defects ... The end was the victory celebrated on Monday last, the greatest ever achieved in the annals of the race.[110]

The teenage Helen Cecil, whose only brother had been killed so tragically at the beginning of the war, nonetheless shared in the general mood of celebration. In a letter written to her mother on 12 November from her Great Wigsell home in Sussex, she described the general scene of jubilation;

> I never thought I should live to be so happy as I am today or that I should ever see East Sussex as it is today. The maids were out hanging up the washing when I sent the news down & they skipped & hopped like young rabbits. Every body was running round for hours telling everybody else and we [her governess and herself] have not expected to be fed, clothed or washed today, but I feel that man does not live by bread alone these days! 5 minutes after the news had reached us it was at High Wigsell, 10 mins. later Robertsbridge was flying flags.
>
> Hawkhurst is a fine sight, arches of flags, real crowds of people, perfect strangers nearly kissing each other in the streets & the joy bells ringing. The school children have cheered till they can't speak & the cottagers have ruined themselves buying flags. All this was absolutely spontaneous ... God save the King is written all over the

village & sung all over Sussex. I feel most perfectly drunk myself.[111]

According to another account, in many towns sexual relations 'between perfect strangers took place promiscuously in parks, shop entrances and alley-ways'. In Oxford, a woman walked up and down the Cornmarket waving a flag, 'with her skirts kilted up to her naked middle, and was cheered as a sort of presiding Venus by the Army and Air cadets quartered in the colleges'. At Cambridge the cadets smashed up the office of the *Cambridge Magazine*, which was the only literary periodical that had embraced the pacifist cause.[112]

In London, the celebrations were especially rowdy. Duff Cooper, returning to the capital with Lady Diana Manners from a visit to the Norfolk country house of their friends, Venetia and Edwin Montagu, described it as being 'in uproar – singing, cheering, waving flags. In spite of real delight I couldn't resist a feeling of profound melancholy, looking at the crowds of silly cheering people and thinking of the dead.' That night he and Diana dined at The Ritz, where there 'was an enormous crowd', and on their return to his St James's Street home, he noted that the streets were still 'full of wild enthusiasm. Diana shared the melancholy with which these filled me – and once she broke down and sobbed.[113]

Lady Desborough spent the morning of 11 November at Avon Tyrrell, which was a military nursing home, with her daughter Monica, who was working there. 'I was so thankful to be with you today – how proud I am of your most splendid 4 years & a quarter, never flinching or looking back,' she wrote in the evening to her daughter. To her friend Mary Wemyss she wrote in a different vein: 'All day the thought of you has burnt in my innermost heart. Victory, & you & I look in vain for our Victors.'[114]

Others, too, shared that more sombre mood. *Country Life* on 23 November 1918 pointed to the general economic and social dislocation that was inevitable after four and a half years of war: 'It will require the whole of the national energy to get things straight again.'

Still more devastating for many was the epidemic of septic or Spanish influenza which had begun to manifest itself even before the war ended. On 23 November 1918, for example, the *Oxford Times* reported that at the small Oxfordshire village of Bladon, at the gates of Blenheim Palace, 'nearly every family' had been affected, and there had been ten deaths. 'The Duke of Marlborough has kindly sent soup every day for the past three weeks to the invalids, besides other comforts to the worst cases.'

Nor did members of High Society escape its ravages. On 12 November 1918, Duff Cooper reported that he was suffering from a mild attack, from which he recovered relatively quickly. His younger sister, Stephanie, was less fortunate. She developed pneumonia and on 9 December 1918, she died, at the age of thirty-three, leaving behind two small children: 'her lungs were full of poison and ... the case was hopeless'.[115] Nancy Cunard, too, in 1919 caught influenza and quickly developed pneumonia. She lay in bed 'weak and furious in her mother's house ... for most of January, February and March. When she eventually recovered she was physically and emotionally exhausted', declared her biographer. Eventually she travelled to the south of France to recuperate. Overall, the epidemic was to kill about 100,000 people in the United Kingdom alone.[116]

It was small wonder that after this miserable end to what had been one of the most testing periods in the nation's history, the survivors looked forward to a revival of pre-war pleasure-seeking. 'The war had ended picturesquely and memorably, at the eleventh hour of the eleventh day of the eleventh month', remembered Loelia, Duchess of Westminster, of her younger self. 'Optimism was in the air. Although in the last four years the flower of the country had been killed and nearly every home mourned a son, a brother, a husband, a fiancé or a dear friend … the hostesses of London … tried to put the clock back to 1914. Wounded soldiers in their blue suits and red ties disappeared from the square gardens and hospital wards became ballrooms again. London was dancing mad.'[117]

2

Adjusting to Peace: 1919–1921

Among the men who returned from the war there emerged a conspiracy of silence, a mutual and unspoken understanding that the horrors witnessed on the battlefield should appear to be forgotten. For landed society the happy world of the years before the war was transformed into one of cynical detachment ... The realization that landed wealth and influence were no longer unassailable seemed to engender among the survivors a brittle, frenetic outlook. Daring and constant diversions were looked for by those who emerged from wartime England.

> Madeleine Beard, *English Landed Society in the Twentieth Century* (London, 1989), pp. 55–56.

Coming to Terms with the Post-War World

When the First World War ended with the Armistice of 1918 and still more following the formal signing of the Peace Treaty at Versailles on 28 June 1919, there was a desire among most sections of the population, and particularly among the social elite, to throw off the anxieties and the sorrows of the last five years and to return to a more carefree existence. For some, inevitably, that was difficult to achieve. Alec Hardinge, who became private secretary to King George V, not only emerged from the war with his health undermined but with his whole approach to life seriously affected, too, in that all his closest friends had been killed and there had also been a heavy toll among his relatives. According to his wife, through these experiences he developed an 'intense loathing for "brass hats" and non-combatant generals'.[1] Herbert Asquith (known as 'Beb' in the family), the former Prime Minister's eldest surviving son, was equally unable to overcome the trauma of the battlefield and to resume his career as a barrister. It was his wife, Lady Cynthia, who was to become the chief breadwinner. Shortly before the end of the war she had been appointed the personal assistant and secretary of the playwright J. M. Barrie, and she not only continued in that role after 1918 but became a writer and journalist in her own right. Barrie proved a generous employer, assisting her financially with the education of her sons and when he died in 1937 she was the principal beneficiary from his will. 'Beb', meanwhile, sought to make a career as a poet and writer, and eventually secured an editorial post with the publishers Hutchinson.[2] He sadly became a heavy drinker.

'Beb's' next youngest brother, Arthur (or 'Oc'), also suffered as a result of the war. He had to have the lower part of one of his legs amputated as a result of a war wound, and suffered other injuries. Although he resumed his business career in 1919, he was never fully fit again and died in 1939 at the early age of fifty-six.[3]

In a different way, the long-serving Conservative MP Lord Winterton was affected, too. He was proud to have seen active service and that cut across his Party loyalties.

It was said that he 'showed more respect for the opponent who had borne arms than for any colleague who had chosen to lie abed on St Crispian's day'.[4] Hence his acid comment in March 1920 after he had been to a large ball attended by the king and queen, 'which is the most disgraceful. To have no ribbons (like Jersey) who has shirked fighting in two wars, or to have 12 like Philip Sassoon without having earned them?'[5] Sir Philip Sassoon, by serving as private secretary to Field Marshal Sir Douglas Haig from 1915, had never experienced front-line combat. Although he, too, was a Conservative MP, in Winterton's eyes, his military shortcomings more than outweighed this, although there may have been a latent anti-Semitism in his comments, too. On at least one occasion in his 1919 diary he referred to Sassoon as the 'Yid Philip'.[6]

Against this background, therefore, *The Bystander* struck an unusually sombre note when it warned its High Society readers against neglecting 'our own poor men, thousands of them, still in hospital here – wrecks of the War, crippled, shell-shocked, and worse'.[7] More broadly, there was also a recognition that the social world itself had changed, and was much more fluid than before 1914. 'The men of the moment were the ex-officers,' wrote a contemporary, Patrick Balfour, 'and a large proportion of them men of a class which, before the war, had no place in the social world'. But now the 'patriotic hysteria of victory allowed no place for social distinctions. No gentleman questioned for a moment the claim of any man with the title of major or captain to be accepted as an equal.' In addition, there was the large-scale infiltration into society of the families of the war profiteers, who were estimated to number around 340,000, as well as by others who had prospered on the home front during the hostilities.[8] To the disapproval of many members of the traditional upper class, they were able to 'buy' their way into the social elite by marriage, or by the purchase of a landed estate, or, as will be seen, by the more direct route of buying a title from a compliant post-war Lloyd George coalition government.

Characteristic of the widely felt desire for a new, more light-hearted approach to life, however, was the enormous upsurge in the popularity of dancing. As *The Bystander* put it on 8 January 1919:

> not even before we thought of war, did we dance here in London as we dance ... now. There is dancing in the mornings – for the newest jazzes and the latest rags must, of course, be learned some time – there is dancing all the afternoons, and there is dancing all the nights at nearly all the restaurants and halls ... They say the shops have netted fortunes selling ten-guinea dance frocks ... And Prime Ministers hardly earn in a year what a black jazz band now rakes in in a season.

Even the middle-aged were drawn into these post-war gaieties. Lady Desborough, then in her early fifties and still secretly mourning the loss of two sons, nonetheless was determined to remain in the vanguard of fashion. In March 1919 she gave a dance at which the guests 'danced "jazz"', in the case of some of them, for the first time. Older and more sober aristocrats, like Lord and Lady Lansdowne and Lady Minto, might deplore the new 'jazz' age and its influence on social relationships, but significantly the Lansdownes' thirty-seven-year-old nephew, Lord Winterton, who had attended Ettie Desborough's ball, took a different view. He had enjoyed it so much that after dining with the Lansdownes he went on to 'a very amusing dance', where he 'jazzed' with a new female friend.[9]

Shortly afterwards Winterton began taking dancing lessons with a specialist teacher at the home of Lady Evelyn Guinness. Later he went for private tuition and found it 'rather amusing'. Despite recurring memories of the battlefield deaths and mutilations he had witnessed, he rejoiced in the fact that he, as a former combatant, had been spared to go to a London ballroom again, to meet 'one's ... friends ... and to dance in a proper spirit of pure comradeship with real pretty girls in an atmosphere almost attuned to heroism by the many empty sleeves among the men'.[10]

The determination to make a fresh start after 1918 was equally apparent among the hunting fraternity. According to *The Field*, by March 1919 many hunts had already relaunched themselves, to the satisfaction of those returned officers who had previously only been able to 'snatch an occasional day' with the hounds during their leave. They included some who had been invalided out of the Army; 'Your enthusiastic hunting man does not allow such disabilities as a lost arm or injured leg to interfere with the sport if he can help it.'[11]

Nonetheless it was the popularity of dancing that dominated the post-war social scene. As Loelia Ponsonby, later the Duchess of Westminster, recalled, 'Supported by nothing but tea or coffee (a glass of sherry would have turned it into an orgy) we fox-trotted tirelessly till it was time to dash home and change into evening dress for a real dance ... Dancing was more than a craze, it had become a sort of mystical religion.' If by chance no formal *thé dansant* was available for Loelia and her friends, they would meet at the home of one of them 'and as soon as tea was swallowed, [we] wound up the gramophone, put on a record and began practising new steps'.[12]

Interestingly, too, there was a return of chaperones. During the war years these had been largely dispensed with for young women who were following independent careers as volunteer nurses, land workers, and motor drivers, or were engaged in other areas of war production. But with the coming of peace, there was a desire, at least among some of the older generation, for a return to this pre-war convention. *The Bystander* in April 1920 welcomed the trend, claiming that they prevented 'boredom, and are responsible for the conveyance of their charges to their domiciles. Men ... are beginning to feel that since women have the vote and claim a sex equality they shouldn't put men to the expense of their taxi-fare, after the dances.'[13] A month later *The Tatler* gave fulsome praise to the 'marvellously well-chaperoned' dance that Lady Falmouth had given for her 'young daughter ... who is eighteen this year. Quite along the old lines, ... with goodly rows of dowagers complete with tiaras ... very young men, with white kid gloves, and clumps of girls standing in the doorways ... Marvellous band, marvellous floor, and ... a marvellous supper.' *The Tatler* even mentioned an advertisement by a 'Lady of Title' who was willing to chaperone a 'Young Girl of Good Social Standing', for a fee. The lady in question had a large house and would escort her charge to Mayfair dances in the afternoon or evening, as well as being prepared to let her own 'Beautiful Ball-room' to families wishing to arrange their own dances. As *The Tatler* commented drily, 'Sign of the times, isn't it? ... Anything to turn an honest penny – or rather, now in the full flood tide of the dance craze – an honest pound or two.' In earlier times such a venture would have 'turned our grandmothers green with horror'.[14] The families expected to take advantage of such an offer were the *nouveau riche*, anxious to assimilate themselves into aristocratic circles.

The more spirited girls resented the restrictions, however, and sought to evade them, if necessary, like Lady Diana Manners, by subterfuge. Edwina Ashley, daughter of a Hampshire landed family and granddaughter of the immensely rich financier Sir Ernest Cassel, fell into this category, too. Although she recognised it was impossible to go to restaurants or private supper clubs in the evening unchaperoned, as her grandfather would be sure to hear of it, she 'discovered small cafés for intimate lunches ... Friends with motors were a godsend.' Edwina learnt to be vague about her precise doings, letting it be assumed she was with a married cousin, whom Sir Ernest considered a suitable chaperone, while she kept that cousin in the dark as to her true intentions. This was unfair to the cousin, who felt 'she should know where Edwina was, and with whom, in case there was an accident'.[15] Even after her marriage in 1922 to Lord Louis Mountbatten, a relative of the royal family, Edwina continued to pursue an unconventional and independent lifestyle.

Dining out became popular again among the social elite, despite complaints about the high prices being charged. In ironic mode *The Bystander*, on 8 January 1919, referred to the manager of a Piccadilly hotel who regretted that he had 'only charged three guineas a head, sans wine, at his New Year's party. For at five guineas apiece he discovered, all too late, he'd still have been turning 'em away! ... Seems as though being a *restauranteur* in this peace year of 1919 is going to be an even fatter job than it was in the war years.' Hotels like the Savoy, Claridge's and The Ritz began to offer dinner and dancing to a clientele who were experiencing a post-war shortage of domestic servants or, with straitened finances, were anxious to limit expenditure on hospitality in a way that was more difficult when lavish provision at home was the alternative. At the Savoy the supper dances were accompanied by cabaret performances, themselves a new departure and one soon adopted elsewhere.[16]

Night-clubs of varying respectability also proliferated at this time. Some, based around Bond Street and Piccadilly, attracted members of the social elite, among them the Prince of Wales. They included the exclusive Embassy, with a high subscription fee. Frances Donaldson remembered first visiting this with her father at the age of seventeen. She recalled the looking-glasses ranged along the walls above the sofas and tables so as to reflect the doings of the high-spirited clientele. The centre of the room served as a dance-floor, although late at night, when the restaurant was full, 'tables placed uncomfortably close together would edge towards the centre of the room, until there was almost no space left in the centre'. At one end was a balcony, which acted as the bandstand. According to Frances, the dominant figure was Luigi, the manager, yet despite his sometimes brusque manner, club members and their friends came night after night, with the food 'always crammed down between dances, drowned with gin-and-tonic, blown over by cigarette-smoke'.[17]

The Prince of Wales attended regularly at the Embassy, often coming with his then mistress and close companion, the Hon. Mrs Freda Dudley Ward, and his younger brother, Prince George, later the Duke of Kent. Mrs Dudley Ward was the estranged wife of a Liberal MP. Petite, dark-eyed and well-dressed, she was the Prince of Wales's principal confidante from 1918 until the early 1930s.[18] In December 1920, she and the Prince of Wales were at a small party also attended by Alfred Duff Cooper. According to him, the prince 'hardly left Freda's side. They say he loves her terribly

... He refused apparently to shake hands with Michael [Herbert] because he is jealous of him.'[19]

One problem for the night-club revellers, however, was the survival of wartime licensing restrictions, under the Defence of the Realm Act (DORA for short). Even when these were somewhat relaxed in 1921 under a new Licensing Act, the concessions were limited. In London, drinks could only be served with food after 11 p.m., so patrons 'submitted willingly to ordering unwanted sandwiches with their drinks and to having their glasses removed at 12.30. In the provinces, the hours were even more restrictive. Furthermore clubs that flouted the law could be raided by the police and the owners fined or have their licences revoked. Those present could be arrested and subsequently fined for drinking after hours. Even the prestigious Kit-Kat Club, which claimed to have thirty peers among its members, was raided on the night following a visit by the Prince of Wales.[20]

In these circumstances, not surprisingly, less respectable night-clubs, often conducted in damp, overcrowded cellars in the back streets of Soho and Leicester Square, sprang up in considerable numbers. They were prepared to risk prosecution in order to boost their membership and their business by breaching the licensing laws. Some earned a reputation as places of ill repute by allowing prostitutes to make contact with potential customers there. In this shadowy world one particularly prominent promoter was Mrs Kate Meyrick, the deserted wife of a Brighton doctor. Initially she seems to have taken up night-club work to pay for her children's education and she began by sharing in the running of a club in Leicester Square. Unfortunately its patrons were not confined to the 'smart set' but included prostitutes and gangsters. As a consequence on 28 January

1920, Mrs Meyrick and her partner were prosecuted, with the magistrate describing the club as 'a sink of iniquity'. Its licence was withdrawn, and Mrs Meyrick was fined £25.[21] Soon after she went into business again, setting up another club, which she subsequently sold, before establishing her famous club at 43 Gerrard Street, under the name of the '43'. Its visitor list included the distinguished and the well-to-do, as well as more dubious characters, such as boxers, jockeys, and the pedlars of sex and drugs. Among the latter were members of a Chinese dope-gang headed by 'Brilliant' Chang. He was a near neighbour of the '43' and Mrs Meyrick claimed she had tried to stop Chang promoting his wares in her club or, indeed, in any other clubs with which she was associated. According to her, at first she did not serve alcohol at the '43', but merely sandwiches and non-alcoholic drinks. Then breakfasts were added to the menu, and soon after that alcohol was introduced. It proved highly profitable. As she later admitted, champagne, which cost her an average of 12s 6d per bottle, was sold during licensed hours at from 22s 6d to 30s a bottle and after legal hours for 30s to £2. 'For beer I paid 4½d per bottle and sold it for 8d during permitted hours and afterwards up to 1s 6d.'[22] She prided herself, too, on the breadth of her clientele.

> There were nights when the '43' might almost have been mistaken for an overflow meeting from the House of Lords, with princes, dukes, earls, and countesses all moving in a light-hearted maze beneath the gay streamers and balloons. On other nights I have seen my dance-floor scintillating with foreign orders, with assorted faces of every hue ... Sometimes the predominant note was struck by the stage, at other times by high finance.[23]

Interestingly, three of her own daughters eventually married into the aristocracy.

Unfortunately for Mrs Meyrick, her cavalier attitude towards the licensing laws led to the '43' being raided for the first time in 1923 and she was fined £300 for serving drinks after hours.[24] On this occasion she was allowed to pay in instalments, but that proved to be the precursor of many such Court appearances, despite the fact that she had apparently paid 'protection' money to at least one metropolitan police sergeant. Ultimately she had six spells in Holloway, prior to her death in 1933. During her absence the '43' and the other night-clubs she owned were kept running by her family and friends. Barbara Cartland, who knew Mrs Meyrick, considered her an attractive personality who displayed 'warmth and originality'.[25] Her more rakish wealthy clients, meanwhile, clearly enjoyed the frisson of mixing with the prostitutes and 'roughs' who were also patrons.

But in the long run the police raids and attempts by the Home Office to clamp down on the clubs did have an effect in diminishing their numbers. During the half-year to June 1924, for example, there were estimated to be forty night-clubs in the Metropolitan area, of which six had been deregistered during that period and a further one had gone out of business. There had also been eight police prosecutions, all of them successful, and on eight occasions premises had been raided by the police, according to the Home Secretary.[26]

The West End theatres, too, were attracting large audiences at this time. 'The stage was very much a part of our life', wrote Barbara Cartland. 'We went to every new show, we discussed it, criticised it and were absorbed it.'[27] Contemporary diaries show that dinner, followed by a visit to the theatre and attendance at a ball provided an evening's entertainment for many members of High Society during the London Season. Typical of such entries was that by Lord Winterton for 29 May 1919:

> Dolly Rawson, the Edward Wyndhams, Miss Barbara Lutyens and young Spicer dined with me and we went to see a moderate play 'Kissing Time' ... Then I drove Miss Lutyens on to the Dudleys Ball which was enormous fun. Most of one's friends old and young and yet plenty of room to dance.[28]

The opera, too, had its ardent supporters, with Lady Cunard among its keenest advocates, inspired by her devotion to the leading conductor, Sir Thomas Beecham (as he had now become) and by her genuine enjoyment of music. Eddie Winterton paid tribute to her 'civic patriotism' in promoting the opera and to her 'kindness of heart', although, like other aristocrats, he had reservations about her general conduct. 'She is a curious character. A bad wife and a worse mother with the worst attributes in some ways of the Nouveaux Riches, and causing almost a scandal by her display of riches.'[29]

For the male members of society there were their clubs, which offered dining facilities, conviviality, and opportunities for gambling as well, in some cases. According to Philip Ziegler, Duff Cooper's 'spiritual home was White's, playing bridge for high stakes, drinking and talking until late into the night'. On Derby Day in 1921 he went to the club to get his hair cut and made a triumphant entry in his diary that the barber had given him a tip for the race. 'I backed it £10 each way, a large bet for me, and it won at 6 to 1.' It was surprising that he considered £10 a large bet to place on a horse when he was willing to lose hundreds of pounds at *chemin de fer* and other gambling games. 'I must confess,' he declared snobbishly to his wife, 'that the only milieu I really like is the "smart set." I hate the provincialism of the respectable as much as I hate the Bohemianism of the unrespectable.'[30] Duff's diary confirms, too, his clandestine meetings with various female friends who had temporarily attracted his roving eye. That applied both before and after his marriage to Lady Diana Manners in June 1919. Typical of many such confessions was that for 1 November 1919, less than six months after the wedding:

> I arranged – secretly to lunch with Diana Capel … I had to lie terribly [to his wife]. We lunched at Sherry's and it was very agreeable. Intrigue of this sort has a fatal fascination. I don't care for her one thousandth part as much as I care for my own Diana, and when I got back to the latter and found her very low with a headache … but believing all my lies, I felt a monster of wickedness and cruelty.[31]

But these pangs of conscience did not prevent another secret assignation with Diana Capel four days later, or his many similar meetings with her and other women with whom he had sexual encounters of varying intensity. Lady Diana rarely displayed jealousy, however, realising that he was intensely sensual. Physically he could not content himself with having just one woman and even before his honeymoon was over; he was seeking extra-marital diversions. He himself recognised his weakness. 'My infidelities are entirely of the flesh,' he wrote on one occasion. 'The long habit of promiscuity asserts itself. I feel guilty of no unfaithfulness, only of filthiness.'[32] As for Lady Diana, her own sex drive was weak, and in some ways the large number of Duff's conquests reassured her that although they satisfied his lust, she alone possessed his love and support.

Like many others in their circle in the early 1920s, they enjoyed an active social life. During the last three months of 1920, for instance, they spent just five evenings alone together at home. For the rest, they went to the theatre fourteen times, and the cinema eight; they had seven weekends away at the homes of friends, as well as paying several visits to Lady Diana's home, Belvoir Castle. They spent four days in Paris, where life became still more hectic, and Duff passed, on average, eight to ten hours a week at White's. When he was so engaged Diana spent time with her own friends. Yet, as Lady Diana's biographer, Philip Ziegler, points out, they never grew apart: 'on the contrary each was amused by and interested in the other's private life and each prised the other's company more and more highly.'[33] Like other socialites they also resumed their pre-war foreign holidays, visiting the Riviera and spending their honeymoon in Italy.

Duff and Diana's participation in Saturday to Monday house parties at the homes of friends was typical of many other members of their circle. These breaks offered opportunities not merely for gossip but for tennis, golf, punting, and dancing, or for quieter pleasures like fishing. There was usually a plentiful supply of alcohol and many opportunities for practical jokes. As *The Bystander* commented, once such tricks would have been the preserve of the young, but 'since grandmothers have taken to wearing short frocks, and grandfathers may be seen in restaurants dancing between courses', guests of the older generation were also joining in. As well as the usual apple pie beds, the ends of pyjama legs and sleeves would be sewn up with double thread and, more unpleasantly, treacle might be smeared on hair brushes.

Barbara Cartland, who attended house parties at that time, remembered playing these tricks herself or being the victim of them, with pillows smothered with flour or a bunch of holly placed strategically at the foot of an apple-pie bed.[34]

Of course, not all house parties were so unconventional. In mid-June 1920 Duff and Diana Cooper went to Blenheim Palace, and Duff was much impressed not only with the grandeur of the Palace but with the fact that the Duke of Marlborough kept 'high state':

> wears his Garter for dinner and has a host of powdered footmen. The dining room is beautiful and so is the bridge over the lake. There was a party of about 20 people. We had the most magnificent bedroom – the best in the house – I don't know why.[35]

But as Barbara Cartland noted sadly, there were many families for whom house parties, to say nothing of stables and carriages, were no longer feasible. With the death or serious injury of a father or husband, incomes were much reduced. In these circumstances, a number of wives and daughters, like Lady Cynthia Asquith, had themselves to seek paid employment. Lady Diana Cooper, too, was keen to boost her finances and to that end was willing to accept gifts in cash and kind from wealthy friends and admirers, both before her marriage and after. Indeed the need became more pressing when, despite the bitter opposition of her parents, she married Duff Cooper. At that time he was a Foreign Office clerk with a limited income and expensive tastes, whom the Duchess of Rutland considered was a mere penniless drunkard with undesirable friends. On the eve of their marriage, however, a wealthy American admirer, George Moore, deposited £500 in Lady Diana's bank account, and also guaranteed her overdraft at the bank. He even took a box at Covent Garden in her name.[36]

Rather more lucrative, however, were her forays into journalism, although, in reality, the articles appearing under her name were penned by Duff. On 20 December 1918, almost six months before their wedding, he and Diana dined with the press magnate, Lord Beaverbrook, who was a long-time admirer of Diana. In the course of conversation he mentioned the new Sunday newspaper, the *Sunday Express*, which he was about to launch. He then offered Diana £200 to contribute four articles to it. She accepted at once and 'he then and there wrote her a cheque for the whole sum', noted Duff, while 'I racked my brain to find subjects for the four articles.'[37] By February 1919 the four had grown to eight and the remuneration had increased to £400. In 1921, Diana even became editress of the English edition of a French magazine, *Femina*, with a salary of £750 per annum proposed. Unfortunately she had no idea how to edit a journal, took little interest in the project, and expected her husband to write most of the articles. Unsurprisingly, the venture collapsed in a few months. More successful were her contributions to the *Daily Mail* and the *Daily Express*, with Duff again doing most of the work. It was her beauty and her fame as a fashion icon that gave her this valuable entré into the world of journalism. For the same reason she was offered 'as many dresses as she [liked] for nothing as an advertisement' by the leading Paris fashion designer, Edward Molyneux, in March 1921. In June of that year Lady Diana also appeared in *The Tatler* modelling hats for Ascot on behalf of 'Rose Bertin'.[38] But most lucrative of all these early money-making activities was her entry into acting for the cinema. Although the two films she made in 1920–21 were mediocre at best, despite her friends loyally reassuring her that her own performances were creditable, Duff Cooper noted on 1 June 1921, that the producer, J. Stuart Blackton, had already paid her £1,000. More was promised, but Blackton was experiencing difficulties, his financial backers having let him down. In the years ahead, however, Lady Diana was to earn many thousands of pounds by appearing on stage. It was her money-making ability which not only helped to cover some of Duff's gambling debts but enabled him to abandon his unrewarding Foreign Office career for that of a Member of Parliament. This led eventually to ministerial office and to his appointment as Ambassador to France.

Few other female members of High Society were able to achieve the earning capacity, or the fame, of Lady Diana Cooper. But for a number of young unmarried women there was a sense of anti-climax when they returned to civilian life after their wartime employment. It was a desire for an occupation that led Lady Marjorie Dalrymple, a relative of the Earl of Stair, to contact Lady Airlie in October 1920, asking her, as a lady-in-waiting to Queen Mary, how she, Lady Marjorie, could get an appointment in royal service. 'I am somewhat ashamed of bothering you thus, please forgive me,' she wrote. 'I suppose my only excuse is that after much occupation during the war one wants to do something, and it is horrid being an idler.' Unfortunately, however, when Lady Airlie broached the subject to Queen Mary, the queen dismissed it out of hand, declaring she did not think Lady Marjorie was 'suitable'.[39]

But these social changes represented only one aspect of society coming to terms with the new post-1918 world order. Beneath the frantic pleasure seeking there were also continuing signs of stress. One aspect of this was a resort to drug-taking by some of the more reckless members of the social elite. Even Lady Diana Cooper resorted to morphia on occasion, to her husband's concern, but perhaps his influence, plus her own will-power, prevented her becoming an addict. Others were less fortunate. There was a growing circulation of different drugs, including opium, heroin and cocaine. On 7 April 1920, *The Bystander* claimed it was in the 'restaurant-haunting, night-club-dancing semi-underworld that the cocaine habit [had] its votaries. The pace is so fast that they can't keep it up without the constant stimulant, and, with so many of them, men and women alike, there is the unending need for money or the fear of the police.' The habit was to persist among some sectors of society throughout the 1920s and it formed the background of Noel Coward's play, *The Vortex*, in 1925. In the case of young socialites like Brenda Dean Paul, it led to years of ill-health and despair as they sought, often in vain, to cure their addiction.[40]

Within society at large there was the continuing need to come to terms with the loss of sons, husbands, fathers and close friends in the war, and among many of the men who had survived there was often a latent sense of guilt. Significantly when Duff Cooper had his 'bachelor' dinner at the Savoy Hotel on 31 May 1919, two days before his wedding to Lady Diana, he confessed the next day to her and to Katharine Asquith how much he had 'missed the dead at it ... How easily would I have replaced the eleven living with eleven dead all of whom – or at least eight out of the eleven – I should have loved better.' Even on their honeymoon in Florence, he and Diana talked about their dead friends until Diana was reduced to tears.[41]

The continuing popularity of spiritualist séances was another sign of the underlying sense of loss. It was claimed, indeed, that in the immediate post-war years, séances had become 'almost as plentiful as dances, with the result that the cleverer mediums [were] booked as far ahead as seats at a popular revue.' However, as *The Bystander* warned, in many cases trickery and deceit were resorted to in order to encourage grief-stricken wives and mothers that contact was being made with those whom they mourned. Some mediums employed as agents 'women in Society' who for a fee would, 'by stories of wonderful manifestations' and accounts of how 'dear Lady So-and-so had a message from her boy', boost attendance at the séances. They were often able to pass on information about the physical appearance or other characteristics of the deceased to assist the medium to defraud the bereaved. In such cases the victim of this deceit might return several times to the medium, unaware that a proportion of the guineas she was paying 'so gladly and lavishly goes into the pocket of the friend who recommended the medium'.[42]

Other families derived comfort from visiting the graves of their dead sons and husbands in the war cemeteries. They included Ettie Desborough, who in May 1919, with her surviving son and elder daughter, Monica, spent a hectic few days in Paris, shopping and attending various social events. Then she and Monica enjoyed a brief break in the peace of the Fontainebleau forest before they visited Julian's grave. Billy, of course, had no grave. 'I dreaded coming back here in a way, as well as longed to,' Ettie confessed to Mary Wemyss, a fellow mourner. 'All the five years seemed to sweep before one.'[43] As Richard Davenport-Hines notes, most of the 'bereaved mothers thought tenderly of one another during their pilgrimages to war cemeteries.' During that same May of 1919, for example, Lady Kenmare visited the grave of her son, Dermot. As she later told her friend, Lady Desborough, it was 'all so beyond comprehension, the wide battlefields, so awful so terrible; the strange hush over all that devastation, the grim ruins, the piteous little crosses standing here and there in utter loneliness; one's mind and soul seemed to break'.[44]

War memorials began to be erected throughout the country and included the unveiling of the Cenotaph in London by King George V on Armistice Day in November 1920. The Desboroughs commissioned their own memorial to their dead sons in the grounds of their Taplow home. In December 1920 they also attended a commemorative ceremony at their sons' school. 'A bronze frieze running along a wall of Founder's Quad recorded the name of 1,157 Etonians who had perished', a figure representing around one in five of the 5,650 Etonians who had served in the First World War.[45] That total took no account of those survivors who had been permanently maimed in body or mind.

The general sense of flux within society likewise probably contributed to the rising divorce rate during the post-war years. Although for women in particular, divorce still carried with it a certain stigma, including exclusion from Court and a refusal of admission to the Royal Enclosure at Ascot, the social penalty was far less severe than had been the case before 1914. Hence by 26 January 1921, *The Tatler* was referring to the perfect 'maze of divorces' that that were taking place. Three months later *The Bystander* claimed that the 'Lord Chancellor ... had to lend a hand in the overwhelming work of the Divorce Courts, such a record crowd is there of petitions'. According to Barbara Cartland, by 1919–20 the number of divorce petitions had risen to 4,874 compared with an annual average of 965 in 1911 to 1913. She considered the war was largely responsible for this, not merely on account of the disruption to family life that long separation had inevitably entailed but because of the 'emotional urgency of marrying a man who might be killed' within a few weeks of the marriage. Then, when the bridegrooms returned at the war's end, the couple found they had little in common. In one case a friend of Barbara Cartland had married a V.C. when he was still in the Army. But 'he seemed so completely different out of uniform in a worn blue serge suit,' she confessed to Barbara, that she had left him. She could hardly believe 'it was the same man! ... but he did look awful'.[46]

In some cases, as with the dukes of Westminster and Marlborough, marriages which had broken up before the war were ended by divorce in its immediate aftermath. To conform to the gentlemanly procedure of allowing a wife to divorce her husband, it was customary for the man to commit adultery by arrangement with a 'professional' co-respondent. The Duke of Marlborough, for example, in February 1920 booked into Claridge's Hotel under the name of Spencer and spent the night with a hired co-respondent, thereby establishing the necessary 'grounds' for divorce.[47] Usually a chambermaid would give evidence that they had spent a night together, but sometimes a private detective would be hired for the purpose, as was the case with the Duchess of Westminster when she divorced the duke.[48] Divorce lawyers, 'winking at the collusive irregularity, were usually able to fix the husband up with a professional "woman unknown" and with chambermaids' evidence'.[49] Ironically in neither case did the ducal remarriages prove a success. The Duke of Westminster's second wife was a divorcee Violet Nelson, whom he married in November 1920. But the social elevation this represented seems to have gone to Violet's head. Her pretentiousness alienated her husband from many former close friends and the marriage ended in divorce in 1924.[50]

The Duke of Marlborough married his long-term mistress, Gladys Deacon, in 1921 but they, too, became estranged from one another in less than a decade, with the duchess growing increasingly eccentric and the duke remaining as self-centred as ever. Until the passage of the Matrimonial Causes Act in 1923, a woman bringing a petition for divorce not only had to prove adultery but also to provide some other cause, such as cruelty or desertion, although for a man adultery alone had sufficed. After the implementation of the 1923 Act, however, adultery by either spouse became a sufficient reason for divorce.[51]

These social trends in the post-war years were joined by another unsatisfactory development, namely the sale of honours by the Lloyd George government. Although Lloyd George was the coalition's Prime Minister, after his split with the Asquithian Liberals he lacked a party machine to provide funds to fight elections or to promote his personal political cause. The 'sale' of titles, in return for a discreet payment to Party funds, was certainly not new in the immediate post-war period, but Lloyd George carried it through more systematically than had hitherto been the case. This angered his Conservative Party allies in the coalition, who saw funds being diverted from their own party coffers to the benefit of Lloyd George. The coalition's Liberal Whip, Freddie Guest, distanced himself from the process by employing a dubious character named Maundy Gregory to arrange the transactions. He in turn organised touts, whom Guest described as 'grubby little men in brown bowler hats', who also shared in the proceeds.[52] Among those taking advantage of these offers were businessmen who had done well in the war and now wished to establish themselves and their families in 'respectable' elite society. Knighthoods were said to cost £10,000 to £12,000 apiece, baronetcies around

£35,000 to £40,000 and peerages were still more costly. Some shrewd businessmen, however, were able to negotiate a deal for a lower payment. To established members of the aristocracy and gentry this blatant means of boosting Lloyd George's personal finances was an outrage. In July 1922, for example, the Duke of Northumberland quoted a letter from one tout who claimed, shortly before the Lloyd George coalition fell: 'There are only 5 knighthoods left for the June List ... It is not likely that the next Government will give so many honours, and this is really an exceptional opportunity.' The recipient was warned that there was 'no time to be lost if you wish to take it'. However, if he decided 'upon a baronetcy', he might have to wait 'for the Retiring List'.[53] In the same House of Lords debate the Marquess of Crewe complained that the number of additions to the Upper House in 1922 had been 'very large'... the number of distinctions conferred had included 10 Peerages, 32 baronetcies, and 141 knighthoods'. *The Times*, too, in commenting on a new annual edition of Debrett's appearing in December 1921, had noted that 'in its five years of office' Lloyd George's administration had 'made the largest number of peerages created by any Government in modern times'.[54] Altogether over the period 1919 to 1922 alone the Prime Minister had recommended thirty-seven peerages. He also created 134 baronets over that period, including forty-four in 1919 and thirty-nine in 1921.[55] Knighthoods abounded, with one contemporary declaring acidly that Cardiff was 'appropriately nicknamed the "City of dreadful Knights"'.[56]

It was not, however, merely the volume of those so honoured that gave rise to criticism but the quality of some of those recommended. As Douglas Goldring declared, they included 'men whose surnames stank' but who 'concealed them under titles which recalled the chivalry of Feudal

England'. Among them were Sir William Vestey (who received a barony) and was described as a 'wartime tax dodger'; Rowland Hodge (made a baronet) who had been convicted for food hoarding; and Sir Joseph Drughorn, who was also awarded a baronetcy despite being 'convicted for trading with the enemy'.[57] Lloyd George himself justified the procedure to a friend. 'You and I know that the sale of honours is the cleanest way of raising money for a political party,' he declared. 'The worst of it is you cannot defend it in public.' The scandal gave valuable ammunition to his enemies and was a factor in his downfall, even if it was not its sole cause.[58] But these developments came at a time when the landed classes felt themselves under growing threat from high taxation, declining incomes, and political condemnation. That undoubtedly added venom to their parliamentary comments. It is to the response of the landed interest to the political and economic problems they faced in the post-war period that we must now turn.

Landownership in the Aftermath of the War

At a time of mounting industrial unrest within mainland Britain and of serious violence in Ireland, where a number of elite families still owned estates, there was a growing sense of unease among the landed classes. That was further fuelled by an awareness of the revolutionary turmoil in Europe, not least in Russia, where the Bolsheviks had first imprisoned and then murdered the Royal Family. Among the more sensitive members of the British nobility and gentry this led to an increasing awareness of the contrasts between the wealth of some of their number and the poverty of many of their fellow citizens. Hence Lord Winterton on 10 July

1919, when he attended the Duchess of Northumberland's dinner and dance at luxurious Syon House, was struck by

> the contrast between the squalor of Brentford and the great sweep of the Park at Syon all kept by police with a magnificent uniformed porter to salute one with a dignified hat raise at the entrance, left 'rather a nasty taste'. – As for the dinner party it was like 'old England before the flood' or perhaps one ought to say 'Old France before the Revolution'. Garters were commonplace, medals banal ... and the dance that followed was very royal & ancien régime.[59]

A few months earlier, when Winterton had dined at D'Eresby House in London with Lord and Lady Ancaster, he had again commented on the wealth and luxury displayed, with the American-born Lady Ancaster 'looking like I know not what in her very artificial get up. One could not help contrasting this with the seething unrest o'er the realm & with Germany, Petrograd, Vienna & the rest. Is it our 1788?'[60] The latter year had marked the beginning of the French Revolution, which had led to the overthrow of the established ruling class in France.

The government, too, was aware of workers' anger and discontent within many of the country's major industries, which had manifested itself in a number of large-scale strikes, as for example on 26 September 1919, on the railways over pay. The government's reaction to this was to call out the troops in large numbers and to begin to enrol 'Citizen Guards'. A plan for emergency road transport was implemented, with drivers registered and lorries requisitioned to provide for the distribution of food.[61] Initially it was feared that the dispute would lead to a general strike. Indeed, a Foreign Office colleague of Duff Cooper expressed a fear that they were at 'the beginning of revolution'. Duff himself noticed that St James's Street was full of policemen and that the Horse Guards Parade was thronged with sailors and motor lorries. He referred frivolously to 'rather a pleasant scent of excitement and revolution in the air'.[62] Some volunteers, including Lord Montagu of Beaulieu, who perhaps bizarrely was a trained engine driver, helped to maintain a skeleton rail service.[63]

Eddie Winterton, coming up to London from his Sussex home, was reassured by the atmosphere of calm that apparently prevailed in the capital. That applied, too, at both the Carlton and the Turf Clubs which he visited. As he observed drily: 'Neither the plutocratic or aristocratic club seem much affected by the strike.' He visited the Chapman Estate in the East End of London also, and again calm prevailed. However, he noted that the womenfolk seemed 'anxious but perhaps no more than they usually do in a quarter where the necessities of life are a perpetual anxiety'. In the end it had been very much a 'day of contrasts!!'[64] The strike ended on 5 October, after the government agreed to maintain existing wage levels for a further year.[65]

More serious was the coal strike which occurred in 1921, when the economy was already moving into recession, after a brief post-war boom. On 31 March in that year the government had ended its wartime control over the mining industry, and sharp wage reductions were proposed for the now deregulated sector. On 1 April the coal strike began, and again there were fears that this would lead to a general strike. Once more that did not occur but already on 31 March the government had declared a state of emergency. Once more the armed forces were mobilised and public parks, including Hyde Park and Regent's Park, became huge vehicle depots. Motor vehicles were requisitioned for the distribution of food and essential supplies, and a special Defence Force of volunteers was created, with 75,000 recruits coming forward in ten days. Fortunately the Defence Force, with its overtones of civil conflict, was never deployed.[66]

But this time, unlike during the brief rail strike, the dispute impinged more seriously on the lives of the social elite. With fuel supplies restricted, the Courts for the presentation of débutantes were postponed, and many balls and other celebrations cancelled. *The Bystander* of 22 June 1921 consoled itself with the fact that Royal Ascot at least was to be held and theatregoing had begun to recover. The strike eventually ended on 1 July, with the miners having to accept defeat.

These disruptions within Britain itself, however, were insignificant when compared to the violence which had broken out in parts of Ireland. The struggle for Irish independence had entered a new phase, with the Irish Free State finally established in 1922. But already in January 1919, following the general election held the previous December, Sinn Fein members meeting in Dublin had adopted a declaration of independence and had set up their own Parliament. If necessary independence was to be achieved by a resort to violence, perpetrated by members of the Irish Republican Army (IRA), which represented the militant wing of Sinn Fein.[67]

The British government responded by recruiting unemployed ex-servicemen as auxiliary policemen. They were quickly labelled the Black and Tans on account of the khaki uniforms and black berets they wore. As Anne de Courcy comments, 'Their reprisals to IRA outrages were as brutal as those of their opponents', and the feelings of bitterness and hatred intensified.[68] Houses owned by Protestant Anglo-Irish landowners were burned down towards the end of 1921. In one case, masked men entered the house of Lady Una Ross at Strangford and forced her and her maids into the garden and made them watch the burning of the house and its contents. At nearby Castle Ward, the home of Lord Bangor, he and his family were defended by B Specials, volunteers enlisted for that purpose. Even Lord and Lady Londonderry at their palatial home, Mount Stewart, were guarded by B Specials and Lady Londonderry slept with a set of day clothes by her bed and a revolver in a bedside drawer when she stayed at Mount Stewart. However, the Troubles did not prevent her and her husband from visiting their Irish property and entertaining guests there.[69]

Even when, in December 1921, articles of agreement for a treaty between Great Britain and Ireland to establish the Free State were drawn up, the unrest continued within Ireland as substantial sections of the political leadership there repudiated the treaty.[70] In the meantime, before the Free State was set up, more than three-quarters of the land previously owned by large landlords had been voluntarily disposed of to tenants. However, under a new Act of 1923 passed by the freshly installed Irish government, the remaining land not yet tenant-owned was vested in a Land Commission which compensated the former owners at a standard price. By the 1920s, therefore, there were virtually no great estates left in Ireland. At best, 'the patricians held on to their ancestral mansion and perhaps the park ... "Landlordism" had disappeared from Ireland.'[71]

It was against this post-war background, therefore, that landowners in mainland Britain considered their options. Although the violence suffered in Ireland was not anticipated, there were other factors causing disquiet and encouraging them to consider diversifying their wealth away from a concentration on land. Foremost among these was the fact that despite a government commitment to guarantee the prices of cereal crops and potatoes under the Corn Production Act of 1917, introduced at a time of serious wartime food shortage, landlords had not benefited. Only the farmers had gained and that remained the case when the guarantee system was renewed under the Agriculture Act of 1920. This led to a willingness on the part of some tenant farmers to consider buying their holdings, should the opportunity arise, rather than continuing to rent. At the same time landowners, who had been prevented from raising rents during the war, had only raised them by about 15 per cent on average after 1918, at a time when their outgoings were increasing sharply.[72]

Then, in 1921, as the disruptions to food production and distribution during and immediately after the war were slowly eliminated, the price of cereals fell rapidly, dropping in the case of wheat from 18s 10d a hundredweight in 1920 to 16s 8d in 1921. For barley and oats the decline was still more severe.[73] The government, fearing it would be faced with a bill of some £20 million under the guarantee system, hastily ended it by passing the 1921 Corn Production (Repeal) Act. Among farmers there were feelings of angry betrayal, and as food prices continued to slide, landowners were obliged to reduce their rents once more, to keep their tenants in business. Sometimes these dropped by as much as 25 per cent during the 1920s. In other cases rents were remitted altogether, in order to ensure that the land remained under cultivation.

It was not, however, merely the unsatisfactory level of rentals that encouraged landowners to contemplate selling at least part of their estates. Rising taxation was another factor.

During the war income tax levels had risen inexorably, and a new super tax had been introduced on incomes in excess of £10,000 per annum. This was retained and increased thereafter. Furthermore it was levied on gross income rather than net, thereby proving especially disadvantageous to landowners who had large outgoings on property maintenance and improvement, to say nothing of their wider philanthropic obligations within local communities.[74] Another factor encouraging the sale of land was the raising of death duty in 1919 to 40 per cent on estates valued at £2 million or more, compared with the pre-war levy of 15 per cent. Still more seriously from the point of view of the landowner, an estate was to be valued at the current selling price of land rather than, as had previously been the case, on its rental value. At a time when land was still very much under-rented and land prices were buoyant, in the immediate aftermath of the war, this made the potential burden of death duties still greater.[75]

Then, too, many owners wished to boost their personal income by investing in assets other than land. The immensely wealthy Duke of Westminster, for example, despite his ownership of valuable real estate in London,

> was sure that the secure future of the Grosvenor fortune must be safeguarded outside … of England. Every decision he made was to protect long-term interests: all the proceeds from the property to be sold and the assets he liquidated went to pay off mortgages and family obligations – £900,000 worth – or to buy land abroad that he thought in fifty or 100 years would still return a safe profit.[76]

He foresaw a continuation of high taxation on landed property and although he was condemned by some critics for his large sales of inherited land and his purchase of property in Australia, South Africa, Canada and elsewhere, he was not deterred. A part of the Eaton estate in Cheshire was sold for £330,000, while in London a number of properties he owned in Pimlico were disposed of for £1.1 million. Nor did he confine his sales to bricks and mortar, accepting a price variously put at between £200,000 and £750,000 for Gainsborough's famous painting *The Blue Boy*, Sir Joshua Reynolds' work, *Mrs Siddons as the Tragic Muse* and a lesser-known Gainsborough painting, *The Cottage Door*. They were disposed of through a well-known contemporary art dealer, Sir Joseph Duveen, who was acting for an American client.[77]

The pressures of taxation, rising costs of estate maintenance, and uncertainty as to the future status of landownership which had encouraged the Duke of Westminster to diversify his assets affected other owners, too. As the 17th Earl of Derby, the so-called 'King of Lancashire', declared ironically in 1923, 'taxation at the present moment is so high that I may call myself a tax collector for the government. At present I am not living on my income. I am living on my capital.' Likewise Lord Clinton in 1919 estimated that on a group of estates with an average gross rental of £20,000, expenditure on income tax, tithe and rates had absorbed £15,800, leaving the owners with an income of just 4s 6d in the pound out of which they must pay for the maintenance of the estate and other fixed outlays. This he compared with 10s in the pound that could be obtained on an equivalent income derived from government bonds or similar securities.[78] Significantly, the Duke of Devonshire, who retained several core estates and four large country houses, was by the 1920s earning more from stock dividends than from agriculture.[79]

These comparisons, drawing attention to the heavy tax burdens faced by landowners, continued to be made over the following years. In July 1921, for instance, in a leading article headed 'Landowners Bled White', *Country Life* examined a number of 'typical' estates selected from different parts of Scotland. In one case the figures showed that whereas parish and borough rates, land tax, heritor's assessment, and other public and parochial burdens had amounted to £2,320 in 1911–12, by 1920–21 they had climbed to £4,838. The costs of management had similarly grown from £1,210 in 1911–12 to £1,677 in 1920–21, while renewals, repairs and improvements had risen from £3,069 at the earlier date to £4,983. Income tax had nearly quadrupled, from £636 in 1911–12 to £2,342 in 1920–21. No personal expenses, according to *Country Life*, were included in these figures.

> The rentals ... are confined to the strictly agricultural parts of the estate. They do not include any rent, whether estimated or actual, for the house, garden, shooting, nor in the outlay is there included any attributable to such 'amenities'.[80]

This estate had been particularly hard hit but *Country Life* maintained that its experience was not unique. It was located in the counties of Moray and Inverness and the accounts showed that overall, net income had disappeared, and had been replaced by a loss of £621. But even elsewhere the return per pound of gross rental that found its way to the landlord also showed a sharp decline. In the case of property in Forfarshire, for example, the decline was from 11s 5d in the pound before the war to 6s 3d in its aftermath; in Perthshire, Stirling and Lanarkshire, the decrease was from

9s 8¼d to 4s 6¾d in 1920–21, and in Argyll, the respective figures were 5s 3d and 2s 7¾d in the pound.[81]

Even wealthy landowners, like Lord Londonderry and the Duke of Northumberland, who benefited from royalties from coal mines on their estates, were hit by other forms of taxation. In 1918, the Duke of Northumberland had a gross income from mineral royalties of £82,450, but of that he received just £23,890 net, the remainder having gone on a 5 per cent Mineral Rights Duty, an 80 per cent Excess Mineral Rights Duty, income tax at 6s in the pound and supertax at 4s 6d in the pound.[82] Hence, as David Cannadine has pointed out, 'The combination of reduced incomes, increased exactions, and eroded confidence meant that most patricians were obliged to economise and to retrench'.[83] For many the answer was to reduce their obligations by selling land, selling or letting country houses, and disposing of other valuable assets, such as paintings, silver and furniture. The latter was especially the case where a country house was sold and its contents dispersed, with some being taken to another of the properties and the rest auctioned. Where houses could not be sold to new owners for residential purposes, they might be disposed of for other purposes, becoming schools, convalescent homes, hotels, country clubs and similar institutions. Taymouth Castle, sold at the end of 1920, became a hydropathic hotel, and Wrightington Hall near Wigan was acquired in 1921 by Lancashire County Council for a convalescent home. On occasion, when all else failed, houses were sold to property speculators for demolition, thereby ending the landowner's responsibility for maintaining them and enabling the site to be developed for other purposes. The raw materials, including valuable wood panels and marble mantelpieces, were often sold separately to those seeking to embellish their own property.

In a few cases they were exported to the United States of America. In August 1921, *Country Life* reported that Carshalton gates were 'about to be taken to America'.[84] In fact *The Field* advised owners to demolish houses which were merely 'incubuses sitting heavily upon impoverished acres that can no longer support them'. [85]

Against this financial background, therefore, it was accepted that an owner could do very well for himself by selling an asset which perhaps yielded him 3 per cent, clearing off mortgages whose burden had risen during the war, and reinvesting the surplus in trustee securities yielding 7 or 8 per cent.[86] In the immediate post-war period, therefore, many landowners embarked on a feverish sale of substantial parts of their estates, both to reduce the burden of their outgoings and to achieve a better return on capital. One of the early vendors was the Duke of Sutherland, who in 1918 had already sold nearly a quarter of a million acres in Scotland. But it was in the following year that what was described as an 'avalanche' of sales began, with the Duke of Sutherland again in the market, offering a further '114 square miles of the Highlands, with Dornoch castle'.[87] He also sold Lillenhall House in Shropshire and the Trentham estate in Staffordshire, this latter realising £333,000. Although he argued that it was 'unwise to have so much capital tied up in land', even after these major dispersals he remained one of the country's largest owners of land.[88] Other important vendors at this time included Lord Aylesford, who sold 2,000 acres of the outlying portions of his Packington estate in Warwickshire for £65,000. That still left him with 17,000 acres. In Lincolnshire the Earl of Yarborough also sold nearly 2,000 acres out of the 50,000 he owned – with just 346 acres in Grimsby alone realising £41,000. Likewise the Marquess of Northampton disposed of part of his Long Compton estate in Warwickshire and 3,000 acres in Devon.[89]

In March 1919 the Marquess of Aberdeen put the greater part of his Haddo House estate on the market, though the tenants were assured that 'the fullest possible consideration [would] ... be extended to [them] so that they [might] not be dispossessed of their holdings'. The sale involved around 50,000 acres, and was important from an agricultural, residential and sporting point of view. According to *Country Life* it covered five parishes in the centre of the county of Aberdeen, and was approximately 15 miles in length: 'the rental exceeds £28,000 a year ... the population on the portion now in the market is between 5,000 and 6,000 inhabitants'; also included were churches, schools and villages. The sporting possibilities, too, were good, with 'low ground shooting and the salmon and trout fishing' mentioned as being of a 'noteworthy order'.[90] This was all sold for £200,000 and was described as 'the largest break-up sale of high-class agricultural land that has ever taken place in the United Kingdom.[91]

Lord Aberdeen's action did not escape criticism, one female correspondent to *Country Life* accusing him of seeking 'to escape the responsibility of being a large landowner'. Furthermore no financial help was proffered to enable the tenants to keep the land when bought.[92]

In September 1919 the Earl of Pembroke sold 7,000 acres of his 40,000-acre Wilton estate, while the Marquess of Bath disposed of more than a third of his Longleat estate in Wiltshire and Somerset, as well as, in 1920, selling outlying estates at Minsterley in Shropshire and Weobley in Hereford. The sale of 8,600 acres of his Longleat property yielded £50,000.[93] However, the largest vendor in 1920 was probably the Duke of Rutland, who sold land in the nearby market town of Bakewell, along with 13,000 acres of his Belvoir estate and nearly 15,000 acres in Derbyshire. Together these comprised half the land he owned in those two localities. He realised £1.5 million from the sales. A good deal of that vast sum was spent on restoring Haddon Hall in Derbyshire, which the duke handed over to his son and heir, Lord Granby, together with the rest of his Derbyshire estate.[94]

In March 1919 the *Estates Gazette* was already commenting on the 'revolution in landowning' that was taking place, and a month later *The Tatler* referred to the passion for selling up 'land and white elephant estates'. It noted that Lord Northampton had given as his reasons for selling his large Cornish holdings the fact that landownership in general had become unpopular, being 'regarded as a monopoly'; that there were doubts over the government's long-term intentions towards landlords; and Cornwall was a long way from his core estate. Further, his family had only owned it 'for the last century or so'. *The Tatler* then added drily, 'One supposes the new war millionaires and people will buy the big houses'.[95] That did happen in some cases, as the *nouveau riche* sought to acquire high-status landed properties. Hence in September 1921, Compton Verney, the family seat of Lord Willoughby de Broke, was sold to Joseph Watson, 'soap-boiler and racehorse owner', who was created Lord Manton about three months later.[96]

A good deal of land was sold to tenant farmers, so that whereas in 1914 around 11 per cent of the improved land of England and Wales had been owned by its occupiers, including the home farms of the major estate owners, by 1921 that had risen to 20 per cent of the land so owned.[97] And while much of the land might be sold off to farmers or to speculators, and a number of country houses converted to other uses, a minority were demolished when it proved impossible to find a purchaser. That was to be still more the case later in the 1920s.

By the end of 1919, therefore, reports on the land market were full of the phrase 'England is changing hands'. *The Times* took up the call in May 1920, when it declared,

> England is changing hands ... Will a profiteer buy it? Will it be turned into a school or an institution? For the most part the sacrifices are made in silence ... The sons are perhaps lying in far away graves ... and the old people, knowing there is no son or near relative left to keep up the old traditions, or so crippled by necessary taxation that they know the boy will never be able to carry on when they are gone, take the irrevocable step.[98]

In reality that was a far too gloomy conclusion. Many owners were selling simply because it was financially advantageous for them to do so, or they wished to divest themselves of some of the responsibilities of estate ownership. Meanwhile *Country Life* joined in the lament at this exodus 'from the stately homes of England':

> Peer and squire, knight and lady, are forsaking the halls, gardens and grounds which, in many cases were built or laid out centuries ago and bear traces of the loving care bestowed on them by a long succession of owners ... We are not so advanced, or so Bolshevik ... as to feel no regret that these ancient associations should be so shattered.[99]

Landowners, it argued, had become disheartened by those who declaimed against property: and had 'got it into their heads that they [were] not popular with the majority ...

Many are as frightened as mice.' Inevitably this post-war land sale bubble soon burst. It had been sustained in the immediate post-1918 period by the buoyant prices for farm produce, the state guarantees offered to farmers for their cereal crops, which had encouraged them to purchase their holdings, and by the desire of some war profiteers to acquire a landed property to give dignity to their new wealth. But by the end of 1920, a general downturn in the economy began to appear and this intensified in 1921, with agriculturists particularly hit by the repeal of the system of guarantees in that year. At the end of 1921 the *Estates Gazette* claimed that during the previous four years around a quarter of the land of England had changed hands.[100] But from that point estate sales slowed markedly, and even early in 1921 *Country Life* was commenting on the growing demand for 'sporting properties, especially those offering a combination of shooting, fishing and hunting'.[101] In July of that year it reiterated the point, claiming that the 'sporting element' was 'becoming of more and more importance' in regard to the sale and letting of landed property, rather than food production.

Elsewhere, and this was especially true of the deer forests and grouse moors of Scotland, owners were able to derive a valuable income by letting their land to English sportsmen or those from lowland Scotland anxious to pursue their shooting interests.

Finally, in these post-war years it was not just country estates that were being sold, but urban land and large London town houses as well. The Duke of Bedford, for instance, sold £2 million worth of his Bloomsbury ground rents in 1919, while Lord Portman disposed of 7 acres of Marylebone, including 300 houses, five public houses and thirty shops, for £94,000. Lord Southampton, who owned land near Euston Station, sold sites on Euston Road for £73,000, and the Berkeley estate, which adjoined the Duke of Westminster's Mayfair property, was sold by the Earl of Berkeley to Sir Marcus Samuel, later Lord Bearsted, in 1919. *Country Life* applauded that sale, commenting that if London land had to be disposed of 'we can desire nothing better than that it should pass into the hands of men of the standing and personal repute of Sir Marcus Samuel.[102]

As regards town houses, the Marquess of Salisbury sold his Arlington Street home for £120,000 in 1919. It had been in the Cecil family for decades.[103] Lord Dartmouth, too, sold his town house in these post-war upheavals, as did the Duke of Devonshire with the sale of Devonshire House. The latter was to be demolished and the Duchess of Albany's ball held there on 14 April 1920, for a Deptford charity, was its swan song before it was 'handed over to the house-breakers'. Tickets cost three guineas and those attending had to wear eighteenth-century dress. According to *The Tatler* it attracted a thousand guests.[104] On the whole, though, it was later in the decade that the large-scale sale and demolition of many of these once great mansions got under way, as their sites were cleared for more lucrative commercial or residential purposes, including flats.

As in the case of the Duke of Westminster and his sale of some of his valuable pictures, so other grandees put unwanted antiques and works of art on the market. In June 1920, *The Tatler* observed acidly that it seemed 'to be the fashion among our dukes nowadays to sell up anything they've got in the shape of loose property; from live stock to antiques. The dukes of Hamilton, Buccleuch, Rutland, and Sutherland have all had sales pretty recently ... And the Duke of Leeds has been getting high prices for his old English furniture and silver'.[105] The following April it returned to the theme, claiming that 'libraries and pictures and art treasures' were 'all going soon there'll be no sign at all of the glories and traditions of the *ancien regime*, and the only people who'll have money will be the New Rich and the Americans'.[106]

So it was that High Society began to adjust to the new world order after 1918. For some it was a time of severe financial pressure but for others there was the establishment of new priorities and new interests. As the biographer of the Duke of Westminster has put it, his property sales 'in no way meant that he was cutting back on his personal pleasures':

> In 1919 he began to purchase blood stock again ... He also bought the 1,000-ton French merchant ship *Belem* and spent more than £100,000 converting it into a luxurious auxiliary motor-yacht, but in August 1920 he put it up for sale. *Belem* was an expensive toy: the wages bill alone was £700 a month ... Soon after the war ended, [the Duke] ... took a polo team to compete in America, and in April 1922 he revived his famous Eaton Polo Week.[107]

Later another yacht was acquired, there were shooting and fishing parties in Scotland and Scandinavia, and parties for polo and tennis at Mimisan, his estate in France. The duke, with his great wealth, was always on the move and could afford to indulge his many whims. But many other aristocratic families, despite their periodic worries concerning financial matters, were still keen to have a 'good time' after the trauma of the First World War, and to enjoy the pleasures that the 'Roaring Twenties' could offer.

3

Community Responsibilities and Sporting Pursuits

Derby ... was a natural, inevitable and highly successful aristocrat. He took it for granted that his employees, his tenants, his neighbours and, indeed, the entire population of the County Palatine, would expect him to live and behave as his ancestors had done in earlier centuries ... He did not himself care for shooting, but the park maintained an abundance of pheasants and he would often fill the house with relations and dependants and provide for them two shoots a day.

Randolph S. Churchill, *Lord Derby, 'King of Lancashire'*
(London, 1959), pp. 106 and 108.

Sport had become the opium of the upper classes, indicating 'some structural defect in the society which over-indulges it'.

Peter Mandler, *The Fall and Rise of the Stately Home*
(New Haven and London, 1997), p. 244.

Community Roles

As many landowners sold off large parts of their estates in the post-1918 period, either to invest the proceeds more advantageously elsewhere or to reduce their debt burden, their former pre-eminence in national politics was also being undermined by the relentless rise of the middle classes. In these circumstances a number ceased to take on the burdens of public office. Admittedly, grandees like the Earl of Derby and the Marquess of Salisbury, as well as enthusiasts like Earl Winterton, continued to exercise power and influence outside their immediate neighbourhood, but for less vigorous or less ambitious aristocrats, it was only in their own locality that they were considered important. The despondency to which this change of fortune gave rise among some of them was expressed by Lord Willoughby de Broke in 1924 when he noted how rarely 'The County' was spoken of at that date

> in the tone of calm and reverent assurance that we heard when we were young ... In these days people do not remain in the country for long enough at a time to steep themselves in its atmosphere. A dinner-party in the country to-day is hardly distinguishable from a London dinner-party ... There is nothing bucolic about such an entertainment ... A flavour of local gossip may percolate mildly through the evening, but if any one really pulls the handle of the parish pump, he or she will be soon voted a bore ...[1]

Of course, a number of landowners continued to serve as magistrates, even if they were no longer the dominant influence they had once been, and they acted as patrons of the living at their parish church. The magistracy now included some female aristocrats after women became eligible for appointment as Justices of the Peace under the terms of the 1919 Sex Disqualification (Removal) Act. In April 1921, *The Tatler* highlighted this rapid increase in the number of 'lady JPs'. Among them at the end of the decade were such titled magistrates as Lady Mount in Berkshire, Lady Slesser and Lady Susan Trueman in Buckinghamshire, and Viscountess Harcourt in Oxfordshire.[2] Lady Londonderry, too, was sworn in as the first woman magistrate for County Durham. Nonetheless she continued her campaign to achieve equal political rights for men and women, and for the election of female MPs. But at the beginning of 1919 that still seemed a remote possibility. As *The Bystander* of 29 January declared,

> There is a consensus of opinion from agents in the country highly adverse to the prospects of petticoats in Parliament. The electors passionately insist on the male article, however indifferent a performer he may be ... We may be sure that no woman will be ... likely for a long time to ... win an election.

Ten months later, however, Lady Astor contested and won her husband's Plymouth seat when he was raised to the House of Lords, and she thereby became the first woman to take her seat in the House of Commons. Lady Londonderry quickly congratulated her, and in response Nancy Astor admitted, 'I feel you realise what a great responsibility it is.'[3] In the event she needed all her natural strength of character and determination to overcome the hostility and prejudice of some of her male colleagues, including a fellow Conservative, Sir Frederick Banbury. On one occasion she tried to stop him from speaking 'by pulling him down by his coat-tails'.⁴ But even Lord Winterton, who was a close personal friend of the Astors, criticised her efforts to promote a further reform of the franchise in favour of women. On 14 April 1920, he noted that a debate within the Standing Committee to amend the Representation of the People Bill had become

> like a Palais Royale Farce. Constant points of order … a scene between Nancy and old Banbury … The position on the Committee is that there are reactionaries … who are opposed altogether to the principle of women's suffrage, extremists like Nancy and the Labour Party who are far too violent in their support of the Bill and moderates like myself. Nancy also had trouble with Joynson Hicks about her seat, the latter resenting her placing a Committee card where he had previously placed a white card.⁵

However, Lady Astor continued to follow her independent line in Parliament and over the course of the 1920s was joined by other female MPs from all three major political parties. At the 1929 general election fourteen women members were elected, including a few aristocrats, such as the Duchess of Atholl and Lady Cynthia Mosley, daughter of the former Foreign Secretary and Conservative grandee, Lord Curson. She, however, represented the Labour Party.⁶

Significantly, too, despite Lord Willoughby de Broke's lamentations, after 1920 the rural elite did recover some of their former political influence within the countryside by promoting 'new paternalistic institutions like village halls, Women's Institutes, the British Legion, war memorials, and Young Farmers Clubs'. Some of these were designed to improve the quality of life of villagers.⁷ Similarly, leading male members of landed society were called on to fill major 'ceremonial' roles within their county by serving as its Lord-Lieutenant or as chairman of the County Council. David Cannadine notes that in Wiltshire, 'power was divided between the Bath and Lansdowne families'. The Marquess of Bath also chaired the quarter sessions until 1923 and served as Lord Lieutenant of neighbouring Somerset. In Shropshire the County Council was chaired by 'a succession of local landowners', while in Berkshire, 'a tightly-knit group of local gentry virtually monopolised the great county offices'.[8] The Earl of Derby was appointed Lord Lieutenant of Lancashire in 1928, and despite his divorce, the Duke of Marlborough continued as Lord Lieutenant of Oxfordshire into the 1930s. Over the Welsh border, Charles Coltman Rogers chaired the county council from 1896 to 1929. He also became its Lord Lieutenant in 1922. In Brecon, Lord Glanusk held both positions before and after the First World War.

Through their background and education these men were well able to perform the official duties associated with such offices and to uphold the county's dignity. At the same time, many landowners preferred to confine their attention to county matters rather than dabble in national politics:

The work was less contentious, much less demanding, much less expensive, and much less risky to reputation than the rough and tumble of parliamentary public life. In the relative calm of the county council chamber, grandees ... could still dominate with a patrician style no longer acceptable in the Lords or the Commons Aloof, Olympian, and detached ... they lent a tone of aristocratic grandeur to the proceedings and elevated the whole level of county council business.[9]

Some leading figures like Lord Crawford played an important

part in the nation's cultural life. As his biographer points out, within a year of his leaving national politics, in 1922, he had 'acquired "interlocking directorships" stretching across the cultural world: Chancellor of Manchester University, President of the London Society, a member of the committee on the mint, resident of the Society of Antiquaries, trustee of the British Museum and Chairman of the Royal Literary Fund'.[10] He also served on the board of trustees of the National Gallery and the National Portrait Gallery, and was unhappy when in 1930 the Prince of Wales was appointed to the board of the former institution. He was fully aware that the prince had little interest in art or in cultural matters generally, being more involved at that time in golf, gardening and dancing at fashionable nightclubs. Crawford's reservations were confirmed when the prince persisted in gossiping to his neighbours during board meetings and in December 1930 he openly admitted that he had attended one meeting primarily because the king had wished him to shoot at Windsor. 'I don't care much about shooting,' he declared, 'but it was a splendid excuse to say that there was an important Trustees' meeting at Trafalgar Square ... Rather a good score, wasn't it?'[11]

Unlike many fellow peers, Crawford had little interest in field sports. He never fished or hunted and rarely went shooting. Even golf, then gaining rapidly in popularity among the upper classes, did not appeal to him. His interest rather lay in the conservation of the countryside than in the destruction of the creatures living in it, and he was particularly active in promoting the work of the Council for the Preservation of Rural England.

Within his local community Crawford also played a part, opening the war memorial in the parish church at Wigan, where his main country house was located and where his mining interests were based. When his son and heir came of age in June 1922, there were great celebrations in the town, with a supper for estate employees on the Saturday, and a garden party for the public officials of the neighbourhood on the following Monday. This was attended by five to six hundred people. They included the Mayor of Wigan, who presented an illuminated address from the Corporation. The next day another garden party was held, this time for tenants and guests from the Wigan Coal and Iron Company, with 'something like 1,500 people attending'. As Crawford recorded triumphantly in his diary, 'Two more addresses ... The weather was brilliant, and everybody enjoyed themselves immensely.' Later, when the family moved to their Scottish seat in Fife there were more celebrations, with two garden parties held for 300 neighbours and 300 tenants, respectively, and with a dinner for around 100 estate workers.[12]

Lord Crawford's close links with the community were shared by some other landowners, for whom the coming-of-age or marriage of the heir or the marriage of another family member became occasions for major local celebrations, much as was the case before 1914. In 1921, when the Marquis of Worcester, heir to the Duke of Beaufort and with strong fox-hunting interests, came of age, the members of the Beaufort Hunt presented him with a motor car. The farmers and tradesmen resident in the area covered by the hunt also gave him a platinum watch and a platinum and gold chain. Two years later, on his marriage, the farmers of the hunt gave his bride a 'diamond and pearl ornament', while the marquis himself received a pearl tie pin. Members of the hunt on this occasion presented the young couple with a cheque.[13]

Significantly, even in the difficult post-war period, most

landowners and their wives and daughters were expected to dispense charity and give personal advice to parishioners. Lady Phyllis MacRae, daughter of the 4th Marquess and Marchioness of Bristol, remembered that at her Ickworth home in Suffolk, it was considered inappropriate for girls such as she to take paid employment, especially when so many people were out of work. Instead

> you were expected to do a lot of voluntary work. You might be a secretary or chairman of the Women's Institute or the Red Cross; you might run the Girl Guides and Boy Scouts. You did not get paid for it ... when I started the Boy Scouts and Girl Guides locally in 1919 ... I had them up at Ickworth every week.[14]

At Wallington in Northumberland, Lady Trevelyan was also a prominent supporter of the Women's Institute, among other organisations. According to her daughter, she 'never failed to visit any house where there was a new baby – she was very close to the people'.

Danish-born Ulla, Lady Hyde Parker, who came to her Long Melford home at the beginning of the 1930s, at first found the duties expected of her very bewildering, since as the wife of the squire various responsibilities were thrust upon her. 'I hardly knew what the Women's Institute was at the age of twenty-two, but I was made President. I had to be Vice-president of the Conservatives at Sudbury ... I was President of the Mental Hospital in Colchester, which didn't really involve much: I had simply to get people from all over the area to give money, and then I sent it on to the Secretary of the hospital ... I was Chairman of the District Nursing Association, and the district nurse used to come and see me.' It was part of the same process that she was expected 'to know everybody in the village' and to patronise the local shops.[15]

Enthusiastic foxhunters, however, might have ulterior motives for the interest and the hospitality they proffered, being anxious to maintain good relations with the farmers over whose land they wished to ride. 'The time spent in a draughty [village] hall lit by a smoky light, slowly discussing the arrangements for the Summer Flower Show on a winter's evening after a tiring day's hunting,' declared Lady Apsley, 'is not wasted.' But *nouveau-riche* businessmen who had taken up the sport after acquiring a country estate did not always appreciate the importance of these extraneous social 'duties'.[16]

Others, too, were unenthusiastic about their community role. Even Lord Winterton, Master of the Chiddingfold Hunt and a keen rider to hounds, admitted in January 1921 that the 'Rent Audit Supper' he provided for his tenants was 'always rather a depressing entertainment'.[17] Gladys, the American second wife of the 9th Duke of Marlborough, similarly carried out her charitable duties in visiting the poor and sick at Christmas in the neighbourhood of Blenheim Palace with a notable lack of zeal. However, she may have been influenced by her husband's arrogant attitude towards social inferiors – as reported by the Earl of Carnarvon, who was at Blenheim for a shooting party on one occasion when the head keeper was ill. The man sent the duke a message to say that he had entrusted the business of the day to his deputy. 'My compliments to my head keeper,' responded the duke coldly. 'Will you please inform him that the lower orders are never ill.'[18] Another visitor was shocked by the unfeeling way in which he expressed a wish that the already high unemployment figures would rise to 2 million.[19] In fact in the 1930s they were to climb well above that level.

The duke, however, seems to have been embittered by the way in which both the population at large and the government in particular had made the landed classes a target for critical comment and heavy taxation. 'The old order is doomed,' he wrote gloomily in *The Times* on 19 May 1919. 'These fortresses of territorial influence it is proposed to raze in the name of social equality.'[20] His pessimistic viewpoint was echoed by Lady Newton of Lyme Park in Cheshire in 1925, when she complained of the 'cruel and ruthless taxation' that made it 'a crime that we should have succeeded to places too large for present-day requirements ... We cannot sell, there are no buyers. We cannot afford to live in our homes, what is to become of them?'[21] In 1919 and 1921 a total of 3,000 acres were sold from the Lyme Park estate, and staff, such as the woodmen, the blacksmith, the wheelwright, the roadmen, the drainers, and nearly all the remaining workshop men were dismissed, in an economy drive. The keepers no longer concentrated on raising game. Instead they built walls, went into the gardens, and carried out some of the tasks formerly performed by the woodmen.[22] In this way the old community spirit on the estate was lost. 'When we came back and saw all that at Lyme we thought, what'd we been fighting for?' was the verdict of one local man.

Although less vehement in their comments than the Duke of Marlborough and Lady Newton, other patricians shared their discontent at their declining status after the war. As Peter Mandler has commented, 'landlords as a class felt wounded and shunned by modern society and were reluctant to "present" themselves as anything in public'.[23] For some that meant they spent less time on their estates than had once been the case, as Lord Willoughby de Broke noted. They preferred to seek their pleasures in London or abroad, and to use their stately homes, where these were retained, as a base for their sporting activities and country house parties. They came to value their privacy and to be reluctant to open their houses to the visiting public as many of their ancestors had done. Mandler claims that nearly three-quarters of the great houses which had attracted thousands of visitors in the late Victorian period were closed to the public by the beginning of the 1930s. That included some of the major show houses of the past, such as Woburn, Belvoir Castle, and Blenheim Palace. The last Earl of Berkeley, who had sold his London property for £2 million, spent some of the proceeds in modernising Berkeley Castle, but then closed it to the public. As he told his wife bluntly, 'I loathe humanity.'

Even those great houses that admitted visitors, like Castle Howard, limited the days and hours they could enter, and warned those who came that they might not walk to the castle 'unless they wish to see through the house on the appointed days'. For this an admission charge of 1s per head was levied. Visitors were also warned against picking wild flowers, swinging on the boughs of trees or playing games in the park.[24]

At Haddon Hall the reaction was more extreme. Initially the Marquess of Granby, heir to the Duke of Rutland, to whom his father had already given the Hall, welcomed visitors while the property was being renovated. He also raised the admission charge, to help cover the cost of the work. But then in 1925, as the restoration was nearing completion, he began to make Haddon less accessible. First he closed off footpaths through the park, on the pretext that charabanc parties had 'left litter about', and had behaved inappropriately. The local authority responded by taking him to court, claiming that the footpaths he had closed were public rights of way. Eventually a compromise was reached, whereby certain outlying paths remained open to visitors but those nearest to the Hall remained closed. In May 1925, Lord Granby succeeded his father as duke on the death of the latter, and from 1926 he closed the house to the public. When he and the duchess moved into Haddon in 1927 it remained shut to outside visitors except for one day a year when it was opened to benefit local charities.[25] It was in these circumstances that early in January 1926 *Country Life* commented drily,

> The country has lately become more conscious of what a loss it suffers if a great landowner departs, but, at the same time, it is difficult for neighbours and villagers to take a real interest in a house if they never have an opportunity of seeing the inside of it. Everybody is delighted that the Duke of Rutland is going to live at Haddon Hall … We feel sure that the Duke, whose interest in architecture and history is bringing him to Haddon, will allow the Hall to be visited freely, as are Knole, Penshurst, Petworth, Chatsworth and so many of the famous houses of the land.

That did not occur and even Chatsworth restricted its visiting times to midweek during a limited period from Whitsun to the August Bank Holiday. In some years, entrance was further reduced by arbitrary closures, according to the family's own needs or whims. Then, too, properties like Knole, which remained open, were often neglected and uninhabited. One visitor drew attention to 'the cheerlessness of the state rooms (and particularly the dust at Knole)', and to 'the silken brocades and carpets sadly faded in places because the family are poor', in the case of Burghley, home of the Marquess of Exeter.[26]

There were, therefore, many ambiguities about the position of members of High Society within local communities and in their attitude towards humbler neighbours. Some, like the Trevelyans at Wallington, took a close personal interest in the lives of parishioners, while others, like Lord Granby (or the Duke of Rutland as he became in 1925) had a more arm's-length approach, reinforced perhaps in his case by the extensive post-war estate sales and by resentment at high taxation. Indeed, for many surviving members of the old landed families and for the *nouveau riche* who had purchased the estates of some of them, it was the sport offered by the countryside that proved the prime attraction rather than the welfare of the villagers.

Sporting Activities

Sport played a major role in the lives of the social elite. In the summer there was cricket, tennis, croquet, and golf, or for the wealthiest there were polo matches and yachting competitions. The yachting week at Cowes was, in fact, seen as marking the end of the London Season, with the yacht races themselves largely subordinated to the cycle of parties held on shore or aboard the largest yachts. It was at Cowes in 1921 that nineteen-year-old Edwina Ashley got to know Lord Louis Mountbatten (or Dickie as he was known to his friends). He was twenty-one and she was the granddaughter and heiress of Sir Ernest Cassel, one of the wealthiest financiers of the day.[27] They married a year later.

On 10 July 1926, *Country Life* noted that the preceding week had seen the culmination of a long series of sporting events. 'There were cricket matches everywhere, there was golf at Gleneagles, running at Stamford Bridge, rowing at

Henley and, perhaps, most attractive of all, lawn tennis at Wimbledon.' Tennis was also popular at country house gatherings. At Chartwell, for example, Mrs Churchill was a noted tennis enthusiast, and the game was a great feature of life there. According to her youngest daughter, the young men attracted to her two older sisters 'were much in favour if they were good players'.[28]

Some house parties were centred around the major race meetings. At Knowsley the great event was the Earl of Derby's party for the Grand National, run at nearby Aintree. In 1921, his guests included the king and queen, the Prince of Wales and Princess Mary. After dinner a film of the race itself was shown, even though it had only taken place a few hours before. The guests were much impressed that such a technical feat was possible.[29]

The Duke of Westminster, too, always held a large house party for the Grand National. In 1930, according to Loelia, his third wife, whom he had married only a few weeks beforehand, this involved conveying his guests from Eaton by a special train. On arrival at Aintree they were supplied with badges which gave entrance to the grandstand. In the evening there was a dinner and dance, attended also by house parties from some of the neighbouring families. Chester Races, held nearer at hand, were similarly marked by a large house party at Eaton. In this case, a fleet of cars ferried the guests to and from the racecourse.[30]

However, it was the Ascot race week which was regarded as the high point of the London Season, with many house parties organised and those grandees who did not own a property in the area often renting accommodation. According to *The Bystander* in June 1925, the larger houses were particularly popular, while at Windsor the king and queen, as always, entertained a large party.[31] For Lady Astor at Cliveden, Ascot was the pinnacle of her social year. The Astors' large house beside the River Thames was filled with guests and their servants, as well as by the Cliveden domestic staff, upon whose skills and efficiency the smooth running of the household depended. That applied to both the indoor and outdoor servants, for Lady Astor insisted that the grounds and gardens must look their best. Frank Copcutt, who came to the estate in 1928, and was soon appointed the decorator, remembered that not only had he to arrange the flowers and plants in the house, but buttonholes and sprays had to be prepared for the racing party. 'There would be a large selection so that the ladies could choose those that went with their colour scheme for the day. The carnations for the men were again in different colours and sizes.'[32]

Rosina Harrison, Nancy Astor's lady's maid, remembered that all the servants 'used to heave a sigh of relief when Ascot week was over'. For most, it meant working for eighteen hours a day during the preceding fortnight, in order to complete the necessary preparations, and with no time off allowed: 'none of us had been out of the grounds, and so it happened year in, year out'.[33] Nor did all the guests choose to go to the races, so special catering arrangements were made for them at Cliveden. Lady Astor herself, indeed, usually attended on one day only, while Lord Winterton did not go at all when he spent Ascot week at Cliveden in June 1920. But he enjoyed the other social diversions on offer. There was usually tennis before dinner and dancing in the evening. On 21 June, he noted, 'Very sad that a delicious week of fun and feasting & innocent enjoyment is over; the whole thing had the Cliveden impress and atmosphere. Hated going back to the workaday world.'[34] The previous August he had visited Cliveden to join in the celebrations for the coming of age of Bobby Shaw, Lady Astor's son from her first marriage to a fellow American. A large party of family and friends assembled and Winterton and the 'younger and more frivolous … went on the river in an electric punt of Bobby's and took our lunch'. The following day he boated, basked in the sun, 'played golf, [ate] and slept'. When he left on 24 August he felt 'much better and rested. There is something very delightful and cheerful and restful about this house with its bright colours, newpin cleanliness and hundreds of books. Nancy and Waldorf … came in after dinner and we played some children's games. Great fun. Nancy in her old form.'[35]

Later in August he spent a week at Barons Court, an Irish country house, where he fished, went boating on the lake and umpired a cricket match between some of the younger house party members plus several indoor servants against a team selected from among the gardeners. 'The House won'. But it was the restful pursuit of fishing that occupied most of his leisure at Barons Court, although he was not very successful.[36]

These different events were welcome additions to the social calendar. However, the two major sports which attracted the rural elite, and those who aspired to join them, were foxhunting and shooting. One writer has seen them as offering 'networks of sociability: an extension of school and Oxbridge, the London Club and (increasingly) the professional association'.[37] Of Lord Redesdale it was said 'he lived for … sport. He fished, he shot, he coursed hares … A day's shooting was what he loved most in the world, and his guns were his most sacred possessions.'[38]

Hunts have been rather pompously described as 'voluntary bodies within rural society, run by enthusiasts' and yet attracting 'a broad penumbra of less-committed sportsmen and women, many of whom shifted allegiance from hunt to hunt'. Hunting and shooting also affected the management and the appearance of the countryside. Foxhunting, for instance, inhibited the use of barbed wire as an inexpensive and effective fencing material because of its potentially harmful effect on horses. Hence negotiations had to be entered into between farmers and hunt committees to arrange for wire to be taken down during the hunting season, at the hunt's expense, and for compensation to be paid where necessary for this and for poultry losses resulting from foxes entering the chicken runs.

Lord Winterton, who claimed to have ridden with thirty-eight different hunts during his career and who was Master of the Chiddingfold Hunt in Sussex for seven years, noted how before the season began he went round local farms to make sure the wire was removed. On 23 September 1919, he did 'some useful work with Eric Bonham seeing farmers about wire'. Two days later he again rode 'round and saw various farmers'.[39] There could be no doubt of his personal commitment to the sport. In his autobiography he described a 'good pack of hounds well hunted' as 'a joy to behold'. Nor did he mind about the nature of the terrain over which he rode:

I enjoy following a good pack of hounds, well hunted, on a first class scenting day after a fox which is making a point in the jungles of my native Sussex or on the moors and amid the bogs of some countries in the West or North just as much as I enjoy riding ... after a pack in similar conditions over the glorious grass of Leicestershire or Northamptonshire ... I have no use for the man or woman who, having been brought up in a good hunting country, says of a difficult 'provincial' one that it is not worth hunting.[40]

In all, by 1928 there were 184 packs of hounds kept by hunts in England and Wales.[41]

Shooting, too, affected the management of the countryside not only through the potential damage to crops caused by large numbers of game birds but by the restrictions imposed on access to land by owners of shoots. This sometimes led to clashes with hunt supporters, who resented the efforts to exclude hounds from entering coverts until 1 February, when the game season ended. There were tensions, too, when gamekeepers, in the interests of their employer's sport, carried out vulpicide. Farmers and other land occupiers had, of course, a legal right to prohibit hunts from entering their land, either to prevent crop damage caused by careless riders galloping over ploughed fields or by their disturbing game – or because, on principle, they disliked fox-hunting. This latter stance was reinforced from 1924 by the establishment of the League Against Cruel Sports. Such moves earned the bitter scorn of those like Lord Willoughby de Broke, who considered hunting 'The King of sports and the sport of Kings', and regarded anyone who opposed it as 'hardly worth considering. His whole outlook would probably be anti-social and un-English in whatever rank of life he is found.'[42] Willoughby de Broke strongly refuted the suggestion that field sports involved the mere killing of animals for pleasure. Such barbarity would have 'no attraction for a true sportsman, for whom the attraction lies in hunting the game rather than in the killing of it ... He is inspired by the instinct of pursuit, the same instinct ... that inspires the literary collector in his field ... The survival of field sports depends upon the survival of the instinct of pursuit.'[43] Such arguments did not persuade the opponents of blood sports, needless to say.

To win over potential opponents, however, hunt

committees were urged by their supporters to make every effort to secure the goodwill of the farming community. In January 1927, *Country Life* warned that hunting 'in a highly cultivated and much enclosed country like England must depend on the good will of landowners and occupiers, and those who pursue the sport must only go upon the lands of those whose consent is expressly, or may be assumed to be tacitly given'. A. W. Coaten, *The Bystander*'s hunting correspondent, also suggested that hunt members should promote good relations by arranging tea parties for farmers and their families or offering inducements, such as clay-pigeon shooting competitions.[44] He conceded there were 'squeamish folk who object to the killing of foxes by hounds' but argued that if the fox were not killed in that way it would be 'shot, trapped, dug out, and poisoned, and would have no chance whatever'. By contrast during a hunt there was always the possibility that it would elude its pursuers and live to fight another day. The detailed diary entries covering Lord Winterton's hunting career suggest that this did happen fairly frequently'.[45]

Coaten also stressed the economic benefit that hunting bestowed by giving employment to grooms, hunt servants, blacksmiths, saddlers, and other tradespeople. Farmers, in particular, benefited from the sale of fodder. Then, too, houses in hunting districts were let for the season at profitable rents, whereas otherwise they would have been left empty, and that would have increased the local rate burden.[46]

It was realised after the war that the heavy tax burden and rising costs would inhibit traditional landowners from pursuing the sport as they had once done. Even in December 1918 *The Field* warned of the effect these restrictions would have on the general finances of hunts, by limiting the number of days that individual members could afford to go out and reducing their subscriptions to the sport. A man who before 1914 had hunted four or five days a week was post-1918 likely to have to reduce his establishment and be content with two days only. 'The one-horse, one-day man may have to give up his favourite recreation altogether.'[47]

In practice, the financial problems of the hunts were largely overcome during the 1920s by various means, including increased subscriptions. In addition, there was a greater use of joint-masterships of hunts, so that the costs over and above those met by subscriptions would be covered by more than one wealthy individual.[48] Even the famous Beaufort Hunt, although it remained under the control of the young Duke of Beaufort, after he succeeded to the title in 1924, reduced its scale of operations compared to pre-war days. Nonetheless they still began hunting in mid-August and carried on to the first of May, going out six days a week. 'We would get off very early in the morning – breakfast at six o'clock, because one was out on a horse by half-past six … Every groom had to do two or three horses, and there was a head groom over them, and two or three rather senior ones.'[49] It was the Master's responsibility to arrange the programme and ensure that good sport was shown.

The infusion of new money from members of the *nouveau riche* who took up the sport also helped with the finances. Among these new members were American socialites like Ronald Tree, who became joint Master of the prestigious Pytchley Hunt in Northamptonshire from 1927 to 1933. Another rich American enthusiast was Mr Strawbridge, a friend of the Prince of Wales, and described in in *The Bystander* as 'the Philadelphia millionaire'. He took a house in Melton Mowbray with his wife for a number of years.[50] At the end of the 1920s, when subscriptions to the famous

Quorn hunt began to fall during the economic depression, Sir Harold Nutting, 'newly rich from bottling Guinness', was co-opted into the Mastership. 'We don't want your personality, we want your purse,' joked his joint Master, Algie Burnaby. During the course of the following decade, Jane Ridley suggests that Sir Harold spent 'around fifteen thousand pounds a year on the Quorn'.[51]

A further financial boost was secured by the introduction of 'capping' for those who came along for a day's sport as the whim took them but who were not regular hunt subscribers. Capping involved the payment of a daily fee to the hunt. It was welcomed by A. W. Coaten in *The Bystander*, when he noted that the North Cotswold Hunt had increased the season's 'cap' for strangers to £2 a day instead of the previous £1:

> Nobody should grumble at this increase. In the Shires, where expenses have increased enormously during the past decade, the usual custom is to take £3 per day from those who hunt occasionally with the premier packs. Apart from the fact that it serves as an acceptable source of revenue, the capping system has the agreeable effect … of keeping down the size of the field, thus minimising the danger of damage to the property of the farmers by irresponsible non-subscribers.[52]

A final influence helping to increase the popularity of hunting was the fact that in 1919 the Prince of Wales started to hunt, mainly in the Shire counties of Leicestershire and Northamptonshire. Between 1923 and 1928 he brought his horses to Craven Lodge, a hunting club in Melton Mowbray, which was the prime centre for the hunting fraternity. The prince was an energetic and sometimes reckless rider and that applied, too, when to his family's alarm he took part in steeplechases. In 1924 he was so badly concussed after a fall at Arborfield that he was confined to bed for a month. But his enthusiasm was made clear to his close female friend, Mrs Freda Dudley Ward, when in August 1920, during an official tour of Australia, he confided,

> This afternoon I rode 6 races & won them all which pleased me because wasn't always riding the fastest horse ... Oh! I'm just crazy about riding races & am more determined than ever to get a chaser & ride in point to points next Spring.[53]

He wanted to succeed by competing on equal terms with other riders rather than being given precedence merely because he was the Prince of Wales. It seemingly did not occur to him that sometimes his fellow competitors might have allowed him to win because he was the Prince of Wales. Despite family opposition, he continued to hunt and to ride in point to points until his father's serious illness in 1928 persuaded him to give up. He then turned his attention to golf and gardening, although he remained a subscriber to the Quorn until 1932. During the 1920s, however, his interest in foxhunting, as well as that of his brothers, the dukes of Gloucester, Kent and York, undoubtedly boosted the sport's social importance.

Inevitably the presence of the Prince of Wales and his entourage made Melton Mowbray the fashionable place for hunting. 'Houses and hunting-boxes in the town and neighbourhood are letting extraordinarily well,' declared *The Bystander*, 'and the season promises to be a record one – perhaps rather a harassing one for the Masters of the Hunts round Melton Mowbray, because of the number of followers ... In November, when hunting begins, accommodation is at a premium.'[54] For many, indeed, hunting had become part of the wider social scene. Hence Patrick Balfour's acid conclusion that the sport had become 'so snobbish as to evince very little of the country sense. Melton Mowbray life is not country life'.[55] That applied not only to the house parties which were arranged during the season but to other aspects of the entertainment offered. This view is shared by Jane Ridley:

The hunting itself was organised as a social event. The Quorn stopped for lunch, when grooms came up with a change of horse and sandwiches. It was not done to carry a sandwich box or flask on your saddle yourself. The army of second horsemen formed a kind of shadow hunt, led by the hunt staffs' second horsemen in red, and followed by a cavalcade of grooms in bowlers and black coats, some of them leading side-saddle horses.

Many ... were really there for the *après chasse*. Evenings in Melton were a whirl of cocktails and fancy dress, poker and adultery. Millionaires like 'Banker' Lowenstein and Lord Furness wined and dined equestrian socialites ... What was 'vice' for the Victorians was 'fun' in the 1920s ... Those who wanted to forget the pain of war sought in hunting a mind-numbing narcotic.[56]

For younger women the sport might give a purpose to otherwise aimless lives away from London. Katherine, Viscountess Mersey, the elder daughter of the 6th Marquess of Lansdowne, remembered that when the family moved to their country seat, Bowood, in 1927, she 'went hunting twice a week' during the winter months. 'On the other days I had nothing to do at all.'[57] Many women also enjoyed the excitement of the chase and a few continued to serve as masters of hunts even when their menfolk returned from the war. Some of the more daring began to ride astride, with cross-saddles becoming acceptable for ladies during the 1920s. Before 1914 such an innovation would have been considered highly improper. But riding astride was cheaper and more convenient than using a cumbersome and costly side-saddle. Cross-saddles were much lighter, so women could ride smaller and cheaper horses, while their clothing was less expensive, too: 'well-cut breeches were far less [costly] than [the] riding habits' worn by those who continued to ride side-saddle, as some still chose to do.[58]

However, it was a sport which had its dangers, as exemplified by Lady Victoria Bullock, the much-loved daughter of the Earl of Derby. In 1927 she was spending some weeks with Lord and Lady Blandford in Leicestershire, so that she could hunt regularly with the Quorn. In November of that year she had a severe fall in the hunting field and died soon afterwards, without regaining consciousness. A month later her grieving father wrote to his son-in-law, 'I loved her, as no man has ever loved his daughter, and with her has gone all joy from my life.'[59] He never fully recovered from the loss.

Nonetheless, there were those who shared the view of the poet John Masefield when he claimed in the 1920s that 'hunting brought all ranks of society together on equal terms in a shared venture ... during the autumn, winter and early spring of each year, the sport is fox-hunting, which is not like cricket or football, a game for a few and a spectacle for many, but something in which all who come may take a part, whether rich or poor, mounted or on foot'.[60] However exaggerated, it was a belief shared by many members of the rural elite.

By contrast, shooting, critics argued, offered none of the wider social and economic benefits that applied to hunting. The labour it employed was limited, with only about 9,000 gamekeepers in England and Wales as a whole in 1921. Even in 1931 that had risen only a little to about 11,000. Thereafter numbers began to fall once more.[61] The beaters employed on shoots were often estate workers, diverted from other duties, or those who were hired within the locality for just a few days while shoots were in progress. And whereas hunts attracted large numbers of supporters and followers, shooting parties were limited to the small circle of friends and acquaintances of the landowner or the shooting tenant. Mrs Mildmay White, the daughter of the first Baron Mildmay, who grew up on the Flete estate in Devon, remembered the relatively small shooting parties who came to her home. These commenced each November:

> We would have about seven or eight guns, friends of my father, who were usually extremely good shots. Each gun had to have a loader and usually brought his own. Shoots were always mid-week, on a Tuesday, Wednesday and Thursday ... The estate staff were beating ... There would be forty or fifty of them going through the woods with the keeper in command ... We had five keepers, and they all had boys to help with the shoot. We used to rear a tremendous lot of pheasants. All the eggs were collected up by the keepers and extra eggs bought, so that the pheasant blood was changed. Then thousands of broody hens were collected and put out in coops all around in the pheasants' big field. They sat on the eggs until they hatched out, and ran in and out of the woods. A tremendous lot of vermin killing went on.[62]

On the Flete estate the womenfolk did not join in the actual shoot, but that was not necessarily the case elsewhere. Although many older 'guns', including the king, disapproved of females shooting, during the 1920s increasing numbers began to do so, as photographs in *The Bystander* and *The Tatler* confirm. At Flete, however, the women

> usually spent the morning either going round the garden or going to look at a church. Then we used to join the men for a tremendous luncheon in one of the keeper's houses, which was quite small ... The food was brought down by the footmen and the butler ... all the food was brought in hay boxes ... by the garden horse. We drank cider and beer, and then there was cherry brandy afterwards. We all used to stay with them in the afternoon ... When shooting was over, we came in and had the most delicious tea, with masses of Devonshire cream, honey, jam, scones and cakes. Everybody would relax and then go to dress for dinner.[63]

The arrangements were still more lavish on the Duke of Westminster's Eaton estate. Twenty gamekeepers were employed and they and their helpers reared about 20,000 pheasants each year. Norman Mursell, who became an underkeeper at Eaton in 1928 when he was fourteen, took part in his first shoots as the 'lad carrying the cartridges for the Duke's gun loader'. The beaters and keepers would meet outside the hall at dawn, with the keepers dressed in their elaborate livery. The senior ones wore

> a green velvet coat, green velvet waistcoat with brass buttons with the Grosvenor crest, and white breeches. They all wore the old hard bowler hat and the head

keeper had that much gold braid round it you had a job to see the top of it. The junior ones just had one piece of braid round it. These hundred beaters, all employees of the estate … were on parade and wore white smocks and red bush hat, a leather belt around the hat and brown leather leggings.[64]

The red hat was designed to warn the guns of their presence and thereby make it less likely they would be shot in error. At Eaton, unlike the policy on many estates, employees were not allowed to take tips from the guests who were shooting. Instead the duke usually sent a £5 note to them at Christmas in compensation. At shooting parties there, as elsewhere, a record was kept of the number of birds killed by each of the guns, and this would be circulated at the end of the day's shooting.[65]

Mursell also described the bitter hostility of the gamekeepers towards poachers, particularly those who took pheasants and thereby destroyed 'our long hard labour for many months and we weren't going to have that. But we were fortunate as we had twenty keepers and we used to have a rota so that there was somebody on duty every hour of the darkness.' He claimed, too, that the security role performed by the gamekeepers was important for the general welfare of the estate because at least one of these men was always about and 'had to be very, very observant,' in order to carry out his normal duties.[66]

However in January 1920, *Country Life* argued that poaching was not only increasing but that post-war poachers were 'much more formidable' to tackle than they had been 'before doing a bit of soldiering'. They were prepared to 'stand up to the gamekeeper or the keeper's master, for the matter of that'. Three years later the journal reported a meeting of landowners and sportsmen in Anglesey, where poaching was rife, due partly to high local unemployment. The aim was to set up a Game Protection Society to check the depredations. As one of the speakers drily pointed out, the poachers never had any difficulty in disposing of their ill-gotten gains. He also claimed that Anglesey had 'long been noted for the number and audacity of its poachers'.[67]

With the break-up of many large estates and the heavy costs involved in running successful shoots, a number of owners leased or rented their shooting rights to syndicates of friends. It was a solution favoured by *Country Life*, which argued that it offered advantages to both landowners and farming tenants. 'As regards the former, half a dozen people can afford to pay more rent and spend more money on upkeep and general care of the land than a single individual, while from the farmer's point of view systematic shooting and destruction of vermin are boons ... [A] shooting party who all pay for the privilege ... want good sport and are willing to pay the price'.[68] Smallholders and others living in the area might benefit, too, by being paid to act as beaters, or they might supply a horse and cart to carry the game, cartridges and the luncheon for the shooting party. Some might even be hired as loaders. But for a syndicate to work well it must have a competent organiser at its head who not only understood the concerns of local farmers but the financial aspects of the scheme. An efficient gamekeeper was also essential and if syndicate members hesitated to recruit a keeper because of the cost of his wages and other factors, *Country Life* warned a shoot would never be successful unless a skilled man was appointed to take charge and to devote himself full-time to its interests.

Partridges and pheasants without a keeper are seldom

more than a quarter of those which his efforts produce. The destruction of vermin, the distribution of eggs taken from nests in dangerous places, the prevention of trespass and the maintenance of cordial relations with the farmers and small cultivators, these items alone account for the increase.

In *Country Life*'s opinion a good keeper was 'first and last, the pivot of the whole scheme, the magician who, even if he cannot make partridges out of stones, certainly produces them where there were none before'.[69] It was accepted that the large-scale shoots of the pre-war era were at an end. Part of the revulsion against the mass slaughter of game after 1918 arose not merely on grounds of cost and organisation but as a result of the human large-scale slaughter which had taken place in the First World War itself. In 1937, the Duke of Portland spoke for a number of other landowners when he admitted that he was 'quite ashamed' of the 'enormous number of pheasants we sometimes killed' on his Welbeck estate in the years before 1914.[70]

That was not a view shared by King George V. He prided himself on his shooting prowess, and revelled in achieving large bags, both at Sandringham and elsewhere. Even in the 1920s around 20,000 head of game were being raised on the Sandringham estate and some of those who visited the estate regarded the king's enthusiasm for killing as 'anachronistic and unbalanced.' Each year, according to the king's biographer, 20,000 head of game were shot at Sandringham, and another 10,000 or so on leased estates. Most were reared pheasants, and there were those who criticised the head keeper, Mr Bland, for this mass killing of what were relatively tame birds. Bland served on the estate for over half a century and both visitors and courtiers commented on the ease with which the birds were shot. 'One sees pheasants everywhere in the park and gardens,' wrote a parson, 'the place is literally crawling with them.'[71]

When the king visited other estates he similarly expected to shoot large numbers of birds. At Elveden, the long-serving keeper, T. W. Turner, recalled that when the monarch paid his regular visits to the estate, 'hand-reared birds would be placed on the beats where His Majesty would be asked to shoot', and any shoots held prior to his arrival would not be permitted to encroach on the area required for the royal party. 'This required the most careful planning. Once the royal shoot was over the whole territory could be freely shot over a second time.'[72]

Unlike his brother, the Duke of York (later King George VI), the Prince of Wales was neither an enthusiastic nor a very successful shot, and he felt this was a handicap for him in his relations with his father. As he ruefully told Mrs Dudley Ward, the king 'was rather inclined to judge people by their powers of shooting, though of course that is silly!'[73]

At Balmoral, too, sport dominated proceedings, not only in regard to the shooting of grouse after the Twelfth of August each year, but also in respect of deer stalking. That was a sport that was valued by Lord Willoughby de Broke as well as by the king. In 1924 the former noted that unlike foxhunting, it had not changed since the war. 'The stalker has to go out on foot, find the deer with his glass, and stalk them by his knowledge of the ground and by his ability to take advantage of the wind, in exactly the same way as his ancestors stalked them on the same hills.'[74] To achieve the best results the services of a skilled ghillie were essential, and Willoughby de Broke's enthusiasm for the sport was shared by *Country Life*. In July 1926, it claimed it was one of the high arts of shooting, for it demands more than a mere capacity to hold a rifle straight and the physical endurance to climb the hills. Stalking at its best involves hillcraft and hunters' craft, and the real hard work is repaid a thousand-fold by the sheer exhilaration of success. No other form of British sport gives the shooting man quite the same thrill as the long-drawn-out period of anticipation when working up to deer.[75]

As for the king, when he shot the heaviest stag ever killed on the leased estate of Abergeldie, he could not resist writing to a friend to tell him of the achievement.[76] Not all of the royal stalking parties were so successful, however. Helen Hardinge, whose husband Alec was one of George V's secretaries, informed her mother on one occasion how the king, the Duke of York and her husband had all gone out for the day on a deer-drive: 'That is what they got: 2 pigeons ... 1 blackcock ... 1 fox (Alec)!!! Rather good for a deer drive!'[77]

George V's pride in his prowess with a shotgun and a rifle also extended to the grouse moor. According to one young onlooker, who had been recruited as a beater, 'every bird that fell to the King's gun was dead in the air before it dropped ... It was shooting as the ordinary first-class shot may dream of shooting.'[78]

Although Queen Mary concealed the fact from her husband, shooting bored her. 'It was so stiff,' she remarked of one shooting party, 'I would have turned cartwheels for sixpence.'[79] She was interested in museums, art galleries and antique shops, and Balmoral offered scant opportunity for her to follow these pursuits.

In September 1921 Queen Mary and her daughter, Princess Mary, escaped from Balmoral for a few days to stay with one of the queen's ladies-in-waiting, Lady Airlie. When arrangements were being made for the visit, the ladies-in-waiting who were with the queen at Balmoral asked that everything should remain relatively informal, so that only 'shooting everyday clothes' would be worn, and the queen was anxious to visit antique shops. 'Are there any old shops in Perth with the sort of little bibelots she likes picking up – little cheap things that might do for the doll's house? Most people take her to the big shops where there is priceless furniture at prohibitive prices.'[80]

The popularity of grouse shooting and deer stalking among the sporting fraternity was particularly important for many Scottish landowners, who relied upon the rental income they derived from letting or leasing their grouse moors and deer forests to outsiders, including American visitors. According to Patrick Balfour, Americans would pay up to £7,000 for three months' shooting in Scotland, and one paid £35,000 for a five-year tenancy of a famous moor. The Cunard Line, to cater for its American clients, leased 'many of the best moors and spent fortunes improving the lodges, installing electric light, building roads and tennis courts'. This all came to an end, however, following the stock market crash in the autumn of 1929. By 1932, declared Balfour, 'gunmakers were facing bankruptcy and Highland lairds a reversion to the simplicity of their former mode of life'.[81]

Although there were grouse moors in the north of England and in Wales, it was Highland Scotland that had the greatest appeal. The railway companies recognised this in the 1920s, when they made arrangements to transport the sportsmen and their gear – and servants – north of the border. In 1922, for example, the London & North Western Railway offered a new facility in connection with their renowned special sleeping-car service. Hitherto passengers for the Highlands leaving Euston at 7.30 p.m. have found that this departure time necessitated their taking an early evening meal in town. With a view to eliminating this disadvantage, the company have introduced a dining-car on this train.[82]

Not to be outdone, the Great Northern Railway Company announced that trains on the east-coast route, from London to Scotland, would be 'augmented as necessary to meet the expected heavy demand for accommodation. For those preferring to travel by daylight, luncheon-car expresses will leave King's Cross at 9.50 a.m.'[83] Nor did advertisers fail to point out the sturdy clothing needed to combat the Scottish climate. *Shooting Times* suggested thick boots with plenty of hobnails, a good tweed suit, flannel shirt and for headgear 'nothing beats a soft felt hat. It turns rain and shades you from the sun'.

Some sportsmen, like the Duke of Westminster, combined an interest in grouse shooting (the duke having acquired a grouse moor in Wales) with an enthusiasm for fishing. According to his third wife, he 'was mad ... about fishing. He had the best fishing in Scotland, on the River Laxford ... A huge loch, Loch Stack, flowed into the river.'[84] One of the duke's mistresses during the 1920s, the famous Paris dress designer Coco Chanel, seems to have shared his enthusiasm. According to the Laxford records, between 1 and 4 October 1927 alone she caught eleven salmon, the heaviest of them weighing 24 lbs. Coco also shared some of the duke's other sporting interests, joining him for cruises aboard his yacht, the *Flying Cloud*, and when staying at Eaton she not only hunted several days a week in the season, but accompanied him to race meetings. Their affair ended in 1929, after about five years, possibly because by then she was too old to bear him the son and heir he craved. She, for her part, had an important career and large income from her business as probably France's most famous dress designer.[85]

The duke, however, did not confine his interest in fishing to Scotland. He arranged many expeditions to Norway, visiting Bosskop in the Arctic Circle on a number of occasions.[86]

Sport Overseas

The Duke of Westminster's fishing trips to Norway were just one sign of the growing internationalism of sport among the social elite during the 1920s. In some cases this merely extended activities available in Britain itself, such as tennis, golf, polo and sailing. But there were other, more exotic possibilities, too, such as big-game hunting in Africa and Asia, while winter sports in Switzerland and Austria appealed particularly to the younger and more energetic members of society. Even New Zealand advertised its sporting credentials, claiming to possess 'the world's Finest Stalking' and to be 'The Angler's Eldorado': 'Rainbow Trout have been taken up to 24 lbs and brown trout up to 10 lbs or more, while fighting swordfish have been killed on rod and line up to 1,000 lbs and over 12 feet in length'.[87]

The desire to resume travelling in Europe after the trauma of the First World War became quickly apparent, not merely among bereaved families making pilgrimages to the graves of their fallen menfolk, but with the fashion conscious going on shopping expeditions to Paris. Holidaymakers, too, increased in number, so that by 17 December 1919 *The Tatler* could report that for weeks past the 'eastward exodus in search of sunshine has been in full swing – to the Riviera,

Italy, Switzerland, and even further afield.' Later, cruises to a variety of destinations were being advertised, while luxury yachts were once more at anchor in the harbour at Monte Carlo, loaded 'with the most inveterate pleasure-seekers.' By early January 1920, Evelyn of *The Tatler* reported that the Riviera was so popular that 'I'm told you can't get a sleeping berth on the trains down there for over a month.'[88] Once they had reached their destination, holidaymakers could enjoy a variety of sports. Early in 1920, for example, Cannes boasted that it could offer tennis, golf, polo and even pigeon shooting, to say nothing of the opportunity to gamble at the various casinos along the coast, including in Monte Carlo itself. At Nice, sailing regattas were organised during the 1920s and race meetings held.

To a lesser extent, Egypt, Algeria and Morocco shared in the new travel boom among socialites. Evelyn in *The Tatler* claimed that Algeria had become an alternative to the Riviera in the eyes of some, offering plenty of tennis and golf, as well as perfect weather. The country was, of course, still ruled by the French.[89] The congenial climate here and in similar destinations offered the well-to-do the opportunity to escape the rigours of a British winter.

The Duke of Westminster indulged his love of travel and of sport overseas not merely by his yachting, tennis and golfing expeditions in southern Europe and his fishing trips to Norway, but by hunting wild boar on his estate at Mimizan. This was situated in an isolated location between Bordeaux and Biarritz, and to establish the hunt he had imported a pack of Welsh hounds and some English horses. Lady Weymouth, who was one of his guests, remembered that the first time she and her husband stayed at Mimizan, there was not only the excitement of the chase but its danger. Some of the men carried revolvers so that they could shoot their quarry when it was cornered. A wild boar at bay was a fearsome creature, and shortly before the Weymouths' arrival one of the huntsmen who had dismounted to despatch a trapped animal had had his thigh ripped open by the enraged beast.

Once the hunt was under way the hounds quickly located their prey and they set off at a tremendous pace:

> After galloping for about three quarters of an hour, twisting and turning through the forest, the hounds broke out into open country ... and after a long run over agricultural land and through muddy farm yards, the quarry was pressed back into the woods, the hounds gaining ground ... Suddenly their note changed to a deeper baying and [the duke] said they must have cornered the quarry ... The ugly monster had his back to a tree; his head was down, and the hounds stood in a circle round him ... I kept well behind as the boar was shot through the head.[90]

The duke subsequently sent her the boar's head, duly stuffed and mounted, as a memento of the chase. What the local peasants felt about these sporting exploits is not mentioned.

For younger and more energetic tourists, Switzerland and Austria, with their winter sports, exerted an appeal, with the season reported to be 'in full swing' at St. Moritz by the beginning of January 1920.[91] A year later *The Tatler* reported that Society had 'migrated in almost greater numbers than ever' to Switzerland, where there was not only skiing and the bobsleigh but skating, with the rink at Davos remaining open the previous year until well into March, so great were the demands made upon it. Among those taking up winter sports was the Prince of Wales, who went skiing in Kitzbühel in Austria and St. Moritz with his friends.[92] For many visitors it was the après-ski socialising in the evenings that was a prime attraction, and *The Field* reported that in Kitzbühel both sports and social entertainment were 'well organized'.[93] In November 1928, in a special 'Winter Sports' issue the health benefits of exercising in 'the dustless cold of high altitudes' were extolled in *The Bystander*.[94]

However, if winter sports in Switzerland and the various sporting opportunities available on the Riviera and along the coast of North Africa offered welcome diversions for many jaded socialites, for the most affluent and venturesome tourists, big-game hunting in Africa, and to a lesser extent in parts of Asia, provided a special excitement. Kenya, Tanganyika, Uganda and the Sudan were all venues for those who wished to go on safari. The Sudan, for example, was said to be 'one of the most easily accessible countries in which Big Game abounds and its large territory affords a most varied choice of shooting grounds'.[95] But it was Kenya that became particularly noted for its big-game hunting and for the professional white hunters who led and organised safaris for inexperienced or nervous travellers, and yet who wished to enjoy what they saw as 'the romance and danger' of shooting wild animals in unfamiliar territory. Robert Ruark maintained cynically that for the professional hunter who led these expeditions it was not so much the location of game and the supervision of the final kill that presented difficulties but the establishing of a camp routine for members of the safari party. The loading and unloading of equipment for what was in effect a small portable city had to be supervised. That included the selection of the campsite, the pitching of the camp, the sourcing of a water supply and the supervision of the skinners who dealt with the animal when it had been shot. Trackers, gunbearers, porters, cooks and body servants had also to be controlled.

The professional hunter thus had to be an expert mechanic, able to repair any motor vehicles in use and to combine

> the duties of a sea captain, a bodyguard, a chauffeur, a tracker, a skinner, a head-waiter, a tourist guide, a photographer, a mechanic, a stevedore, an interpreter, a game expert, a gin rummy partner, drinking companion, social equal, technical superior, boss, employee, and handy man ... [He] lives in the pockets of his clients for long weeks, and unless he is a master of tact, nobody is speaking to anyone else when the safari pays off in Nairobi.[96]

Many high-status people went on safari, including members of the British Royal Family. In 1924–5 the Duke of York and the duchess visited Kenya, Uganda and the Sudan, and seemingly on their recommendation the Prince of Wales went big-game hunting in East Africa in 1928 and 1930. On the former occasion he was accompanied by his brother, the Duke of Gloucester. In 1930, for some of the time his travelling companion was his then mistress, Lady Furness. [97]

The firm of Safariland, founded in Nairobi in 1903, supplied all that was needed by way of tents, transport and general camping equipment from its shop in Nairobi and its branch in Piccadilly in London.[98] A rival enterprise, Shaw and Hunter, likewise offered to provide all that was required for expeditions to Kenya and Tanganyika, its advertisement enthusiastically claiming these to be 'the sportsman's paradise for Big Game Hunting'.[99]

The specialist white hunters included Pat Ayre, who lived in Kenya and accompanied the Duke and Duchess of York on the Kenya leg of their 1924–5 safari, and Pat Rattray, who 'captured the heart of the daughter of Lord Furness' when she went on an expedition with him. They later married. Then there was Danish-born Bror Blixen, who with his wife ran a coffee farm in Kenya, and combined his skills as a safari organiser with a reputation for hard drinking and womanising. Denys Finch Hatton, brother of Lord Winchilsea and a close friend of Karen Blixen, Bror's wife, was likewise a very competent leader and he and Bror arranged the Prince of Wales's safari in 1930. They subsequently earned the prince's high praise for their efficiency and their pleasant personalities.[100] In the late 1920s Blixen and Philip Percival, another well-established professional hunter, founded their own safari firm called Tanganyika Guides.[101] Others at work during that decade included J. A. Hunter, who advertised in *The Field* in 1927, offering to outfit and conduct big-game shooting parties to Kenya, Tanganyika, Congo and Uganda. He was also prepared to undertake 'Museum collections and photography' and he combined these activities with work as a game ranger.[102] Unlike many of the other professional white hunters both he and Blixen praised the contribution of the African trackers upon whose skills they depended for the location of the rarer game animals that their clients were seeking as trophies.[103]

As one writer has wryly expressed it, much of the pleasure of this kind of sport 'was the shooting of alpha-male animals by alpha-male humans ... The preservation of ... tiger skins, alligators and crocodiles cannot be disassociated from male boastfulness.'[104] Nonetheless on many safaris female members of the party took pride in their skill in killing game, too, and that included the Duchess of York.

This issue of personal pride was borne out by contributors to *Country Life* when they recounted their safari experiences. In January 1921, Raymond Kent, for example, reported his pleasure in achieving his ambition to kill a large bull elephant

– 'a good tusker', as he put it. 'No other sport that I know of produces the exhilarating, self-satisfied and contented feeling which follows a successful day's hunting for big game,' he declared. He also described the 'great sport and exciting experiences' obtained 'by sitting up for lions during the night.'[105] Later in the same month, another *Country Life* contributor, W. D. M. Bell, warned that in order to prevent the wholesale slaughter of elephants, restrictions had been imposed and a licence to kill two animals in a year would cost the hunter between £40 and £80, so it was important to be selective when making a kill. The following September, in another *Country Life* article, Bell claimed to have killed sixteen lions personally, arguing that as a game animal the lion afforded 'first-class sport'.

Early in 1921 the Duke and Duchess of Sutherland and Lord and Lady Maidstone embarked on their own joint safari to the Sudan. They left England early in January and travelled to Khartoum where they had arranged to hire a small river steamer to act as their base for the trip. These could be chartered at a fixed rate and included catering facilities, servants, transport, forage for the animals and attendants, bearers, skinners and camp equipment for expeditions on land.[106] Among the highlights of the safari mentioned in *Country Life* was the shooting of bull elephants. Even the Duchess of Sutherland killed one and was duly photographed beside its carcase. In all, they shot six elephants, this being their allocation for the trip. Other trophies collected by the Sutherland expedition included a hippopotamus and a rare white rhinoceros, which the duke particularly wished to secure. Lord Maidstone made his own contribution to the total, killing among others a male buffalo with a 'good head', which he presumably intended to display on a wall when he returned home, and a large crocodile.[107]

However impressive the Sutherland safari might have been, it paled into insignificance when compared to the four-month tour undertaken by the Duke and Duchess of York. As an enthusiastic sportsman the duke was much attracted by the idea of shooting big game. The duchess initially had some qualms, confessing to a friend,

> I am feeling slightly mingled in my feelings about going to Africa, as I hate discomfort, and am so afraid that I shall not like the heat, or that mosquitoes will bite my eyelids ... or that I shall not be able to have baths often enough ... On the other hand I think it is good for one to go away and see a little LIFE.[108]

In reality her fears proved groundless, and despite the long marches she undertook and the discomfort of blistered feet, she later described the whole expedition as 'Wonderful. Best bit of one's life.'[109]

The couple left England on 1 December 1924, with five other members of the party, including the duchess's friend Lavinia Annaly, who also acted as her lady-in-waiting, and the duke's equerry. They reached Mombasa shortly before Christmas, and left by train for Nairobi. On Boxing Day they were at last able to drive north to set up their first camp on Siolo plain. Here they were joined by their official safari companions. These included two professional white hunters, one of whom was Pat Ayre, and Captain Caldwell of the Kenya Game Department. They remained at the camp for three weeks, but soon began undertaking short expeditions from it. On 29 December, the duchess excitedly described to her mother how they had

> got up at 4 ... to try & get a lion. It was thrilling. They

had left a rhino and zebra out, & as it was getting light we crept up behind bushes & found two lions growling over the zebra ... We all shot together but it was still too dark to see properly, and they were off like a streak of lightning ... I saw about 12 giraffes the other day.[110]

The duke subsequently went out for a day's hunting with Pat Ayre, looking for lion or eland.

After this the strenuous part of the safari began. They travelled on foot, moving camp almost every day, and walking over some very uncomfortable terrain. They covered at least 12 miles a day, rising at about 4.30 a.m. and then hunting until 10 a.m. or 11 a.m., when they rejoined the camp, 'which has moved after us like magic', noted the duchess. They rested until about 3.30 p.m. before resuming their expedition. On one occasion the duchess reported seeing 'thousands of zebra – I shot two dead with two shots for lion kills. Hated doing it.' Later, as she honed her shooting skills, she informed the king, who she knew disapproved of women with guns, that she had taken to shooting with a rifle. 'I do hope you won't dislike me for ... I enjoyed it so much, and became very bloodthirsty.' Her victims included large birds 'for the pot', a buck and 'a rhinoceros which nearly broke my heart'.

On 4 February they returned to Nairobi at the end of the Kenyan part of the safari. They then moved on to Uganda, where they met two new professional hunters and a new safari manager. Their first camp was in the Semliki Valley and the duke noted ironically that they must have presented a remarkable spectacle in the dawn light, for the expedition's procession 'seemed unending, as we have 600 porters'.[112] In Uganda they had their first sight of elephants, and the duke shot a large bull with impressive tusks. By this time he had accumulated a sizeable number of trophies, which in those days was the chief aim of any African safari. However, unlike the Duke of Sutherland, he was unwilling to kill a rare white rhino. 'It is not at all difficult to shoot,' he noted, 'but only three or four are allowed to be shot a year as they are becoming scarce. I did not want to shoot one on hearing this, but they wanted me to get one.'[113] In the end he did so.

Early in March they moved on to the Sudan, where they joined a river steamer, although from time to time they left the boat to travel inland in search of more wildlife. Finally, on 6 April they disembarked from the steamer. The 'idyllic days in the wild' had ended and they returned to Khartoum. From there, on 9 April, they travelled to Port Sudan, to begin their journey home on SS *Maloja*. They finally reached Britain on 19 April.

The duchess found it difficult at first to adjust to her usual daily routine. 'It's awful coming back to the social and unnatural atmosphere again!' she wrote in her diary, soon after her return. London seemed drab after the months in the wild, while the restrictions of her daily round as a senior member of the Royal Family and at Court were 'more stifling than ever'.[114]

Perhaps inspired by the experiences of the Yorks, the Prince of Wales made two private visits to East Africa in 1928 and 1930. Unlike his younger brother, he was not an enthusiastic shot, although he did go shooting on occasion. However, even in 1921–22, when he was in India, Lord Cromer reported: 'One of the tragic things about this tour is that HRH is not really keen on big-game shooting or shooting of any kind.' He preferred polo and that had apparently caused 'puzzlement and hurt among his Indian hosts'.[115] Nevertheless he did go tiger shooting and secured some of the expected trophies. In East Africa in 1928, likewise, his equerry claimed he was 'definitely bored by shooting and fishing', even though he counted among his victims an elephant. He called the shooting of this 'easy and unexciting'. When he returned in 1930 he took with him a cine camera as well as a rifle. As Edward Steinhart has pointed out, on these royal safaris an important change was 'the downplaying of hunting pure and simple. Although plenty of animals would fall to the Prince's gun,' he had not come merely to 'collect heads. His main concern was to observe, to photograph and to film big game.'[116] Nonetheless, as Steinhart added drily, 'His own considerable total of animals killed, especially on his second safari, belies the idea that big game shooting was not of major significance.'

The prince's use of the camera rather than the gun may have encouraged a more general trend towards 'camera safaris', which became increasingly popular in the 1930s. However, as early as 1928, a contributor to *The Field* pointed out that while on his first safari in Kenya he had used a rifle, that was to be the only time. He had subsequently replaced it with a camera:

I can say that from my experience the camera affords more fun and excitement, more interest and chances of greater knowledge than ever can be attained by the rifle. Those who contemplate going on a shooting safari in the near future will, I hope, in the end see how little is really gained by the slaughter of these ... interesting creatures and how much can be gained by the use of the camera.[117]

As for the prince himself, the term 'sport' needed to be expanded beyond the mere hunting of wild animals, in that in 1928, true to form, he rode in horse races, played golf, and watched the annual cricket match between the officials and settlers in Kenya. He and his brother, the Duke of Gloucester, engaged in a number of flirtations, and it was said that the prince's 'high jinks' meant he did not get to bed before 3 a.m. each day. On this occasion the trip was cut short after nearly three months when the serious illness of the king led to the two princes being recalled to England. This may account for his second visit in 1930 with Bror Blixen and Denys Finch Hatton, when he enjoyed what Edward Steinhart has labelled a truly luxurious 'champagne safari'.[118]

4

Social Rituals

That nebulous thing called London Society was larger
than it had been before the war, but it was still exclusive
and difficult for outsiders to enter ... People gave dances
for their daughters and the daughters of their old friends,
and, if one did not get married, one went on being asked
to dances for years.

Loelia, Duchess of Westminster, *Grace and Favour*
(London, 1961), p. 88.

Family was essential; and to debs from good families the
rest simply didn't count.

Quoted in Angela Lambert, *1939: The Last Season of
Peace* (London, 1989), p. 6.

Growing Up

In many respects the 1920s was a decade of change, with
the development of new social attitudes and a growing
acceptance of technological innovations, such as the wireless,
the refrigerator and the motor car. There was an increasing

use of electricity, and families hit by declining incomes and a heavier tax burden moved 'from mansions to mansion flats'.[1] That view of change, however, scarcely applied to the methods adopted for the rearing of the children of society's elite families. As Angela Lambert has commented: 'From cradle to Christening, from nursery to schoolroom' children participated 'in a series of rigidly prescribed social conventions that had changed little over the last hundred years.'[2] Hence, much as had been the case before 1914, babies were speedily handed over to nursery staff soon after they were born, and it was the nanny rather than their parents who provided their day-to-day care. Mothers with a busy social life had little desire to devote time and attention to the nurturing of children and, in any case, most of them lacked the necessary expertise. As one head nurse dismissively commented, 'the parents didn't know how to look after children ... They couldn't relax, couldn't let themselves go.'[3]

It was perhaps indicative of this approach that Mary Soames, the youngest daughter of Sir Winston and Lady Churchill, should describe her mother during the 1920s as having

> no real understanding of the childish mind or outlook, and [she] applied her own perfectionist standards not only to manners and morals, but to picnics and garden clothes. Consequently, although all her children loved and revered her, they did not find her a fun-maker or a companion for their more untidy, knock-about activities.[4]

Mary spent her childhood in a small house in the grounds of the family estate, Chartwell, where she was brought up by her mother's first cousin, Maryott Whyte. She was a trained Norland nurse and acted as a nanny-cum-governess to all four Churchill children. Although the children went to school – in Mary's case to a day school near Chartwell – it was Maryott who brought 'stability and orderliness' to their lives. She was to remain with the family for over twenty years.

Some nannies, however, were very snobbish, so that those employed in titled families considered themselves a cut above fellow nurses who were recruited by less prestigious parents. Often, too, when they acted as a surrogate mother they came to regard themselves as the real decision-makers in the upbringing of 'their' children. Daphne Weymouth, who had her first child in 1929, remembered that the little girl's nurse firmly informed her that 'she did not approve of parents interfering in the nursery'. However, when the woman was found to be keeping the baby 'tightly wound up in shawls with her hands bound down to her side', Daphne summoned up all her resolution and dismissed her after three weeks. Ironically the final breach took place not over her treatment of the baby, but over the fact that she refused to allow dogs in the nursery.[5] After this, Daphne took great care in selecting a new nurse, with Grace Marks the chosen candidate. She remained with the family for the rest of her life, finally retiring to a cottage on the Longleat estate after Daphne's husband had succeeded as the Marquess of Bath.[6] Over the years Nanny Marks experienced problems with other staff members, notably with the cook over the issue of nursery meals, and with one of the governesses, who was determined that the nurse should not interfere with the children's education. She sought by various means to undermine the nanny's influence but ultimately had to accept defeat.

Edwina Mountbatten, who spent her pregnancy in a

frantic social whirl, dancing at night-clubs, visiting the theatre, and meeting her friends, unsurprisingly lost no time in passing her infant daughter to Nanny Woodard after her birth in February 1924. Edwina seemingly took little interest in the baby. Instead she concentrated on her own recovery, so that she could resume her hectic social round. With the aid of electric massage, three weeks after the birth she was ready for her first outing. Soon after that, she and her sister-in-law, Nada Milford Haven, went to Paris to purchase new clothes. From there they visited a friend at Antibes in the South of France. Edwina returned to England in April when Dickie Mountbatten himself came home on leave, and their daughter was christened Patricia Edwina Victoria a few days later. As Edwina's biographer notes, few photographs or press cuttings relating to Patricia's birth or christening have survived: 'Edwina's album for 1924 had dozens of snapshots of her friends, playing tennis, hunting, yachting, winning cups at polo, many of herself, three of Simon, her black spaniel, but only nine of Patricia in the first months of her life. Edwina consigned her daughter to experts.' It was indeed her father who gave the little girl love and attention rather than her mother.[7] Paradoxically, that seems to have made Edwina jealous and when her second daughter, Pamela, was born in April 1928, she was determined to retain the younger child's affection, to the exclusion of her father. So when Dickie returned to England from Malta in July 1929, he was excluded from the nursery, Edwina giving as an excuse that the nanny thought his visits disturbed the baby. 'Dickie was upset but believed what he was told and stayed away. Edwina's albums had no pictures of Dickie and Pamela together. Mother and daughter, yes; father and daughter, no.'[8] Nonetheless it was upon Nanny Woodard that both little girls depended for their day-to-day care.

Other socialites would probably have sympathised with Nancy Astor's sentiments when she referred to Frances Gibbons, the Astor children's long-standing nurse, as her 'strength and stay' and the 'backbone' of her home.[9] That meant that if other servants displeased the nanny, they would be dismissed by Lady Astor, who took the view that if they could not 'get on with Nanny Gibbons' they must go. Edwin Lee, the Astors' long-serving butler and the real linchpin in the running of the household, nevertheless conceded ruefully that it was useless to oppose Frances Gibbons.[10]

Like many of the nurses employed in these elite families, Nanny Gibbons was loved by her young charges. As was the case with the Churchill children, such women brought stability and affection into their lives when, often enough, they had little contact with their parents. At best they might be brought down once a day to the drawing room for a brief stay after tea, or parents sometimes paid short visits to the nursery. Only a few remained long enough to play with their offspring. Many children, like the young Churchills, accepted that although their mother was 'devoted and conscientious' in her contacts with them, it was her husband and his interests that 'came first'. 'We never expected either of our parents to attend our school plays, prizegivings or sports' days', wrote their daughter, Mary. 'We knew they were both more urgently occupied.' Mrs Richard Cavendish, whose father was at Court and whose mother was a daughter of Lord Bellew, similarly recalled that her parents were away from their Oxfordshire home at Compton Beauchamp for most of the time. This was where the children were based and the parents visited only at weekends:

When we were tiny children it was absolutely straightforward: Nanny Abbott took charge of us and during the week we did exactly what Nanny said. We had walks, and then we rode our ponies ... and had a few lessons ... [At] weekends there were grand visitors and we were shoved into smart clothes. We were much too young to see what was going on in the dining room, but we used to hang about on the back stairs and get food and delicious things when they came out of the dining room.[11]

It was Nanny Abbott who took them on visits to their grandparents, usually when their parents had other engagements, where they were thoroughly spoilt. And it was she and a nurserymaid who went with them on seaside holidays: 'We would go to places like Frinton. We used to go shrimping and paddling ... And Nanny, who never let on when she was at Compton that she was able to cook, cooked like a dream. My parents would come down to see us once or twice during our seaside holidays – they loathed coming ... They'd come down for about three minutes and go away again. They'd done their duty.'[12]

Like many other girls in her social circle at that time, and much as had been the case before 1914, Mrs Cavendish did not go to school but was educated at home by governesses. They rarely stayed long 'because we were so nasty' to them. The schoolroom was a converted billiard room and neighbouring children from similar families came to share in their lessons. She and her sister also attended dancing classes in nearby Faringdon and when they were older they went to Oxford twice weekly for lessons in French, dancing and skating. During the holidays a French governess was recruited and this was a practice followed by Lady Astor for her children and by Lady Redesdale for the young Mitfords. While the governess was with the latter family, they were supposed to speak only French during meals.[13]

As a consequence at those times there was largely silence, though in later life Nancy, the eldest daughter, was to become an ardent Francophile.

Unlike Mrs Cavendish's mother, Lady Redesdale took a personal interest in the rearing of her children, although in their earliest years she depended on the nanny, Laura Dicks (nicknamed 'Blor') for their care and training. All of the Mitford girls kept pets, and two of the older children, Pamela and Diana, had hens, the sale of whose eggs provided them with pocket money. Nancy had goats whose milk she sold to the estate's home farm. Their mother also took up chicken farming on a considerable scale and was so successful that she later claimed she had paid the governess's £120-a-year salary from the egg money.[14] Somewhat unusually, Sydney Redesdale herself gave lessons to her children up to the age of about eight, and according to Jessica, one of the younger daughters, she was a far better teacher than the governesses she employed. Nonetheless these varied greatly in quality. The first to be employed was a Miss Mirams, who had the daunting task of not only teaching four children of varying ages and abilities, but of giving special tuition to the only boy, Tom, in readiness for his entry to a preparatory school.[15] When he eventually went to Lockers Park at the age of nine he proved to be advanced for his age and, unlike many other boys going away to school for the first time, he seems to have enjoyed the change. As he had grown up with older sisters, and especially with the eldest, Nancy, who was a great tease and something of a bully, he was well equipped to cope with the minor difficulties of prep school life. He was sufficiently good at games to enjoy them, was normally near the top of his class, and at the appropriate age he passed effortlessly on to Eton.

Tom Mitford's education, moving from preparatory

school to public school and then on to university, was one common to most of the boys in his social class. For the girls, however, schooling at home, with perhaps additional classes in dancing, French and music or other accomplishments was still widespread, as we have seen. Inevitably, too, as Helen Vlasto remembered, they had to accept the strict stratification which took place within the household. In Helen's home the different floors seemed to divide the house into different worlds.

> We children belonged at the top of the house ... Right down below the ground floor, with its elegant public rooms, lived the maids, surrounded by kitchen, scullery, pantries, store cupboards, and a massive coal cellar ... One thing ... linked the top of the house with the basement, and vice versa, and that was the speaking tube. 'Go and whistle down and ask Cook nicely for another plate of bread and butter, there's a good girl,' Nurse would say ... After tea was the time for washing sticky fingers and faces, and for a quite painful hair-brushing from Nurse, in her hurry to get us going downstairs. This was the lovely time for doing things with our parents, and often for being polite to visitors in the drawing room.[16]

Even as adults such girls remembered the rules their nanny drilled into them such as, 'Bread and butter first, then jam', or 'No such word as can't.'

It was, however, a sign of changing attitudes that an increasing number of girls' day and boarding schools were established from the close of the Victorian era. Towards the end of the First World War, Loelia Ponsonby, for example, attended Heathfield, which was considered at the time to be the most fashionable girls' school in England, with fees to match. She did not consider the education she received to be particularly good, and regarded the highly religious headmistress as distinctly eccentric. The girls had to attend prayers twice daily, 'putting on strange, starched caps, rather like nurses'. In sexual matters she remembered they were 'absurdly innocent'. 'Most of us knew nothing at all about the "facts of life", even though we were fifteen or sixteen years of age'.[17] She left after two years, with few regrets, probably because her parents were experiencing 'one of their recurrent financial crises for I ... just lived at home and rather languidly did a correspondence secretarial course ... people said it would always come in useful'. Then, soon after the war ended she 'came out' as a debutante, noting drily that 'till one came out, one was a child ... speaking when spoken to, dressed in any old clothes (it went without saying that well-dressed children had common mothers) and of course no male friends.'[18]

Lady Astor, too, sent her only daughter, Phyllis (known as Wissie in the family) to school. Initially she chose a day school, Notting Hill High School, which Wissie attended during the week while her parents were in London. After about a year, however, in August 1922, Lady Astor decided that this was not in her daughter's best interest. Originally it had been intended that she should stay on 'until she was ready for college if she was anxious to go there'. But Wissie showed little interest in pursuing an academic career. This was not, however, the reason for her mother's change of heart. Because she was living in a large, busy household, with weekends often spent at Cliveden and with her mother either occupied with her parliamentary duties or her social activities, Wissie became stressed. Nor had she many opportunities to get into the fresh air, as would have been the case if she had stayed in the country. Her mother therefore decided that she should attend North Foreland Lodge, St Peter's-in-Thanet in Kent as a boarder. This was fairly close to the Astors' holiday home at Sandwich and it catered for girls between the ages of twelve and nineteen. According to its prospectus, it aimed to 'develop their characters and power of thought and, while rousing intellectual interest to keep in sight the domestic and social life in which they will take part on leaving school'. At the same time care was taken 'to train them in habits of responsibility, order, and courtesy'.[19] These objectives met Lady Astor's own requirements that her daughter should be taught 'unselfishness and a steadiness of purpose', which, as she told the headmistress, Miss Wolseley-Lewis, 'I feel you will be able to do, better than I can under the circumstances.'[20]

The headmistress was to prove a stabilising influence, anxious that Wissie should fit in, for as she told Lady Astor, girls shrank from being 'different'. 'Perhaps it seems to them an instance of the hated taint of "swank"!' Initially Wissie's school reports suggest that she was still under strain. At the end of the summer term in 1924, for example, when she was around fourteen, her form mistress called her 'Good and helpful ... but still excitable', while the headmistress considered she had 'made a real effort to do better work and to be more self-controlled'.[21]

Phyllis Astor seems to have stayed on at the school until 1928,when at the age of eighteen, she embarked on the important social rituals associated with 'coming out' and being presented at Court, thereby marking her entry into the adult world.

Unlike the Astors, Lord and Lady Redesdale strongly disapproved of girls receiving a formal education. They believed that they got nothing from going away to school 'except over-developed muscles and an argumentative disposition.'[22] Their daughter Nancy particularly resented this decision.

She felt for the rest of her life that it had hampered her intellectual development. In practice, as she had access to a good library at home and her governesses taught all the children along the lines recommended by the Parents' National Education Union (PNEU), her education was 'thorough and reliable'. The PNEU system catered for children learning at home and each summer and Michaelmas term examination papers were sent out which the youngsters had to sit, much as they might have done at school. The papers were then sent to London to be marked.[23] It seems more likely that Nancy simply wanted to get away from the restrictions of the parental roof. Not until she was sixteen, in 1921, did her opportunity come, when she was able to attend a school of sorts conducted at Hatherop Castle, just over the Gloucestershire border from her Oxfordshire home.

Hatherop Castle was owned by a Mrs Cadogan, who had several daughters of her own to educate. She therefore invited a small number of girls from neighbouring 'superior' families to join them. They lived in the servants' quarters and were looked after by the family nanny, who acted as matron. The rooms were spartan and very cold in winter, and the academic programme sketchy, with French taught by Mlle Pierrat, and the rest of the curriculum covered by a highly competent young woman called Essex Cholmondeley. Mornings were devoted to lessons, and after lunch Miss Cholmondeley read aloud to them while they lay on the floor, presumably to rest and perhaps to improve their posture. The afternoons were spent in walking, sketching and netball, according to the weather. In the summer there was swimming and tennis. Once a week the largely unmusical Nancy had a piano lesson, and piano practice was a regular part of her routine.[24]

Nancy remained at Hatherop for a few months only but during that time she formed a friendship with Mary Milnes-Gaskell which outlived her brief 'school' career. She and Mary joined a troop of Girl Guides and her enthusiasm for this was such that when she returned home she set up a troop in her home village of Asthall for the local girls. Her two reluctant oldest female siblings, Pamela and Diana, were recruited as patrol leaders. After about a year, however, her interest waned, much to her sisters' relief.[25]

In April 1922, seventeen-year-old Nancy, like a number of other daughters of the social elite, was sent on a cultural tour of Europe, visiting Paris, Florence and Venice. It was organised by the headmistress of a school in Queen's Gate in London attended by one of her friends, and was carefully chaperoned. In many respects it was a substitute for attendance at one of the many Continental finishing schools favoured by the parents of other girls at around this time. Angela Lambert, tongue in cheek, has described these schools as bestowing a 'light dusting of culture' while instilling 'the rudiments of feminine skills like arranging flowers' and bringing their pupils into contact with a selection of well-bred girls of different nationalities.[26]

For Nancy Mitford this Continental tour proved a life-changing experience and one during which she felt that she had really grown up. The main disadvantage, from her point of view, was that she realised that her clothes were much less smart than those of her companions and she was not allowed to wear any powder, as they did. But on that point her father was adamant: 'paint, however discreet, was not for ladies. Nancy had been allowed one concession, to wear her hair up, and that was enough.'[27]

Edwina Ashley, the future Edwina Mountbatten, by contrast, was sent at the end of 1919 to Alde House at Aldeburgh, which called itself a Domestic Science Training College. Its aim was to instruct 'batches of twenty girls at a time' in the rudiments of competent housekeeping. It was something of a halfway house in that its pupils were no longer girls but were not yet quite women. Like the others, Edwina took turns working as a scullion, in the laundry, and as a housekeeper, ordering meals, paying wages, and getting in stores.[28] From her point of view its two main benefits were that it taught her that she was able to organise other people into an effective team and she learnt about the details of housework and was thus better able to manage her own household after marriage and to judge the competence of her servants. She remained at Alde House for a few months only and then, like Nancy Mitford, although on far more luxurious lines, she went on a Continental tour, with a chaperone and accompanied first by her cousin, Marjorie, and then by a school friend. Her grandfather, Sir Ernest Cassel, had had three objects for Edwina to fulfil on this tour – shopping, culture, and integration into society. The trip began with an extensive clothes-buying spree in Paris and a visit to the Louvre, while in Rome she took in the city's ancient sights, had lessons in music and Italian, and learned to mix in upper-class Italian society. Above all, despite feeble protests from her chaperone, she discovered it was 'pleasant to do exactly what she wanted, especially if it was risky'. According to her cousin Marjorie, it was during this visit to Italy that Edwina 'discovered men'. At the beginning of 1920 she returned to England to prepare for her formal introduction to London Society the following May.[29]

For the sons of these elite families, the educational path

was a good deal clearer. Attendance at a public school, after a spell in a preparatory establishment, was the usual progression. Eton, Harrow and Winchester were the schools favoured by the wealthiest and most prestigious families, but a growing number of other public schools had by this time made their appearance. In all of them academic pursuits were seemingly regarded as secondary to sporting prowess, while bullying and fagging were among the ordeals the younger boys had to endure. Patrick Balfour, for one, claimed he learnt nothing at school except to be 'rendered fit to black any man's boots. (For in fagging I cleaned a dozen or so pairs per day.)' According to him the atmosphere at Winchester, which he attended, was 'primarily athletic'. Athleticism was 'the primary' instrument in the manufacture of character as the public schools conceive it.'[30]

At Lancing, too, the young Evelyn Waugh joined in a variety of sports, even though he had little interest in them. His main desire was to be successful, and that meant engaging in sport. Also present there, as in the other public schools, was a strong homosexual influence, despite the fact that such practices were still illegal. As Waugh's biographer notes, although Lancing may have been more 'overtly religious than some public schools', that did not mean its moral standards were particularly high. 'For most boys the years at public school were years of erotic and romantic passion and many of Evelyn's contemporaries were engaged at one time or another in the pursuit of love, conducting amorous affairs with younger boys with or without physical expression.' Evelyn himself was not averse to talking 'filth', as sex was called, in the changing rooms, but he seems to have kept aloof from physical encounters at this stage. In that respect he differed from Tom Driberg, a fellow pupil, who 'went on the downs with older men, and on Sunday

151

evenings organised competitive masturbation sessions in his dormitory'.[31] Driberg was eventually asked to leave the school but both he and Waugh then went on to Oxford University.

Oxford in the 1920s has been described as a city of 'sports cars and motor-bikes, jazz and gramophones', and of smart young men in plus-fours – although those with strong 'aesthetic' tendencies wore polo-neck jumpers and Oxford bags (that is distinctive wide-legged trousers). Then there were the 'young bloods' of the Bullingdon dining club 'who hunted, played polo and got spectacularly drunk on an income of £3,000 a year'.[32] As a reaction against the solemnity of the war years, frivolity and childish behaviour, often accompanied by heavy drinking, were commonplace. For many it was also fashionable to pretend to be homosexual, if such a pretence were needed.[33] Many of the leaders of the most reckless social group were former Etonians, and subsequently they were to be prominent in the exploits of the 'Bright Young People' during the mid- to late 1920s.

Daphne Vivian visited Oxford in the mid-1920s with her friend, Lettice Lygon, daughter of Lord Beauchamp. She often went to parties given by Lettice's brother, Hugh, and remembered the whole atmosphere as vibrating 'with a fantastic ephemeral life ... The young men who were the leaders of the so-called aesthetes of that period have since become legendary figures'. They included men like Harold and William Acton and Brian Howard. Howard, who was to be particularly prominent in the exuberant London social scene of the 1920s, was described by Daphne as a

> sinister impresario, epigrams crackling from his lips ...
> It was Brian who made a tailor fashionable at Oxford,
> it was Brian's taste in ties and shirts that predominated

... The Charleston and the Black Bottom had just been introduced into England. Brian decided that we should all become proficient in the steps of these dances, and encouraged us all to take lessons in London.[34]

Howard was considered to be 'one of the most extravagant of the aesthete-homosexual circle at Oxford.'

Not all outsiders were prepared to tolerate the irresponsible and high-spirited doings of the more extreme undergraduates, however, and that was true of John Fothergill. He kept the Spread Eagle Inn in Thame, which was favoured by many leading figures of the day as well as by some of the undergraduates from nearby Oxford. In 1926, Fothergill noted in his diary,

It's hard to be governess as well as cook, but it's only by great vigilance that we've won a reputation amongst the better-class undergrad, or, rather, lost it with the worser. The fool or bounder seldom comes now, or if he does he behaves as nowhere else. One has to watch him from the moment he comes into a charming dining-room with his hands in his pockets ... It's no pleasure to go and tell eight 'hearties' in the common-room that people in the hotel might be bored with the sound of their hunting horn, or that I don't like girls who are not sisters or suitable companions, or not to swing on one leg on an eighteenth-century chair. The other day I told some lads who seemed to be blowing up for the idiotic to go to those places in and around Oxford where the furniture was made for breaking ... To make this an Eton or Stowe of public-houses will be no joke, but it's got to be done ... Yet to have to dinner the pick of charming or clever youths is a vast privilege and a knowledge.[35]

This last comment by Fothergill was a timely reminder of the presence of the large number of undergraduates at Oxford, Cambridge and other universities who completed their academic courses blamelessly, without attracting any of the notoriety of the exuberant few.

The London Season

During the three months from May to the end of July, when the London Season was in full swing, there was a feverish round of social and sporting events, including the all-important presentations at Court of debutantes and young married women. The latter were probably being presented for a second time after their marriage.

For the debutantes the advent of their first Season meant important personal changes, not least in their wardrobe. 'I used to have awful clothes before I grew up', recalled Katherine Viscountess Mersey, who was a daughter of the 6th Marquess of Lansdowne. 'When I came out, everything had to come from a very good dressmaker or a very good tailor ... I rather enjoyed having some nice clothes at last.'[36]

Loelia Ponsonby remembered, too, the fluctuating fashions during the 1920s, although paradoxically it remained essential to wear a hat all the year round. That applied even when playing tennis, or gardening, or lunching in a restaurant. Hems rose and fell, while waistlines wandered 'high and low, but throughout the twenties bosoms and hips were definitely *out* ... We squashed ourselves into tight bustbodices ... As plastic surgery developed it was rumoured that in Paris you could get your curves operated on.'[37] According to Frances Donaldson, girls not endowed with flat breasts and boyish figures were constantly on a diet. As skirts became very short, 'to be born with fat legs or thick ankles was an innate disaster'.[38] As Patrick Balfour wryly commented, during the decade the 'modern woman herself grew each day slimmer and slimmer'.[39] Cosmetics were still frowned upon in conservative circles, but increasingly girls used face powder and although at the beginning of the decade nobody wore bright lipstick, this, too, was becoming accepted by its end. When Loelia Ponsonby first saw Alice Bingham, owner of the fashionable Rose Bertin hat-shop, wearing a hat trimmed with large red cherries and with 'lipsalve as it was called, to match', she was shocked. It seemed impossible that 'Englishwomen should ever take to such a garish fashion but of course we all did'.[40]

There were other signs of female emancipation, too, notably the short hair revolution, with the adoption of the shingle and the bingle. This ran parallel to the abbreviated skirt lengths. Parents, particularly fathers, seem to have objected to the new hair fashion, considering it a violation of women's crowning glory. But as both Daphne Vivian and Nancy Mitford discovered, after initial anger when they first had their hair cut, parental hostility evaporated fairly quickly.[41]

Other symbols of women's growing independence was their ownership of cars, with wealthy young women like Edwina Mountbatten driving all over the place in their own vehicles, albeit not always very safely. According to her biographer, her 'frantic travels often ended abruptly. She tipped the two-seater Rolls into a ditch, was caught speeding at 34 miles an hour over a crossroads and prosecuted for dangerous driving.'[42]

These were the new trends that had to be taken into consideration when debutantes and their mothers were preparing for the excitement of the London Season. They also needed to be aware of the most up-to-date fashions promoted by the French couturiers and their many imitators. As Frances Donaldson observed, to be really well dressed 'was to be dressed by one of the great French dressmakers ... no departure from the style of clothes that were portrayed in such magazines as *Vogue* was conceivable for those who wished to conform to the standards of fashionable London'.[43]

Many girls had other anxieties about their wardrobes, too, wondering what to take when they went on a country house visit lasting several days. 'Even for a shoot in Scotland – a seven-day shoot – you had to dress for every day of the week. And naturally that meant a different hat; and a hat box ... There were very rich people who had marvellous clothes, but on the whole one just scraped through', commented Lady Marjorie Stirling, a daughter of the 8th Earl of Dunbar.[44]

For girls entering the adult world for the first time, the Season had three main benefits. First it enabled them to get to know other young people within their social milieu, and to be introduced to 'eligible' young men. That remained true even though initially many of them found the formalities involved daunting, once they had moved beyond the security of their domestic circle and that of long-term family friends. Loelia Ponsonby described the misery she had experienced owing to her shyness, and the 'paralyzing terror of being noticed or drawn attention to in any way' that she had felt. These included 'ghastly moments of humiliation' when attending a ball. Once 'the band struck up a new dance all the guests surged into the ballroom and set off with fresh partners ... but a pathetic jetsam of girls was left standing partnerless in the doorway feeling the cynosure of all eyes. One imagined that when the Dowagers put their tiaraed heads together they were saying *what* a pity it was that the Ponsonby gal had so little success.' One means of escape was 'to take refuge in the ladies' cloakroom between the racks of coats and endure the contemptuous glances of the maids'.[45]

A second purpose of the London Season was to serve as a marriage market. As one writer has commented, 'the girls were not allowed by their mothers to forget that, in the end, making a good marriage was the underlying aim of the Season'. To this end the girls were carefully guided, to make sure that they associated only with the 'right' kind of young man. As Lady Mary Dunn put it, parents 'wanted to see their daughters taken care of, and wanted them to live a life to which they'd been brought up.'[46]

That restrictive policy was not always easy to implement. As in the immediate post-war period, so throughout the 1920s, many of the more spirited girls adopted ingenious ways of eluding parental surveillance. Daphne Vivian, for example, borrowed a latchkey from her lady's maid, and had it copied. Then when she had been brought home by her chaperone, she would sneak out again as soon as the coast was clear to meet her friends and to visit night-clubs, usually of the unconventional kind such as Mrs Kate Meyrick's '43' Club where she knew she was unlikely to meet people who knew her family.[47] Night-clubs were regarded as particularly unsuitable for young girls, being seen as places of sexual danger, 'dark and secret ... their gloom pierced only by arabesques of cigarette smoke and the stimulating or melancholy music of jazz and the blues.'[48] By then women had themselves taken to smoking as a matter of course, no matter how much the older generation disapproved. For the young it was seen as a sign of sophistication.

The third benefit debutantes derived from the Season was in familiarising them with the formality of life at Court, as epitomised for most of them by the protocol involved in their presentation. That included the strict dress code to be observed and the way they were to conduct themselves during the presentation ceremony itself. Specialist teachers, such as those at the Vacani School of Dancing, were consulted by anxious mothers, to ensure that the girls learnt to curtsey in the correct manner.[49]

Court ceremonial under King George V and Queen Mary followed a rigid pattern – something against which the Prince of Wales, in particular, often railed. It may also have been the reason why only after many months of hesitation the young Lady Elizabeth Bowes Lyon agreed to marry the king's second son, the Duke of York. As she wrote to her sister, shortly after the engagement was announced, 'The King & Queen are both so charming to me, but it's most terrifying!'[50] It was significant, too, that one sympathetic lady-in-waiting wrote to her friend, Lady Airlie, 'I do feel that she is giving up all the adventure of life.'[51] Even for Lady Elizabeth's parents, the Earl and Countess of Strathmore, it meant many changes. 'I *can't* tell you how sorry I am for the parents', the lady-in-waiting told Lady Airlie. 'I don't believe they had really the least realized before coming [to Sandringham] how different things really are & that – gild the pill as you may she *will* be royal now.'[52]

For the relatively few other young people who went on to have close links with Court life, even if they did not marry into the Royal Family, it was important that they understood what was expected of them. Helen Hardinge, who was married to one of the king's private secretaries, remembered being advised by one of the ladies-in-waiting how she was to conduct herself. As she subsequently wrote,

The Court at Windsor was a very formal one and most

particular in its routine [it] meant that exactly what one
was to do, where one was to go, and how one was to
behave at any given moment, was clearly laid down. To
feel reasonably secure, one just had to learn the rules.[53]

When she was invited to dine at Windsor Castle for the first
time after her marriage she noted that it was the king who
chose the menu and selected the music played during dinner.
At the end of the meal he rose to his feet as a signal for the
ladies to withdraw. 'We had to curtsey to him and follow
Queen Mary ... out of the room.' The queen then seated
herself on a sofa 'in her own special corner of the Green
Drawing Room ... and various ladies were brought up to
talk with her, one at a time'[54] At first Helen found it all very
intimidating, but she learnt to fit in and to play her expected
role with suitable discretion and decorum. However, she did
confess to being upset when she was told by 'one or two
of the older members of Queen Mary's entourage' that it
was thought wise that Lady Elizabeth after her engagement
should not see too much of long-standing friends like Helen,
once she was married to the Duke of York.

The older ladies were afraid that we should not treat her
with enough dignity. And I was so anxious to be courteous
and to behave properly towards her, that I became very
formal and decorous – so that it took the Duchess of York
some time after her marriage to come to terms with all our
conventional efforts to treat her correctly.[55]

Indeed, as she confessed to her mother in September 1923,
after she had attended a large royal gathering at Balmoral,
with the young duchess among those present: 'I did such
a deep curtsey to her ... that as she is tiny I very nearly

couldn't get up again. It puts one's eye out so having first the Queen and then her', because, of course, the queen herself was tall.[56]

However, for most debutantes entering adult society for the first time, the niceties of Court life had limited immediate relevance. Some of them, like Daphne Vivian, may have had what was called a 'little Season' before they came to London. Perhaps they had visited friends in the country or had attended Hunt balls and dinner parties in their immediate neighbourhood. Lesley Lewis, who returned from her Paris finishing school in about 1926, when she was almost eighteen, recalled that initially she followed the example of her contemporaries and went hunting, played tennis, and visited the country houses of friends. 'I did my stint in local good works such as the Red Cross, helped whenever help was needed at home and at all odd moments read voraciously.'[57] She attended parties held by neighbours who 'with great kindness' enabled her to work off some of her 'gaucherie'. She had limited cash and so found it embarrassing when she stayed in a country house on her own to know how much to tip the maids or the chauffeur who drove her to the railway station. Then, too, she was self-consciously aware that however pleasant the servants might be in the house where she was staying, she had 'an uncomfortable feeling of being under surveillance', especially since she had no lady's maid of her own. 'It was thought essential to have proper equipment of matching brushes to be set out on the dressing table. We were usually packed or unpacked for, and clothes were laid out on the bed before dinner', with one of the housemaids in the home where she was staying carrying out the duties of a lady's maid. But, she confessed, there was always a worry as to whether your underwear would 'come up to scratch and was there enough of it?'[58]

1 Members of a hunt taking advantage of the return of peace to ride out shortly after the signing of the Armistice on 11 November 1918. (*Country Life*, 7 December 1918).

2 Lady Diana Cooper, the former Lady Diana Manners, advertising 'Icilma' face powder in 1927. (*Daily Sketch*, 17 August 1927)

3 The gramophone provided music for many small impromptu parties during the dancing 'mania' of the 1920s. (*The Bystander*, 16 June 1926)

4 Brenda Dean Paul, one of the leading members of the 'bright young set', in the 1920s. (From Brenda Dean Paul, *My First Life* (n.d. *c*. 1935))

5 The former Loelia Ponsonby, looking rather solemn after her marriage to the 2nd Duke of Westminster ('Bendor' to his friends) on 20 February 1930. She was the Duke's third wife and the ceremony took place at the Registry Office off Buckingham Palace Road.

6 *Vogue* was the leading fashion magazine of the 1920s. This front cover depicted a model with the desired slim 'boyish' physique.

7 Demonstrating the tango in the affluent surroundings of the Savoy Hotel.

8 King George V sailing his yacht *Britannia* in a race during Cowes week, which was the culminating event in the London social season. (From *The Queen*, 22 January 1936, published to mark the king's death).

THE RESULT OF A BEAT—SOME OF THE GUNS AND THE BAG.

9 A shoot at Kilverstone in November 1928. The Maharajah of Patiala was among the guests admiring the large bag of pheasants. (*Country Life*, 17 November 1928)

A PAIR-HORSE GAME CART WITH SPECIAL RACKS IS NEEDED FOR BIG DAYS.

10 The game cart collecting pheasants after the Kilverstone shoot in November 1928. (*Country Life*, 17 November 1928)

11 A member of Sussex shooting syndicate in 1924. (*Country Life*, 2 February 1924)

12 The Duchess of Sutherland beside the elephant she had shot as a trophy on her East African safari in 1921. (*Country Life*, 23 July 1921)

THE DUCHESS OF SUTHERLAND WITH THE ELEPHANT SHE SHOT.

13 Fulke, the teenage 7th Earl of Warwick, enjoying winter sports *c.* 1928. Fulke was born in 1922 and succeeded to the title on the death of his alcoholic father on 31 January, 1928. (From Frances, Countess of Warwick, *Life's Ebb and Flow* (1929))

14 *Vogue* showing an attractive outfit for winter sports, which enjoyed a great upsurge in popularity during the 1920s.

Above left: 15 The all-important presentation at Court. A debutante, Miss Penelope Crofts, dressed for the first Court in 1926 and wearing the obligatory ostrich feathers on her head, as well as a train. (*The Bystander*, 16 June 1926)

Above right: 16 The demure Miss Audrey Yarrow was to be presented at the first Court in 1926. (*The Bystander*, 16 June 1926)

Enterprising Hawker. "BUY A NICE BLOOD ORANGE, LADY; ALL SWEET AND JUICY."

17 A debutante with her disdainful mother waiting to be admitted to Buckingham Palace for her presentation at Court. (*Punch*, 22 May 1929)

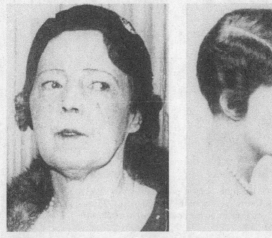

Above left: 18 One of London's leading society hostesses: Lady Cunard, known as Emerald to her friends from 1926. (From Patrick Balfour, *Society Racket*, 1933)

Above right: 19 The wealthy American-born Laura Corrigan who pushed her way to the top of London society in the 1920s. (Patrick Balfour, *Society Racket*, 1933)

20 A member of the nursery staff and the lady's maid with the children of the Earl and Countess of Lichfield and their friends at Shugborough Hall, Staffordshire, in the 1920s. (Arts and Museum Service, Staffordshire County Council)

21 Contrasting Mayfair interiors at the end of the 1920s. The upper room reflects the clutter of an earlier era. The lower room depicts the lack of elaborate ornamentation in the modern age, with some Art Deco furnishings. (Patrick Balfour, *Society Racket*, 1933)

22 The butler was a key figure in ensuring that a large household ran smoothly. John Henry Inch in the dining room at Nidd Hall, Yorkshire, where he was employed by Viscount Mountgarret and his mother during the 1920s. There was a total indoor staff of sixteen, including two liveried footmen. (Arthur R. Inch)

POLICEMAN. "Yer can't go there, Miss; it's a one-way street."
LADY. "But I only want to go one way."

23 *Punch* mocking a woman driver, as females began to exercise their greater independence.

Alfieri

"THEY ALSO SERVE—"

Miss J. Leveson-Gower convoying "sausages and mashed" at one of the Hyde Park canteens. The volunteers were as good trenchermen as they were workers

24 A 'High Society' helper during the 1926 General Strike. Miss J. Leveson-Gower working as a volunteer at one of the temporary Hyde Park canteens. (*The Bystander*, 26 May 1926)

Sport and General

NOT IN THE CURRICULUM

Volunteers from the Universities who temporarily exchanged the pen for the platelayer's hammer

25 Two undergraduate volunteers working as platelayers on the railways during the 1926 General Strike. (*The Bystander*, 26 May 1926)

THE FREAK-MERCHANTS; OR, THE BRIGHT YOUNG PEOPLE.

THEY USED TO THINK THAT THE DEAR OLD BOTTLE-AND-PYJAMA PARTY WAS QUITE ORIGINAL—

TILL THEY WENT ONE BETTER WITH THE BATHING SUPPER-PARTY—

26 *Punch* poking fun at the excesses of the 'freak' parties organised by the 'Bright Young People' in the 1920s. (*Punch*, 4 November 1929)

THE FREAK-MERCHANTS; OR, THE BRIGHT YOUNG PEOPLE.

— THEN THEY HOPED THEY HAD TOUCHED THE HIGH-WATER MARK OF ORIGINALITY WHEN THEY HELD
A "BABY" PARTY IN A PUBLIC SQUARE.—

27 *Punch* drawing attention to the 'Baby Party' held in July 1929, which caused much annoyance to the residents of Rutland Gate in London. (*Punch*, 4 November 1929)

28 The Mozart Party organised by David Tennant on 29 April 1930, at the New Burlington Street Galleries. When they left in the early hours some of the guests saw workmen digging up a gas pipe in Piccadilly. Patrick Balfour is shown standing on top of a mound of rubble, while Cecil Beaton has seized a pneumatic drill. The former Elizabeth Ponsonby, now Elizabeth Pelly, was standing to Beaton's right. (Patrick Balfour, *Society Racket*, 1933)

29 *Vogue* continued to provide the latest fashion news into the 1930s and beyond.

"One more traffic block, darling, and I'll have finished my jumper."

30 A sign of things to come. A London traffic jam. The woman driver has brought her knitting along. (*Punch*)

In 1927 Lesley embarked on her first London Season. She was to be presented at Court by an aunt rather than her mother, since her uncle and aunt had a more extensive social circle than her parents. As an eighteen year old she found it 'an exacting performance' since she had little experience of the kind of world she was about to enter.

First there were several fittings with a French dressmaker who afterwards put in *The Times* your name, her name and what you wore. My dress was white chiffon over a pink slip and as skirts were then very short and waists very long, the belt area was round my hips and I had great difficulty in not showing my knees. To my shoulders was attached a silver lamé train which in due course was frugally turned into another dress. With other girls I was made to practise with a table-cloth how to curtsey without getting entangled in a train, and to move off crabwise so as neither to turn my back on the royal couple nor fall flat on the carpet ... I carried a borrowed white feather fan and at the back of my head, secured by a pearl bandeau across my forehead, rose three ostrich feathers from which hung a length of tulle. I had white kid gloves above the elbow and silver brocade shoes with straps across the instep. My aunt, in a grey dress with a lace train, wore some splendid diamonds of her own but had also borrowed my mother's and a sister-in-law's ... George V and Queen Mary enthroned on a dais among the uniforms, brocades, medals and jewels of an entourage which included some well-known public figures, provided a climax I have never forgotten ... This was one of the last Courts for which cars were allowed to queue up in the Mall instead of waiting in the Palace quadrangle. The milling East End crowds were good-naturedly enjoying the show and their forthright comments were kindly, but times were hard ... for the urban poor in about 1927 and the display seemed tactless.[59]

To take part in this ceremonial a large cash outlay was needed, something which many of the families could ill afford, at a time when incomes from landed estates were shrinking and much of British industry was in the doldrums. Some mothers economised by holding joint dances to launch their daughters, thereby halving the cost. Others chose the cheaper alternative of holding a ball in a hotel.[60] But others again, according to the gossip columnist Patrick Balfour, were prepared to spend up to £1,000 on a single large ball for their debutante daughter, to which fellow debutantes and eligible young men were invited. Balfour calculated that since few families still owned large houses in London, merely renting a property – perhaps a large flat – for the Season, they would have to hire somebody else's house for a night. That might cost £150. Then a band had to be ordered from a band agency, there would be 'a cartload of flowers from a florist, servants and champagne from a catering company', and the expense of sending out some hundreds of invitations. Balfour argued that wiser or thriftier mothers had discovered that it paid better 'to enter the marriage market in a more informal and personal spirit', and to lay out the thousand pounds in various smaller entertainments, including theatre parties, supper dances in restaurants, and Saturday to Monday gatherings in a country house.[61] He was not alone in his reservations. Lady Mary Dunn, too, considered it was all 'somewhat overdone ... The amount spent in one night would have kept a whole family for a year.'[62]

Yet, despite such criticisms most parents felt they must follow the traditional course. Daphne Vivian's father had very limited means and she realised that he could only afford to finance her in London for two Seasons. Even then she felt guilty in case it resulted in the family having to sell her beloved Cornish home. In the event she was to have a third Season, but this time it was paid for by an aunt.

In May 1922, the Vivians moved into a house they had rented for 15 guineas a week. They took with them six servants, including Mabel Creek, Daphne's lady's maid. She was to remain with Daphne long after she married. As with other debutantes, she acquired an extensive trousseau, helped by the contribution of a rich uncle of her stepmother, who agreed to double the amount originally set aside for expenditure on her wardrobe. This enabled her to go to some top London dressmakers, including Lucille, the prestigious establishment owned by Lady Duff Gordon.[63]

As the Vivians' circle of friends in London was limited, Daphne at first received few invitations to parties and balls organised for her fellow debs. Her stepmother responded by leaving visiting cards on all prospective hostesses of dances. In addition, an aunt agreed to give a small dance for Daphne at the end of the Season. 'People soon heard about this, and so began to ask me to their dances. I realised that Society was conducted on a strictly cutlet-for-cutlet basis.'

It was Daphne's father rather than her stepmother who chaperoned her at the various parties she attended. Most of the other debutantes were accompanied by their mothers or other female relatives, who sat on gold chairs placed round the ballroom, gossiping to their friends and keeping a close eye on the dancers. In those circumstances her father's arrival was welcomed since he 'ran a shuttle service', taking one lady after another to supper 'and giving them a turn round the room'.[64] He enjoyed it, too, being always a keen partygoer.

Daphne's particular friends were two half-sisters, Diana Duncombe and Beatrice Beckett. They were unusually emancipated in that they were allowed to go to dances on their own. 'Until I knew them,' wrote Daphne, 'I was not allowed out by myself even in the daytime, but had to be accompanied by a maid.' However, when she went out with Beatrice and Diana she was allowed to go without any other escort, on the strict understanding that they stayed together.

During the Season Daphne was constantly warned against getting a reputation for 'wildness', although as she subsequently recalled, the young men she met that first summer were far from wild. 'The entry in my diary after my first dance reads: "Disappointed in the London young men – rather a spotty, weedy crew."' She was presented at Court, 'wearing a silver dress with a train and white feathers in my hair'. She also went to Ascot, where she much enjoyed being permitted to lunch alone with young men. Nevertheless, she returned to her Cornish home at the end of the Season feeling rather deflated because she had not received one serious marriage proposal.[65] In later years that changed and she became involved in several flirtations before she became secretly engaged and then married to Henry Weymouth, heir to the Marquess of Bath. The two had first met when he was at school at Harrow, and their friendship was resumed when they attended parties in Oxford, where he was an undergraduate. The secrecy was needed because of parental opposition on the grounds that they were too young to make such a long-term commitment. In 1926, however, shortly before Henry was due to depart for the United States of America, where he was to spend some months, they decided to marry anyway. While he was away Daphne wore her wedding ring on a chain round her neck. On his return the following year both families agreed the match could go ahead, quite unaware that the two were married already. The official ceremony took place on 27 October 1927, at St Martin-in-the-Fields in London amid much pomp and ceremony. Daphne's dress was designed by the young Norman Hartnell, and the pages who attended her wore Hartnell-designed medieval doublets of red velvet and gold.[66]

Meanwhile, the four Courts which were held in 1922, when Daphne came out, were the first since 1914 that had something of their pre-war splendour. During the war all presentations had been suspended, so that by 1919 a large backlog of aspiring debutantes had built up. In that year the Lord Chancellor decided that to meet the exigencies of the situation, instead of holding Courts, three special Buckingham Palace garden parties would be held during the summer, to which 15,500 people were invited, including several thousand debutantes who had missed out during the war.[67] *The Bystander* declared this decision was a grave disappointment 'to many young matrons and maidens ... Presentation in a walking dress, with just a little "bob" to Majesty' hardly matched the evening splendour and glamour of a formal presentation.[68] The policy was attributed partly to the need for economy after the disruptions of war, but doubtless it enabled the backlog of debutantes to be dealt with more speedily. For those who feared they might not meet the king and queen, reassurance was given that the mere receipt of an invitation to a garden party would be regarded as equivalent to a presentation. This latter point was important for the debutantes in that permission to enter the prestigious royal enclosure at Ascot was only given to those who had been presented at Court.[69] As *The Bystander* commented slyly in 1929, one of the chief attractions of this privilege was being able 'to pass those green velvet-coated guardians at the white gate that leads from the paddock', thereby 'exciting envy in the hearts of those of one's friends who cannot do so ... The woman with an enclosure badge who can wave to her dearest friend on the other side of the railings can be said really to have lived.'[70]

That comment drew attention to the underlying spirit of rivalry and petty jealousy that also characterised much of the London social scene. This competitiveness provided valuable material for the growing number of aristocratic gossip columnists who appeared on the scene from the mid-1920s. The first signed social column, detailing the doings of 'High Society', appeared in the *Sunday Express* in 1926 when Lord Beaverbrook recruited Lord Castlerosse to write his 'Londoner's Log'. The following year Lady Eleanor Smith carried out a similar role in the *Weekly Despatch*, and others followed quickly in their wake, including Patrick Balfour himself.[71] In the late 1920s he became 'Mr. Gossip' in the *Daily Sketch*, and in 1939 succeeded to the title of the 3rd Baron Kinross. As Balfour admitted, in this way 'Society people are making money ... by recording each other's doings in the Press.' Hence if the well-to-do wanted to maintain their reputation they must be careful not to 'behave like a fishwife in somebody's drawing-room. There may be a social columnist present, who will record your antics.' At the end of the decade *The Times* gave space to those who were protesting at the unscrupulous tactics adopted by the gossip writers, who attended events merely in order to pass on any revealing details and tittle-tattle they had picked up to their eager readers.[72] The protests were to no avail for the social columns were too popular.

In the interim the traditional Courts began to be held once more from 1920, although initially they were 'shorn in some small measure' of their previous magnificence by the decision not to permit the wearing of feathers and a full Court train.[73] Not until 1922 did the ostrich-feather headdress and the train again make an appearance, and even then they were somewhat modified in that the length of the train was reduced, and to meet the changing fashion for shorter skirts, the floor-length gowns of pre-war days were no longer the norm.

It was, however, part of the strict Court protocol that divorcées were excluded. Hence a divorced mother could not present her daughter, but must find a friend who would perform the service for her. Loelia Ponsonby, whose own presentation at Court was delayed until 1925, even though she had 'come out' six years before, remembered her mother also sponsoring another debutante whose mother had been divorced. As a token of gratitude, the mother provided Loelia with a dress from the famous French designer, Patou. Unfortunately, despite its high cost, it proved a disappointment. Since she was unable to return to Paris to have a fitting, it was 'a shocking fit'. Later, when worn as an ordinary dance frock, she thought it looked hideous.[74]

The second wife of the 9th Duke of Marlborough was affected by this 'no divorce' rule even though she had not been married before. But the duke had. The fact that she had been his mistress before they married perhaps further blighted her prospects. Consequently, when he asked his cousin, the Duchess of Devonshire, who was Queen Mary's Mistress of the Robes, to make the presentation, she promptly refused: 'Oh, no .... I really couldn't go that far.' Eventually, almost two years after the marriage, he prevailed on Lady Birkenhead to make the presentation. But the duchess remained very much on the fringes of society both in Oxfordshire and in London. As she noted in her diary, she had not been invited to a garden party at Buckingham Palace because 'H.M. ... [was] terrified of articles published re divorced men's wives going to court!!!'[75] Yet the prohibition does not seem to have been universally applied since Lady Astor, who had been divorced many years before in the United States, was able to sponsor not only her own daughter, Wissie, on 8 May 1928, but two other ladies as well. All were instructed to wear 'Court Dress *with* feathers and trains'.[76]

Soon after receiving the invitation for herself and Wissie to attend the Court, Lady Astor and her daughter went to Paris to order a new wardrobe. Unlike Loelia Ponsonby, when some of the clothes proved unsatisfactory, Lady Astor soon complained. Thus a dress ordered from the famous couturier Molyneux for Wissie was condemned as 'colourless' and ill fitting. 'Lady Astor wonders if you would be willing to take this back', wrote her private secretary to the fashion house. That Molyneux agreed to do. In addition he was to provide 'an interlining' for a navy blue coat Lady Astor had ordered for herself. Their Court dresses were ordered from Madame Louiseboulanger, another couturier, and cost around 3,000 francs each.[77]

In addition to acquiring a new wardrobe, there was Wissie's coming out ball to arrange, with hundreds of guests to invite and the celebrated Ambrose and his orchestra to provide the music. It proved 'a great success', but for Lady Astor, the numerous social occasions on which she must chaperone her daughter, combined with her parliamentary duties, put her under a good deal of pressure. As she confessed ruefully to one friend: 'Life is a changed thing for me since my daughter is out.'[78]

Clementine Churchill, too, found chaperoning her debutante daughters tedious. That was not merely because of what her youngest daughter has called her 'un-social nature and early-to-bed habits', but through her contacts with fellow mothers. 'They are really rather a depressing back-biting tribe & I have to sit for hours with them...', she confessed. 'I'm thinking of taking a cookery book to Balls. I could be hunting up tasty dishes ... to try, instead of listening to their gossip.'[79]

For non-debutantes, on the other hand, the many social events associated with the London Season offered opportunities for marital infidelities, for those so inclined. That was true of Lady Edwina Mountbatten and her friend, Jean Norton, who had become the close companion of the newspaper tycoon Lord Beaverbrook. Edwina, bored by her husband's frequent absences on naval duties and seemingly by his lack of expertise as a lover, by the mid-1920s was beginning to seek sexual satisfaction elsewhere. One of her biographers claims that by this date her 'promiscuity was legendary among her friends and acquaintances, to whom moral discipline was foreign anyway.'[80]

Edwina's first serious relationship seems to have been with a long-standing friend, Hugh Molyneux, but when in October 1925 he left England for India, a replacement was readily found. He was Laddie Sanford, a wealthy American polo player and man-about-town who was regarded as a 'bounder' by many male members of London society. He was said to know 'every *demi-mondaine* in London'. Edwina's affair with Laddie lasted for some years, but she also became involved with Mike Wardell, manager of the *Evening Standard*, a good-looking member of the Beaverbrook circle. It was in these circumstances that her cousin, Marjorie, described ironically how a servant at her London home, Brook House, announced that he had shown Lord Molyneux to the morning room and Mr Sanford to the library, 'but where should I put the other gentleman?'[81]

When Dickie Mountbatten learned of Edwina's infidelities he was bitterly hurt and shocked, but ultimately he reluctantly accepted the situation. After all an open scandal and marital break-up would not only have been humiliating for him but would have seriously damaged his naval career and perhaps his connections with his royal relations. As Edwina's sister declared, when attempting to defend her promiscuity, both girls had been 'brought up to consider the media, ... and only a tight little coterie knew if there was a love relationship between individuals.'[82]

Meanwhile, if extramarital affairs were largely hidden from public view in the 1920s, except for those in the know, they did not impinge on the lives of the debutantes in their first Season. However, in 1927 they did have a new ritual added to their presentation year, at the instigation of Lady Howard de Walden. This was the introduction of Queen Charlotte's Ball. The innovation apparently arose from Lady Howard de Walden's post-1918 interest in London's maternity hospitals, of which there were seemingly only two in London at that time. Queen Charlotte's concentrated on catering for unmarried mothers, who were given priority over others when having their first child. However, the facilities available were sadly deficient. A large new hospital was needed and Lady Howard de Walden set about raising the necessary funds by holding concerts and dinners, but most of all by inaugurating Queen Charlotte's Birthday Ball. This was held on the first Tuesday in May and, under her presidency, it quickly became established as part of the Season's traditions. A card issued for the ball pointed out that Queen Charlotte, the wife of King George III, had been the 'first influential lady to take a personal, compassionate and practical' interest in the plight of poor women, 'ill, in childbirth, or homeless'. The ball was intended to 're-enact her Birthday Party, with a Birthday Cake and a Guest of Honour' to represent the queen. To her the 'Maids of Honour', selected from the current year's debutantes, made obeisance.[83] All those connected with the ball gave their services free, so that Jackson's of Piccadilly donated the giant cake, and each year a different cosmetic company provided presents for the Maids-in-Waiting, drawn from debutantes from a previous year, and the current year's Maids of Honour. The 'Guards of Honour were the favoured girls who actually dragged the cake into the ballroom'. The morning of the great day was spent in rehearsing the ceremonial under Lady Howard de Walden's critical eye. As Angela Lambert comments, if '228 girls [were] to sweep in pairs down two staircases and curtsey in twos to the Guest of Honour and a cake, it [had] to be done with military precision, otherwise laughter ... could ruin the effect'.[84] The cake was decorated with candles representing the number of years since Queen Charlotte's birth. By the end of the decade, therefore, Queen Charlotte's Ball had been accepted as an integral part of the process of 'coming out'.

Leading London Hostesses

Among other changing aspects of the London social scene during the 1920s was the emergence of a new kind of 'High Society' hostess, ambitious to make her mark, and sometimes of American origin. Before the First World War it had been the wives of the great aristocratic families, like the Cecils and the Greys, who had ruled society. Grand hostesses of this kind had entertained as naturally as they breathed, for it was part of the tradition in which they had grown up. Many exercised political influence, too, at a time when females were without the parliamentary vote, through the opportunities they gave Party leaders to meet together at the dinners and weekend gatherings they organised. However, following the economic upheavals after the First World War that situation changed. Town mansions were sold along with some country estates, and as incomes declined so the authority wielded by the nobility and gentry waned. Many families played a very limited role in the London Season itself, perhaps renting a property for a brief period or making a special effort when a daughter was to be presented at Court, as happened in the case of Daphne Vivian's Cornish family. In 1933 Patrick Balfour lamented the fact that 'the pageantry of the aristocracy itself [was] no more'. Even the great houses – Devonshire, Grosvenor, Dorchester and the rest – where they had once resided, had gone 'and with them the principle of large-scale formal entertaining for which they stood'.[85] A few years earlier Lady Milner had similarly noted with regret that the 'Great Hostess' had 'passed with the great House'.

By the 1920s, only Lady Londonderry, of the old aristocratic families, was still entertaining on a lavish pre-war scale, arranging large receptions at Londonderry House and allowing her home to become the social headquarters of the Conservative Party. Regular celebrations were held to mark the opening of Parliament, and on those occasions she would stand, a statuesque figure, at the top of the impressive staircase, to receive her guests. By her side stood the Prime Minister of the day, if he were a Conservative or, in the case of David Lloyd George, because he headed the post-1918 coalition government. On these occasions she was resplendent in the magnificent Londonderry jewels, and exuded an impressive aura of power, wealth, glamour and high status. At the first of the receptions held after the war, on 18 November 1919, 2,500 guests were reported to have attended.[86]

But Edith Londonderry exercised influence in smaller and more intimate ways, too, through the charities she patronised and, in particular, through the weekly meetings of the Ark Club. This had continued from its wartime inception, with each member having the name of an animal, bird, insect or other creature, including mythological beings. She herself retained the name of Circe, while her husband was called 'Charley the Cheetah'. Some said he had earned the label through his well-justified reputation as a notorious womaniser.[87] But there were new recruits as well, including Ramsay MacDonald, the first Labour Prime Minister. His close friendship with Lady Londonderry angered many members of his Party and of the trade union movement. They saw it as fraternising with the enemy, since most of the Londonderry fortune was derived from their Durham coalfields and Lord Londonderry was in no way noted for his enlightened attitude towards the miners. As one Labour MP caustically commented, a few months ago 'we sang the Red Flag. Now he whistles the Londonderry Air.'[88]

The friendship between MacDonald and Edith Londonderry had first arisen in 1924, shortly after he became Prime Minister. It developed as a result of their mutual love of the Scottish Highlands, with MacDonald addressing her in his letters as 'My dearest Ladye' or 'My dearest Friend of all'.[89] However, as one of Lady Londonderry's biographers has suggested, her letters to him also revealed a desperate need for affection, which may have been linked to the loneliness and unhappiness she felt at her husband's serial infidelities.[90] By the end of the 1920s they were meeting frequently, and MacDonald found relief from the pressures of office in her sympathetic and intelligent company and in the cultured world she gathered round herself.[91]

Other aristocratic ladies, of course, continued to offer hospitality to their friends, and for those participating in the London Season, regular attendance at dinner parties, balls, the theatre and other events remained very much what was expected of them. Yet the relentless round of activities could prove irksome, as the diary of Lady Jean Hamilton reveals. Thus in late February 1927 she was dining with Lord and Lady Middleton and noted gloomily that her fellow guests had been 'a lot of dull grand people – terribly cold house ... We shivered over a dying fire together until St John came and dragged me off.'[92]

But this kind of traditional aristocratic hospitality was overshadowed in the 1920s by the emergence of a new kind of hostess for whom the need to entertain in order to secure impressive social connections became the prime motivating influence of life. As John Lehmann commented, a 'great hostess and creator of a salon needs an unflagging curiosity about other people, a flair for making them feel at home, or at least stimulated in her circle, almost unlimited time to organize her entertainments ... and plenty of money'.[93]

During the 1920s four of these new-style hostesses became particularly prominent in the eyes of their contemporaries. They were the Hon. Mrs Greville and Lady Colefax, who were both British, and Lady Cunard and Mrs Corrigan, who had been born in the United States, though in Lady Cunard's case she had lived in England from the mid-1890s.

Although the social circles they wished to cultivate differed considerably from each other, all four shared a desire to shine and to be able to boast of their wide range of impressive friends and acquaintances. As such, they became recognised as important figures on the London social scene. Lady Cunard, indeed, became something of a celebrity herself, not only for her gaiety and wit, but for her determined promotion of the arts, particularly of opera and the theatre. According to her friend Daphne Fielding (the former Daphne Weymouth) it was chiefly through her efforts that the Old Vic theatre was saved.[94] She spent enormous sums of her own fortune to launch further seasons of opera, and according to Cecil Beaton, who much admired her, she 'tirelessly bludgeoned her rich but vandalistic friends into subscribing for boxes at Covent Garden'.[95] It was said that she lived for 'music, literature, conversation and romantic attachments probably in that order.'[96] As regards romantic attachments, although she had a number of male friends and admirers, her one great love was the conductor Thomas Beecham, later Sir Thomas, whom she had first got to know in 1911. She remained devoted to him for the rest of her life, despite his blatant infidelities and the fact that when they met both were married to other people.

In 1926, recognising the new, more vibrant spirit of the age, Lady Cunard changed her Christian name from prosaic Maud to Emerald, declaring that emeralds were her favourite jewels. Thereafter almost all her friends referred to her by her new name.[97] The interesting people she gathered round her dinner table and her own ability to maintain the flow of conversation along witty and light-hearted lines attracted, among others, the Prince of Wales, much to the disapproval of his mother, Queen Mary. According to Kenneth Clark, who became Director of the National Gallery in London while still in his twenties, her luncheon and dinner parties 'were a curious mixture of handsome young men, accepted wits like Lord Berners, a few writers ... and clever, spiteful women', with a leavening of more serious people, such as ambassadors.[98]

Yet, not all of her guests appreciated Lady Cunard's conversational style. Even Kenneth Clark felt that because everyone was afraid of being labelled a bore, it was impossible to stick to a point long enough to develop a train of thought. Virginia Woolf described her dismissively as 'a ridiculous little parrokeet-faced woman', while to Lady Cynthia Asquith she was like 'an inebriate canary'. The sharp-tongued Margot Asquith considered her 'a crucial supervisor of Fun', but then added, 'I don't know how good a brain she really has because she has never used it. Massage in the mornings, music in the evenings, talk, telephone all day. She is a little pagan.' However, Margot admitted that despite her faults she was loved by most people because she was 'a really kind woman – never wants any thing as much for herself as for you.'[99]

Crucially, though, it was Margot, now Lady Oxford, who in 1930 caused the final breach between Lady Cunard and her wayward daughter, Nancy. Nancy spent most of her time in the 1920s in France, merely coming to London from time to time. She had long resented her mother's breach with her country-loving father, Sir Bache Cunard, and the relationship with Sir Thomas Beecham. Nancy herself, however, had become involved with a black musician, Henry Crowder, while living in France. The two came to London on a visit in 1930, despite the racial prejudice that still existed, and it was this that provoked Margot's intervention. On arrival for lunch one day at Lady Cunard's she shouted, 'Well, Maud, what's Nancy up to now? Is it dope, drink, or niggers?' The remark was offensive and to compound it Margot insisted on calling her hostess Maud rather than Emerald, as she preferred.[100] The information about her daughter's new friendship came as a great shock to Lady Cunard. After telephoning other friends to confirm the veracity of the story, she had her daughter and her black lover followed by detectives, to Nancy's fury. As a consequence, in 1931 Nancy published privately a bitter pamphlet, which appalled her High Society friends and acquaintances by its relentless denunciation of her mother, whom she had long referred to with contempt as 'Her Ladyship'. In it she claimed that while her mother could be as 'hard and as buoyant as a dreadnought ... one touch of ridicule goes straight to her heart'. She called her mother's mode of entertaining pure 'hypocrisy' combined as it was with snobbery and gossip. 'Her Ladyship's ... snobbery is quite simple. If a thing is *done* she will, with a few negligible exceptions, do it too.'[101]

Emerald, for her part, maintained a stoic dignity, treating the whole affair as a sign of her daughter's mental instability.[102] The two were never to be reconciled. For the rest, Lady Cunard continued her active social life and her devotion to music and literature. Daphne Fielding, who first got to know her in 1926, remembered her with affection. She recalled that she would 'always appear slightly late at her own parties, poking her head round the door to peer with an expression of pleased surprise at her assembled guests. Then she would enter the room "like a jewelled bird uncaged" ... The young men I met at her house were far more entertaining than any of the Guards officers, budding stockbrokers and sporting characters who had hitherto been my lot at debutante dances and hunt balls.'[103] Nor did her 'conversational alacrity and versatility' desert her when she grew older.

The other leading American-born hostess of the 1920s was the exuberant Mrs Laura Corrigan. She was very different from Lady Cunard in her lack of education – her malapropisms were notorious – and her unabashed neglect of intellectual issues. She derived her great wealth from her American steel magnate husband, who seems to have played little part in her determined assault on London's social scene. Cecil Beaton considered she conquered London society through the 'calculated spontaneity' of her parties at which 'the most eminent or fashionable guests somehow were generally those fortunate enough to win the tombola prizes of gold cigarette cases'.[104] Humbler guests would find that their prizes were more modest. Her extravagance was such that when she hired an all-star cabaret to entertain her guests, they were paid more for their brief appearance at her party than they received for a week in the theatre.[105] She even won over her rival hostess, Lady Cunard, by taking an expensive box at Covent Garden Opera House and making a large donation to Sir Thomas Beecham's pet project, the Imperial League of Opera.[106]

Despite the fact that many of Laura Corrigan's aristocratic guests secretly mocked her for her ignorance and the fact that she always wore a wig, apparently because she had lost her hair early in life, they came to appreciate her for her personal qualities of kindness and absence of malice. They were also amused at her unconventional behaviour. Loelia Ponsonby remembered seeing her stand on her head at a party (having previously tied a scarf round her skirt for modesty's sake) while assuring everyone that it was both 'delightfully comfortable and good for the health'. On another occasion, when she had persuaded some of her guests to perform cabaret turns for the benefit of the rest, she ended proceedings by performing the Charleston as an exhibition dance, while wearing a top hat and red-heeled shoes.[107]

On her first arrival in London Mrs Corrigan had been unable to penetrate the exclusive world of the social elite.

Then she learned that Mrs Keppel, who had been King Edward VII's close friend, was planning to live abroad. She was seeking a tenant for her large Grosvenor Street house in consequence and Laura's immense wealth ensured that cash was no impediment to a successful transaction. The price was to include the services of the experienced butler, Mr Rolfe, his wife, who was the cook, and the full complement of twenty indoor servants. For an extra sum Mrs Corrigan gained access to Mrs Keppel's visitors' book.

Mr Rolfe proved a particular asset. He not only sought to attract former friends of Mrs Keppel so that they paid a call on his new mistress but he advised her to contact Charlie Stirling, who was a nephew of Lord Rossmore. He had family connections with many other aristocratic families and was employed as social secretary by the Marchioness of Londonderry, who had her own impressive personal connections. Stirling agreed to help Mrs Corrigan for a generous fee and Lady Londonderry, too, assisted her career by accepting an early invitation to her house. The fact that the Marquess and Marchioness of Londonderry were prepared to accept her hospitality soon led others to follow suit. Lady Londonderry was even able to open the doors of Buckingham Palace for her. As Brian Masters comments: 'George V and Queen Mary would have nothing to do with her until Lady Londonderry persuaded them.'[108]

Through her relentless pursuit of royalty and members of the aristocracy, Mrs Corrigan's social circle gradually became more exclusive. But, as Patrick Balfour drily noted, she did not entertain people because she liked them nor, unlike the pre-war great hostesses, did she invite them 'from a sense of responsibility or duty or habit'. She had no interest in what they might tell her concerning politics or art or intellectual matters. Instead she made Society itself her object in life. She entertained because 'she [was] ambitious – to entertain'.[109] Her philosophy was perhaps best summed up by a remark she made shortly before she died in 1948, when she declared, 'as a little girl I often dreamed of knowing all the kings and queens in the world. And I've had my wish.'[110]

The Hon. Mrs Greville, too, used her personal wealth and determined character to force her way to the top of society, although she was initially aided by the well-established connections of her husband, a younger son of Lord Greville, and a friend of King Edward VII. Mrs Greville, known to her friends as Maggie, was the illegitimate daughter of a wealthy self-made Scottish brewer, William McEwan. She had a good education and was eventually to inherit her father's fortune. Following the deaths of her husband and father, she devoted her organising ability and intelligence to the running of the firm of McEwan & Co. and to becoming a leading member of High Society. Like Mrs Corrigan, she particularly favoured royalty and the upper ranks of the aristocracy. In this connection sly comments were made that she never failed to have cinnamon-flavoured scones available at teatime in case Queen Mary should call.[111]

Contemporary reports of the 1920s confirm Mrs Greville's royal successes. In 1922 she entertained the Prince of Wales; two years later she gave a huge ball 'at which the crowd was so dense that the King and Queen of Italy had to sit in their car outside while … footmen cleared a way through the assembled guests'. The Queen of Spain was a particular friend, and it was maliciously claimed that Mrs Greville allowed scarcely a day to go by 'without some royal name-dropping'. However, she achieved her greatest triumph in 1923 when the Duke and Duchess of York chose her luxurious country house, Polesden Lacey, for their honeymoon. Thereafter she and the Yorks remained close friends and the latter were often entertained at Polesden Lacey.[112]

In appearance, Maggie Greville was short and fat, but despite her plebeian appearance she took great pride in the social influence she wielded and in her own status, stating firmly that she would 'rather be a beeress than a peeress'. But the grand dinners she gave for statesmen, diplomats and members of the royal families of Europe, as well as the excellent food she provided, were balanced by other, much less attractive, characteristics. She was an expert in spreading malicious and cruel gossip, and she delighted in the reverses suffered by her rivals. On one occasion she crushingly observed of Emerald Cunard: 'You mustn't think that I dislike little Lady Cunard,' adding 'I'm always telling Queen Mary that she isn't half as bad as she is painted.'[113] Emerald's response was to mock the oversized quail that Mrs Greville served at dinner, claiming they had been 'blown up with a bicycle pump'. To the former diplomat, politician and author, Harold Nicolson, Maggie Greville was 'nothing more than a fat slug filled with venom', while the Duke of Portland considered her 'poisonous; if she heard a nasty story about some one, she would embellish it and make it even nastier'.[114] Only the Royal Family were exempt from her vitriol. Cecil Beaton, then a leading society photographer and theatre designer, described her bitterly as 'a galumphing, greedy, snobbish old toad who watered her chops at the sight of royalty and the Prince of Wales's set'.[115]

Yet, despite her malevolence, many accepted her hospitality. She was a shrewd judge of those likely to rise in the world and it is significant that Kenneth Clark, who became Director of the National Gallery before he was thirty, was a regular dinner-party guest, together with his wife. His recollection of those gatherings was unflattering. He considered them 'the dullest I can remember, stuffy members of government and their mem-sahib wives, ambassadors and royalty'.[116] Yet her connections with the social elite were apparently sufficiently attractive to encourage him to continue to accept her invitations.

The fourth of these leading new-style hostesses of the 1920s, Lady Colefax, differed from the others in that she came from a solidly middle-class background and was of relatively modest means. Her husband had been a very successful patents lawyer before 1914, but by the 1920s his increasing deafness and the depressed state of trade meant that his opportunities to practise were much curtailed and their income reduced. At the end of the decade, indeed, it was Sibyl Colefax herself who sought to overcome their financial problems by going into business. Nevertheless, throughout the 1920s she continued to entertain regularly at her attractive, though not particularly large, family home, Argyll House, in Chelsea. Despite the limitations on her income she was determined to attract to her table the leading figures of the day, particularly those whom Loelia Ponsonby has labelled 'the intelligentsia'. They included people prominent in the worlds of literature, art and music, as well as some leading politicians. Kenneth Clark called her need to attract celebrities 'an addiction as strong as alcohol or drugs'.[117] She issued hundreds of invitations and even her younger son, Michael, admitted she could not be described as 'an effortless hostess; in fact the force which she generated in organizing her parties was hydro-electric'.[118] Only when her guests had arrived did the dynamos cease to hum and there was an atmosphere of repose. 'If, sometimes, she attempted to manage her friends,' declared Michael, 'they accepted the discipline gladly, knowing that she gave them in return her passionate and sometimes combative, loyalty.'

The less charitable regarded her in a different light. She was called 'the most persistent and successful lion-hunter' that London had ever known:

> Every eminent person, every famous name, everyone whose achievements had attracted attention or whose position inspired awe, sooner or later was inveigled to her oval dining-table. Resistance was futile. Sibyl Colefax issued another, and another, she would mount up scores of them if necessary, until the prey eventually succumbed ... through sheer weariness. Thus by attrition did the collection of famous guests grow to unrivalled dimensions.[119]

Daphne Fielding described how one regular recipient of these missives, the maliciously witty Lord Berners, 'impishly adapted a Victorian toy he owned, a large japanned head of a blackamoor, so that when a button was pressed it opened its mouth and spewed out a stream of these invitations'.[120] A particularly desirable potential guest might receive three or four invitations at the same time, written in Sibyl's sprawling, almost illegible hand, each for a separate occasion. Not being acquainted with someone she felt she ought to know was her greatest anxiety, and her 'self-esteem rose in proportion to the number of celebrated persons she assembled around her'.[121]

Yet even her critics admitted Lady Colefax was well-read and was a knowledgeable connoisseur of art. One of her closest friends was Bernard Berenson, the American-born art expert whom she and her husband visited several times at his villa near Florence. She had first met Berenson in 1894 when, aged nineteen, she had visited Italy with her mother, and they had kept in touch ever since.[122] Sibyl also appreciated music, and on a wider basis she was always concerned to promote the best interests of her friends and guests. Michael Colefax claimed she would often introduce young people to those who, she thought, might advance their careers. In a letter to her husband she once wrote, 'What differentiates me from most people is that I enjoy *liking* more than disliking – I enjoy *love* more than hate – I enjoy describing & praising far more than decrying and abusing.'[123] In that respect she differed greatly from her fellow hostess, Mrs Greville, and even from the mischievously witty Lady Cunard.

Sibyl went to great lengths to serve excellent food to her guests, aided by her skilled cook, Mrs Gray, and her entire daily round was centred upon the luncheon and dinner parties she was to hold, or her other social commitments. At the beginning of the 1920s, she wrote to Bernard Berenson, 'We've of course slipped back into the Ballet, Opera, dining whirl which is very pleasant and I don't pretend not to enjoy [it].'[124]

Yet among those who accepted Lady Colefax's hospitality, sometimes, as in the case of Virginia Woolf, with reluctance, there were many who mocked her persistence in issuing invitations, and derided her 'lion-hunting' technique. On 1 May 1925, for example, Virginia Woolf told a friend that she was about to take tea with Lady Colefax. She 'interests me, as you would be interested by a shiny cupboard carved with acanthus leaves ... so hard and shiny and bright is she; and collects all the intellects about her, as a parrot picks up beads'.[125] Yet when the two met alone for tea at Virginia's house, she admitted Sibyl was 'so nice'. She only glittered 'as a cheap cherry in her own house'.[126] The diplomat, Sir Ronald Storrs, who declared his dislike of Sibyl's habit of 'capping everything with a more celebrated but less well-fitting cap', also conceded that she was at her best 'in total company of two'. Then she 'was not peering round fearing she might be missing somebody or something else'.[127]

A number of guests commented, too, on her inability to create spontaneity and light-heartedness at her luncheon and dinner parties. To Sir Ronald Storrs she was a 'convenor rather than a chairman' of her parties, while Lady Desborough declared she knew how to get her guests to her table 'but she does not know what to do with us when she has got us'.[128] In that respect she received little help from her husband. One socialite said of Sir Arthur Colefax that he was deaf but 'unfortunately the reverse of dumb ... boring beyond belief'.[129] Even Sibyl herself, despite her affection for him, recognised his deficiencies in that regard.[130] But she herself was accused of talking ceaselessly without saying anything memorable. On one occasion, her rival hostess, Lady Cunard, declared mischievously, 'Oh dear, I simply must stop. I'm becoming a bore, like Lady Colefax.'[131]

As she became more prominent on the London social scene, Sibyl became aware of the snide comments made about her. In 1929, in a letter to her friend, Harold Nicolson, she had evidently expressed her deep hurt at this treatment. In response he sought to console and reassure her:

Of course people are ... malicious, but are they malignant? After all, Sibyl, the central fact is that ... Argyll House is a feature in the intellectual life of today & that it will be thought of and remembered long after the disagreeable sneers are forgotten. I do not pretend that I *have* not heard people say that you are autocratic & dictatorial (poor Sibyl!) in arranging your parties. But the point is I have never heard anyone of importance speak of you

except with admiration & I have heard many of the men
& women whom we most admire affirm again & again
their friendship towards you & the debt they owe you.[132]

On a wider front, after her first visit to the United States
in 1926, she became an enthusiastic supporter of efforts to
strengthen Anglo-American relations. She had gone there
initially to see her elder son, Peter, who had recently taken
up employment in America, but thereafter she regularly
entertained American friends and acquaintances when they
came to London. Soon her transatlantic connections were
to become as important to her as her English friends.
According to Michael Colefax she would give two or three
dinners each year from May to July specifically for special
friends from the United States.[133]

In the end, despite Sibyl's 'lion-hunting' tendencies and
her tireless pursuit of celebrities, as her son Michael declared
in an account of his mother's life, her true nature was shown
'in her abhorrence of the vulgar, in her quick enjoyment of
any form of beauty, in her detestation of publicity, malice or
intrigue ... If Sibyl met anybody, liked them & sensed that
the feeling was reciprocated it was a friendship for life. The
exceptions were very few & far between.'[134]

It was, then, in their very different ways that all four of
these new-style 'great hostesses' made their contribution to
the vibrancy of London's social life during the turbulent
twenties. With the onset of economic depression at the
end of that decade their role, and that of others like them,
inevitably became more subdued.

5

Domestic Affairs and Breaking the Mould

No one who considered herself a lady expected to have to do any housework. If one had a servant at all one did not even pull a curtain or open the front door when the bell rang.

> Loelia, Duchess of Westminster, *Grace and Favour*
> (London, 1961), p. 94.

The upper classes now began, almost as a matter of course, to go into business. Only thus could they save the fortunes of their class.

> Patrick Balfour, *Society Racket: A Critical Survey of*
> *Modern Social Life* (London: 1933), p. 78.

Domestic Issues

During the 1920s the domestic life of many elite families underwent a change, as they moved away from the elaborate and lavish arrangements that had been common before 1914 towards a more cautious and cost-conscious existence.

For some that meant from the middle of the decade the purchase of new, more functional art deco furniture and fittings, with their rectangular shape and avoidance of excessive ornamentation, which made them easier to clean. They appealed to those consciously seeking a more modern image or who were now living in mansion flats rather than their own large houses. They were also a response to the approaching era of mass-production and the machine age.[1]

Very often the changes were accompanied by a reduction in the number of domestic servants, to match more restricted incomes, and a greater resort to labour-saving devices and commercial services. These latter included an increased use of hotels and restaurants as venues for luncheons, dinners and receptions by hosts and hostesses whose own domestic resources were too limited to provide large-scale hospitality. The *nouveau riche* also appreciated the facilities they offered since such locations removed the uncertainties involved in organising their own parties. At the Savoy, Stanley Jackson described 'a new-rich ostentation' jostling 'the remains of Edwardian magnificence'. He claimed that during the decade the hotel's fourteen banqueting rooms were continuously booked for an endless series of luncheons and dinners. 'Throughout the 'twenties it was rare to see fewer than seven or eight hundred people in full evening dress, dining and dancing every night at the Savoy.'[2]

Few with straitened finances were as fortunate as Lady Diana Cooper, who was able to rely on rich friends to provide game, salmon and champagne for the lavish parties she and her husband, Duff, held at their Gower Street home. 'Immense expenditure in effort, frugality in money, was Diana's rule', it was said, and 'the result gave happiness to everyone, including the donors'. Like many successful hostesses, she was fortunate in having an exemplary butler, named Holbrook. Though, ironically, she was sometimes angered by 'the bland satisfaction' with which this paragon anticipated her requests. 'We need some more coal, Holbrook', she would say, only for him calmly to respond, 'I took the liberty of ordering it this morning, my lady.'[3]

In other cases hostesses economised by organising cocktail parties, which became part of the London social scene from about 1922, or they arranged afternoon games of bridge. However, in the case of bridge enthusiasts like Margot Oxford, expenditure on the game could far outweigh economies made elsewhere. In July 1927 her stepdaughter, Violet Bonham Carter, expressed fury at the size of 'Margot's bridge bills (40£ last Sunday)' and the pressure this 'completely irresponsible extravagance' was placing upon the restricted income of her husband, the former Prime Minister.[4]

Yet, despite these developments, numerous aspects of social life continued much as before. That included a continued emphasis on the importance of observing the rules of etiquette in relationships with friends and acquaintances. They covered such questions as the paying of calls, the leaving of visiting cards, and the importance of observing a correct precedence of rank when arranging seating at a dinner party. 'Society, for its own protection, has built up a definite code of manners and customs which must, to some extent, be observed by any one desirous of being welcomed by well-bred people', declared Lady Troubridge. Nevertheless, it was also important to remember that 'the practice of etiquette' implied more than 'a knowledge of the conventions regarding the giving and accepting or refusing of invitations, the number of cards to leave ... or the correct use of titles ... : [it] must be built upon the fundamental principles of respect and kindly feeling for others.'[5]

Certainly Loelia Ponsonby recalled how, after 1918, afternoon calls 'and card-dropping still went on, although not to the same extent as in Edwardian days. It was unusual to write and thank for a dinner or a dance, but the polite left a card.'[6] She also remembered how the ladies who came to lunch with her mother 'deplored Modern Times. They said how crippling the taxes were, how dreadful the housing shortage, how expensive the shops ... Above all they complained about the servant problem.'

As a government report had noted as early as 1919, after the war, girls were reluctant to return to the restrictions on daily lives and on dress connected with residential service, while many parents, too, discouraged daughters from taking up the work.[7] As a consequence there were loud laments about both the shortage of domestic staff and the generally uncooperative behaviour of those recruited. 'No peace even down here', wrote the exasperated Earl Winterton about servants at his Shillinglee country house. 'I hear Crowe has been misbehaving himself. D--n all modern servants, I say.'[8]

According to Loelia Ponsonby, however, the new circumstances meant that advertisements for domestic workers in the newspapers and elsewhere began 'to adopt a conciliatory tone. "Good wages. Good outings," they promised, adding as an attraction, that they had electric light.'[9] Landed families and other established aristocratic households normally had less trouble in recruiting servants than their *nouveau-riche* counterparts. Lily Milgate, who was employed by several well-to-do families between 1922 and 1930, mostly as a housemaid, considered that the

happiest time of my life was from the age of 14 to 22 for these years were spent in the stately homes of England before the decline set in of the real gentry and noblemen and before their lovely houses were opened to public eyes. I feel now that I was privileged to have lived in such mansions and to have seen & touched the wonderful treasures they contained.[10]

Similarly, Mrs Boyce, a farmer's daughter from Northamptonshire, who became a lady's maid to Lady Millicent Palmer at Cefyn Park, in North Wales, preferred to work for a titled family:

If they were just money-made people, well, nobody wanted to go there, they didn't know how to treat a servant. It had got to be breeding, especially for housemaids and lady's maids and footmen; they were very particular where they took a job. The good old aristocracy of England, they treat you as a jewel.[11]

Then she added, somewhat shamefaced, 'So we're a lot of snobs all of us really.'

Nonetheless Loelia Ponsonby argued that despite the complaints, in practice 'we all continued to live with what now seems a vast quantity of servants ... [The] houses were the reverse of labour saving. Coal needed carrying, grates blacking, wash stands needed cans of hot water brought and slops carried away. Nothing was in a handy or convenient position. There were flights and flights of stairs and few taps. Ceremonies had to be observed. One dressed for dinner though the skies fell.'[12] Furthermore, for those wives who led an active social life or, like Lady Denman, were involved in various administrative and charitable ventures, efficient servants were essential. 'When my mother was made Grand Dame of the British Empire,' declared Lady Denman's daughter, 'she said that she could never have achieved what she had done had it not been for the excellence of her staff, who took all worries off her shoulders and organised everything. All she had to do was to say how many people were coming for the weekend ... [The] servants all felt part of the family.'[13]

Where large parties were held in private houses, the problems involved in arranging these remained as great as they had ever been, even if, as sometimes happened, outside caterers were hired to help, and temporary staff were brought in. Gordon Grimmett was one of these, after he lost his place as one of the Astors' full-time footmen, in 1924. It was a way of earning extra money to supplement his salary as a floor manager in one of the Lyons Corner Houses. Occasionally he went as an auxiliary matching footman to Arlington House, which meant that he and the other footmen were all of the same height and build. 'We were chiefly there as ornaments, for after we had dinner we lined up in the beautifully dim-lit corridor and just stood there for the rest of the evening ... Nevertheless there's something artistically satisfying in wearing full livery and carrying it well.' He and the other auxiliary footmen were paid the substantial sum of £2 5s a night for a dinner and ball, or a little more if they had powdered hair. But there was 'always a deduction. At the end of the evening when you went to collect and sign for your fee you threw five bob back to the butler and got a, "Look forward to seeing you again" for your pains.'[14]

Cecil Beaton attended one of these large receptions, given by Mrs Guinness, where the guests were so numerous they were

> literally overflowing into the street ... all the people one has ever known or even seen – up and down the big

staircase, in the ballroom, along the corridors – 'Hutch' singing in the ballroom while we all sat on the floor – Edythe Baker playing to some of us in another room downstairs – Oliver Messel in the same room giving a ludicrously lifelike imitation of a lift-attendant describing the departments on each floor – Lady Ashley shining in a glittering short coat of silver sequins over her white dress – glimpses of the Ruthven twins – of Noel Coward ... impression after impression, before one sank and sank ... to the supper room.[15]

Where house parties were held, mistresses normally arranged the allocation of rooms for the guests in consultation with the housekeeper, and would discuss with the chef or cook the proposed menus. The butler would be informed of day-to-day engagements, including the number expected to lunch or dine. This could be a considerable responsibility, especially if extra guests unexpectedly arrived. In 1920 the Astors' newly promoted butler, Edwin Lee, recalled how early in his career he had to arrange a dinner for forty people, followed by a reception for up to 2,000, at his employers' town house, 4 St James's Square. So nervous was he at the prospect of this, and so meticulous was his general approach to his work, that he held rehearsals with his underlings to give himself peace of mind.[16] Later he became the key figure in organising most aspects of the Astors' hospitality, and that included coping with Lady Astor's volatile and demanding character. Only once did he threaten to leave, after becoming exasperated at her unreasonable conduct and lack of appreciation. He announced that he would go at the end of the month, but quick as a flash Lady Astor saw she had gone too far. 'In that case, Lee, you must tell me where you're going because I'm coming with you.' That broke the tension, and, according to the butler, they both 'ended up laughing and she was easier in her behaviour towards me for quite a while'.[17]

Even in small households, like that of Lady Colefax, their reputation for a high standard of hospitality depended on the skills of their staff. The Colefaxes relied on three servants, namely the parlourmaid, Norah Fielding, who had been with Sibyl from the age of eighteen, the cook, Mrs Gray, who came in the early 1920s, and the chauffeur, Briance. Like her mistress, Fielding enjoyed entertaining and she took sole charge of Lady Colefax's visitors' book. Mrs Gray had a well-earned reputation for being an excellent cook, serving simple dishes but making them from the best and freshest ingredients.[18]

Some newly married mistresses found difficulty in carrying out the duties their changed status required. That was true of Gladys Marlborough, the Duke of Marlborough's second wife, whom he married in 1921. Prior to marriage she had lived mainly in Paris and she soon became disillusioned with her new position, declaring gloomily to a friend, 'I married a house not a man.' Life at Blenheim Palace was organised on a grand scale, with forty servants employed inside and around the same number outside. These numbers were boosted when guests arrived with their own staff, who also had to be accommodated. The footmen were all at least 6 feet tall and wore maroon coats decorated with a good deal of silver braid. Their hair was powdered daily with a mixture of violet powder and flour, and they were paid an extra amount to enable them to purchase the violet powder. But, as Gladys confided to Lady Ottoline Morrell, who lived in the nearby Oxfordshire village of Garsington, 'The mere thought of those huge rooms makes my acheing legs ache more'. Another of Gladys's friends, who was staying at

Blenheim, was struck by the way in which the staff worked so quietly and invisibly that life in the household was conducted in 'majestic silence'. This she found disquieting:

> I heard the fire crackling in my room without having seen it lighted, the curtains were drawn and breakfast was brought up without my being awakened, and at ten o'clock *The Times* was insinuated under my eyes ... By eight o'clock in the morning the lawn was rolled, the dead leaves removed and the flower stands filled with fresh flowers.[19]

Gladys herself found the atmosphere oppressive. As an animal lover, she particularly disliked the regular autumn shooting parties, or, as she put it, the time when the household was 'murderous with heavy people & talk of guns, game etc'. The contrast between the life she had enjoyed in France and this 'intellectual wilderness' was brought home to her, and as a diversion she took up gardening, spending hours pruning the roses and beginning work on a rock garden. Not surprisingly by the late 1920s relations between the duchess and her husband had reached a very low ebb, with frequent rows about the servants. Marlborough accused Gladys of upsetting them and causing them to leave. As the duchess's biographer notes, a situation soon developed 'in which neither party could do anything right'. At one dinner party, indeed, 'she produced a revolver and placed it beside her. A rather startled guest at her side inquired: "Duchess, what are you going to do with that?" to which she replied: "Oh! I don't know, I might just shoot Marlborough."'[20] By the early 1930s the marriage was virtually over but there was no divorce, as the duke, in the interim, had converted to Roman Catholicism.

Fortunately, few newly-weds had such an unhappy experience as Gladys Marlborough, but many found problems arising from their sheer lack of knowledge on how to run a home. Helen Hardinge recalled ruefully that a few months before her marriage in 1921, she had begged her mother to allow her to learn how to cope with domestic matters in the family home, but her mother 'could not bear the idea of anybody else doing it but herself'. The outcome was that almost as soon as she became responsible for her own household Helen ran into debt, and subsequently settled this by selling a small amount of her jewellery. Then, because of her lack of confident leadership, the domestic routine became disturbed by quarrels among her three senior servants. As a result they each insisted on eating their meals separately in different rooms. 'I was only saved from ... disaster by my father-in-law's old cook, who ... had been lent to me for a time. Most of what I learnt about housekeeping, I learnt from her.'[21] Yet even after this she continued to rely on her mother for guidance when hiring new staff, as in September 1924 when she informed Lady Milner that she would be needing a cook and a kitchenmaid at the end of the following month. 'I think your cook would do perfectly', and a proposed wage of £65 a year 'would be quite all right'.[22]

A number of mistresses in the upper ranks of society, however, unashamedly left the running of the household to their senior servants as a matter of course, despite the risk that such a policy could lead to extravagance and even dishonesty if the staff members concerned were careless of the family's best interests. Mary, Duchess of Buccleuch, who married in 1921 and moved with her husband and family between the various houses they owned, openly admitted that she relied 'enormously' on her staff:

One had a housekeeper in each house, and a very good head butler, who travelled from house to house, and he nearly always had a second butler, who also travelled with us. Men staff always did, but the housekeeper remained in each house. And one usually had a travelling housemaid ...

I left the menus and the ordering of the food entirely to the cook – I had rather a good cook, luckily, so I left a great deal to her ... She had her own department – she never came out of the kitchen. She had her own sitting room and ate there, fed by her own minions.[23]

Similarly Patricia, Viscountess Hambleden, a daughter of the Earl of Pembroke, remembered the large retinue of servants at Wilton, her family home. 'We had an absolutely marvellous butler called Mr Smith ... he had everything under control and nothing ever worried him. Everything was done impeccably ... and the same for the housekeeper and cook ... I think most people had butlers. I can only think of one person who had parlourmaids, and everybody rather noticed it ... [It] wasn't quite the thing to have parlourmaids.'[24]

At West Wycombe Park in Buckinghamshire, Lady Dashwood, who married in 1922, remembered the butler ruling everything in the household: 'He was very very grand – and then the cook considered herself even grander, but wasn't, I suppose ... The butler, the cook and the housekeeper were the king pins.' One of the cooks, a Mrs McKay, who had trained at The Ritz and obviously took great pride in her skills, firmly refused to allow Lady Dashwood to learn to cook in her kitchen. Presumably she considered that would have undermined her own status.[25]

However, other mistresses of stately homes took a much

stronger line. Lady Astor, aided by her private secretary, not only kept a firm grip on household expenditure, but insisted on any additional items required receiving her approval before an order was placed. Bills were queried, and any infringement of the rules led to a sharp reprimand. Typical of this attitude was a letter written in the 1930s to the then housekeeper, reproving her for hiring a temporary housemaid for the busy Ascot week. The letter was written by the private secretary and pointed out that the 'engagement of temporary servants without [Her Ladyship's] knowledge and consent is something about which [she] is very particular, so do be sure not to make this mistake again.'[26] In addition to supervising the housemaids and still-room maids, to ensure they carried out their duties satisfactorily, the Cliveden housekeeper had a number of other responsibilities. These ranged from taking care of the household linen and china to preparing the guest rooms for visitors, making large quantities of jam, bottling fruit, inspecting the three bothies, or hostels, where the Astors' unmarried gardeners and stable workers lodged, and ensuring that Greenwood Cottage, an estate property often let to family friends, was ready for occupation. Lady Astor also refused to recruit any Roman Catholic servants.

The head gardeners at Cliveden, too, were soon admonished if they failed to supply sufficient vegetables, fruit and flowers to meet the household's requirements, and that included despatching produce during the week to London when the Astors were in residence there. Lady Astor also kept a keen eye on the appearance of the gardens, drawing attention to any faults. In 1928, for example, she compared the horticultural skills of her long-standing head gardener, William Camm, adversely to those of her friend Sir Philip Sassoon's head gardener, telling him that Sir Philip's tuberoses were 'much fuller and an altogether better specimen than those grown at Cliveden'. She told Camm to consult the Sassoon gardener to find out how he achieved these results.[27] Seemingly this was done, for two months later she was congratulating her head gardener on the 'beautiful tuberoses' he had grown.[28] Camm was first appointed in 1906, when the Astors moved to Cliveden, and he remained head gardener until his death in February 1929.

Michael Astor, one of Lady Astor's younger children, confirmed that his mother was 'an expert and meticulous housekeeper ... nothing escaped her notice'. Scarcely was breakfast over before she was downstairs, dealing with the day's housekeeping arrangements. 'Monsieur Gilbert, the chef, in his white jacket and carrying his menu book, would come into her boudoir to discuss the meals. After this it would be Lee, or the housekeeper, or the gardener who had come in to arrange the flowers.'[29]

Clementine Churchill, too, had to keep a firm grip on household expenditure during the 1920s since her husband found it impossible to economise, especially after he acquired his country estate of Chartwell Manor in 1922. According to her daughter, Mary, their precarious financial condition 'had a wearing effect on her nerves, and the perpetual back-log of bills, and the struggle she had to get even the local tradesmen paid, were the cause of gnawing worry and mortification'.[30] The lavish hospitality they provided at Chartwell was only possible because of her husband's prodigious literary output. If that had failed, their financial position would have been dire. Clementine could rarely afford to employ a highly trained cook so she often recruited a talented kitchenmaid, whom she would guide herself. Mary claimed that she never grudged the time or trouble she spent 'planning and discussing the food with her cook'. In all, to ensure that life at Chartwell was 'easy and comfortable, eight or nine indoor servants were needed: two in the kitchen; two in the pantry; two housemaids; a personal maid for Clementine (who also did a good deal of family sewing); a nursery-maid; and an "odd man"'. He was responsible for looking after the boots, boilers, dustbins and similar miscellaneous tasks. In addition, there was a nanny or governess and 'always two secretaries ... Outside they employed a chauffeur, three gardeners, a groom for the polo ponies (until they were sold), and a working bailiff' on what they called their 'farm'. The turnover of indoor staff was fairly rapid, partly because of the remoteness of the house from any bus stop. This was a further worry and expense for Clementine, since she had to recruit and instruct a stream of new servants. Her feelings of frustration were scarcely helped by Winston's cavalier attitude towards these staff changes, as in September 1928, when he told his wife not to 'worry about household matters. Let them crash if they will. Servants exist to save one trouble, & shd. never be allowed to disturb one's inner peace ... Nothing is worse than worrying about trifles.'[31] But Clementine well knew that if things had gone 'crash' and the household routine had been seriously disrupted this light-hearted acceptance of the difficulties would not have long survived. Hence her worries over expenditure and her horror of unpaid bills.

Other mistresses of High Society households, too, spent much time over their accounts. Lady Redesdale, faced with her husband's periodic financial difficulties and erratic patterns of expenditure, would carefully record every penny she spent. Her youngest daughter, Deborah, claimed that when she totted up the totals at the end of the year, a few pence unaccounted for caused her 'major anxiety and we knew to keep out of her way.' She was determined that her children should be as good at managing the finances as she was and to that end started them off with a few pence weekly as pocket money; we 'graduated at the age of twelve to what was grandly called "an allowance", eleven shillings a month'. Out of that they had to buy stockings, gloves, sweets, gifts and 'any other extras' they needed. The amount was increased until at the age of seventeen they were allowed £100 a year. This had to cover most of their travelling expenses as well as their wardrobe. Lady Redesdale also ordered food over the telephone from '"Wicked Old Harrod" (her name for expensive but reliable Harrods), which was delivered a couple of hours later in a silent, electrically driven van'. But she walked to the shops herself to make certain of her purchases, too, something which few fellow members of the social elite were likely to do.[32]

Lesley Lewis's mother was another careful mistress of her household, spending hours at her desk dealing with household orders and bills, or writing out character references for servants. As a child Lesley claimed she was paid three pence a dozen to docket the household receipts, 'which were kept for seven years ... The day-to-day tradesmen's accounts were entered by hand in leather-covered books.'

There was a special storeroom in Lesley's home where were kept various items like soap, floor polish, brushes and broomheads, as well as marmalade in large stoneware jars. These products were ordered in bulk at six-monthly intervals from the Army and Navy Stores in London, after Lesley's mother had consulted the butler, cook and head housemaid about their requirements. Jam was ordered seasonally from the Tiptree jam factory, and general groceries came from the nearby town.[33] As in most well-organised households, the stores were distributed only by the mistress, or with her explicit permission, at certain specific times, usually once a week.

Even Pamela Cavendish's mother, who spent relatively little time at her Compton Beauchamp home, took care to organise the distribution of the stores. She also made her daughters share in this. As in Lesley Lewis's home, many items were ordered in bulk and were distributed once a week, with the staff departmental heads making a list of what they needed. According to Pamela, if they asked for too much, she would say, 'What have you been doing with it? I think that's too much.'[34] In this way outgoings were curbed.

As most reminiscences confirm, there was a clear division between the family and their servants, even when the latter were on apparently good terms with their employers. This difference was underlined by cynical servants like Eric Horne, who claimed in 1932 to have spent fifty-seven years in service 'with the Nobility and Gentry'. He commented on the

> vast abyss between gentry and servants. Servants are looked upon as part of the furniture of the house; live furniture, nothing more. If the live furniture is in the town house and is wanted in the country house, or vice versa, it is simply moved there. If a piece of the live furniture gets broken in body and health, the gentry simply say: 'Chuck it out and get another. It's all the same to us.'[35]

He drew attention, too, to the backbiting and jealousy that existed among the staff themselves in many large households.

Ironically the distinctions that existed between family and servants were also reflected in the hierarchy which reigned below stairs. This extended from their daily work routine to their dress and eating arrangements. Lily Milgate remembered that when she was offered a place as under-housemaid by Sir

Charles and Lady Wyndham at their Bruton Street home in London, her interview was conducted by Miss Meek, the head housemaid:

> she looked me over without speaking (all these Upper Servants had that habit of looking you up and down as if you was something the cat brought in ...) ... She didn't bother to ask me my name, she simply stated 'Her Ladyship always likes the under-housemaid to be called Mary' so Mary I became ... That's a funny thing about the names. The gentry always wanting to change them, even the footmen, if one had the name Horace they would instantly rechristen him James or John.

Mrs Milgate remembered, too, the snobbery attached to the eating arrangements in most grand houses. For the majority of the meals, the senior staff ate in the housekeeper's room, waited on by a very junior member of staff. But for the main course of the principal meal of the day they would join their subordinates in the servants' hall. According to Lily Milgate, in her London household it was supper that was the 'big event of the day':

> All the staff assembled for this meal except the kitchen people, they always kept to themselves and [ate] in the kitchen.
> First came the butler with the housekeeper. He sat at one end of the long refectory table, she sat at the opposite end. The butler was dressed in full evening dress ... The housekeeper wore a black silk dress, sometimes relieved with lace and always jewellery ... Next came the lady's personal maid and dressed much the same as the housekeeper, next came the first footman, his uniform was

the same as the butler's with one exception. All footmen [had] yellow and black striped waistcoats. They sat one side of the table looking like wasps at a feast, at the end of their row came the odd job man, then the Hall boy who waited on us at table under the keen eye of the butler who corrected him if he made a mistake or forgot any small item or spilled water as he filled our glasses. This was ... to give him his first training to being a footman and last not least at the end of the row was the boot boy.

On the other side of the table sat the maids, the head housemaid with her three inches of lace on top of her head (I always thought this rather ridiculous but it showed rank), then the other maids according to position.[36]

It was customary for the junior servants to remain silent while their seniors were present, and they were expected to lay down their knives and forks when the butler had finished eating. Then the senior staff would proceed to the housekeeper's room to eat their pudding and the atmosphere would at once become more relaxed.

The servants employed in these prestigious households were recruited either through recommendations from friends and relations or through one of the 'superior' servant registry offices. Lady Astor, for example, used Mrs Massey's Agency, which had offices in London and Derby (the latter town being where the agency had originated). Mrs Milgate consulted another exclusive registry, the Mayfair Agency in North Audley Street in London. It was comparatively rare for staff to be recruited from the immediate neighbourhood of a country house, except perhaps for the most subordinate positions, such as those of hall boy or scullery maid. This was partly because of the high degree of efficiency employers required from their domestics and partly because they did not want gossip about the household to be circulated within the local community.

Discipline was strict, with the senior staff expected to keep their juniors in order and to ensure that they obeyed instructions without quibbling. At Shugborough in Staffordshire, a kitchenmaid employed by the Earl and Countess of Lichfield remembered that the chef never moved from his position at the table when he was working: 'everything had to be within his reach'. Anything he needed she had to fetch, and when he first appeared in the morning, she was expected to curtsey and say 'Good morning, Monsieur'.[37]

All the jams and preserves required at Shugborough were made in the still room, as was the practice elsewhere, and cakes and biscuits were baked there. Every morning the first task in the still room at Shugborough was to produce the hot rolls needed for breakfast. The last thing at night the maids would prepare the 'calling trays' for Lord and Lady Lichfield and their family and guests in readiness for the early morning tea. The following morning the trays would be prepared for collection by the housemaids to distribute, so that the head housemaid would take in the tray to the Lichfields themselves, and the second housemaid would be responsible for the trays for any married members of the family staying at Shugborough. The other housemaids would distribute the remaining trays. However, in some households a valet and a lady's maid might take in the trays for the master and mistress, respectively. According to one of the still-room maids who worked at Shugborough in the mid-1920s, their normal working day extended from 5 a.m. to 10 p.m.[38]

Much the same was true of the housemaids, whose laborious duties included cleaning the huge carpets at

Shugborough with a hand brush and dustpan. The wooden surrounds were polished with beeswax and a 'donkey', which was a solid stone block with a thick felt pad beneath it and a long handle to push and pull it. When the dust had settled from the floor cleaning, the furniture and fittings were dusted and rubbed, the latter being carried out with a silk cloth or chamois leather. At 8 a.m. the housemaids took off their 'dirty' aprons made from a heavy cotton and prepared themselves to deliver the morning tea. Small wonder that the Shugborough housekeeper remembered the pressure under which they were all working: 'Everybody was running, you didn't have time to live.'[39] Yet she enjoyed her life there. 'It was just a world of its own. I never knew about the outside world. I devoted my whole life to it.'

The long hours and, often enough, the heavy physical labour required from the Shugborough maids were reflected in the experience of those employed elsewhere. Doreen Whitlock, who was a housemaid at Priestlands House near Lymington in Hampshire, began work as the third housemaid at the age of fourteen. There was a total staff of nine indoor servants and she shared an attic bedroom with the kitchenmaid. Each morning she began work at 6.30 a.m.

> sweeping on my knees with dustpan and brush the front stairs carpets, cleaning and laying several large fireplaces, polishing brass fenders, all on a cup of tea, but a good breakfast followed at 8 a.m. I swept, on my knees, all the carpets in all the rooms and carried heavy buckets of coal, wood etc. ... Once a year Mrs Tillyer Blunt [her mistress] would, with her lady's maid, have a week in Worthing, which meant we did a big clean up. We housemaids had to pull all the huge carpets on the front lawn and with a hand carpet beater ... on my knees, I did the beating ...

Once a week the lady would come below stairs with her
bunch of keys and open the store cupboards to give Cook
her allowance of things to cook with ... Also cleaning
items were measured out such as soda, black lead and
lemon and sand for the kitchenmaid to clean all the
copper pans hung around the kitchen. As a housemaid
I was given Brasso, soap and beeswax to make my own
floor polish.[40]

As she noted drily, '"Priestlands" was a lovely house,
and the owners, Major and Mrs Tillyer Blunt, were very
wealthy, not that this was apparent from our tiny wages'.
Nevertheless she remained at the house for six years, until
she married in 1935.

For those who wished to make a career in service, and
to become butlers, housekeepers, or cooks, it was normally
necessary to move around fairly frequently in their early
days, in order to gain experience. However, it was important
to move only to another elite household, if they wished to
serve wealthy or high-status employers. Gordon Grimmett,
for example, began his career at Longleat, home of the
Marquess of Bath, as a lamp boy. After a year he was
promoted to third footman:

I learnt now how to serve at table, how to clean silver,
how to welcome and valet guests, how to appear as if by
magic, how to seem not to listen to conversations, how
to put rugs round ladies' knees in carriages or cars with a
steady hand, as well as the thousand and one things that
are in a footman's inventory of duties.[41]

Subsequently he was appointed second footman by the
Astors and came under the influence of Edwin Lee. 'He

was perhaps a hard taskmaster, sometimes to be feared but always respected, and a word of praise from him would keep a man happy for a week. There was no job in the book that he couldn't do, and do superbly.'

Every morning Gordon and the other footmen would go down to the still room to collect the morning tea trays to be distributed round the rooms of the male guests. Curtains had to be opened and the sleeper gently awakened. Then their clothes from the night before were collected and taken to the brushing-room, where they were sponged, brushed, folded and hung up. This was followed by laying the breakfast table and bringing in the various dishes, both hot and cold, as well as constantly 'running to and fro with fresh toast and hot rolls'. After breakfast the silver had to be cleaned, and then came hall duties. At the Astors' London house the duty footman would be 'stationed all day in the front hall sitting in a large leather chair. There were constant callers ... to see either Lord or Lady Astor'. Along with this there was the running and taking of messages, despite the availability of telephones in the household. For this he was paid £32 a year, plus 2s 6d a week to cover the cost of beer and of his laundry. Lady Astor, as a strict advocate of the temperance cause, did not supply alcohol to her servants.[42]

During Ascot week and at weekend parties the footmen had the task of valeting perhaps six gentlemen who had no servant of their own. A list of the guests concerned would be put up in the brushing-room and Grimmett admitted that this was studied with interest, before a selection was made. That decision was made not on the grounds of rank or importance but upon 'their reputation as tippers. This reputation was based not only on our own experience but that of the underground telegraph of the below stairs world.' Generous tips could add considerably to a footman's earnings. Ernest King claimed that when he was employed by Mrs de Wichfeld, as a valet to her second husband, tips from guests whom he also had to valet meant this extra income 'never came to less than sixteen pounds a week', which was a very large sum indeed in the 1920s.[43]

But servants employed by the social elite had rules to observe, too, including restrictions on contact with the opposite sex. For maids this meant 'no followers' were allowed in most cases, and there were also prohibitions on sexual relationships between fellow members of staff in the majority of households. That applied at the Astors' Cliveden, where Gordon Grimmett fell in love with Poppy, the third daughter of the head gardener. She was employed to help with the flower arranging in the house, but when their relationship was discovered, Gordon was dismissed. He and Poppy then married soon after and he was fortunate to find a new position at one of the Lyons Corner Houses.[44]

Yet while there were these clear rules and regulations to be observed by those employed in elite private service, there were also instances where warm feelings existed between a master or mistress and a favourite servant. Lady Jean Hamilton told one evidently surprised fellow guest at a dinner party of her 'wonderful' lady's maid, McAdie, and how she had 'great power in our household, and stage-managed me ... I told him she looked after my money and kept my accounts, and when she doled out pounds to me, asked me, when I came back without them, what I had spent the money on.'[45] She also depended heavily on the maid's ministrations when she was unwell, and particularly when she suffered from serious asthma attacks. So when McAdie suddenly died in April 1927, her mistress was devastated. Six weeks later she was still lamenting her loss: 'I dread ...

a quiet life and no McAdie', she wrote in her diary, even though she had recruited a 'nice new maid'.[46]

Similarly, Rosina Harrison, Lady Astor's lady's maid, joined her staff at the end of the 1920s and remained with her until she died in May 1964. Under the terms of her mistress's will she received an annuity of £500 per year. It was the largest single bequest made by Lady Astor to any of the servants.[47] Similar generosity was displayed by General Sir Dighton Probyn, Comptroller of the Household of Queen Alexandra, from his far more modest resources. Out of an estate with a net value of £6,405 he left £1,000 to his valet 'and excellent servant', Edwin James Nichols, in his will.[48]

Employment Opportunities and the Social Elite

Throughout the 1920s, as had been the case before 1914, some members of High Society were involved in various business undertakings, alongside their traditional connections with the land and the running of their estates. In addition, a number of manufacturers and financiers had been raised to peerages, baronetcies and knighthoods both before 1914 and in the immediate aftermath of the war, under Lloyd George's premiership. There were, too, major landowners whose agents arranged for the renting, leasing or development of urban land, especially in London, or who exploited coal and other minerals, as was the case with Lord Londonderry. In this context it should be remembered that the ownership of wealth was itself still very highly concentrated at the end of the 1920s, much as it had been in Victorian and Edwardian times. One estimate suggests that the top 1 per cent of British wealth-holders accounted for around three-fifths of the nation's wealth in the second half of the 1920s. That compared with just over two-thirds of national wealth owned by this tiny minority of the population before the war.[49] Many were substantial landowners and prominent members of the social elite, like the Duke of Westminster and Lord Londonderry. In all, in 1923, 242 peers owned between them 7.362 million acres. They formed around a third of the total adult membership of the peerage at that date.[50]

However, in the post-war era, with declining rental incomes from land and a rising tax burden, there was an increased incentive for many upper-class men to seek additional incomes, away from traditional outlets like the military and the Church, which, since Victorian times, had been regarded as suitable occupations for those waiting to succeed to a title or for younger sons and members of the squirearchy. Hence in 1923 it was estimated that in addition to the industrialists and bankers who had been ennobled in their own lifetime, there were 272 peers holding directorships in 761 public companies of different kinds. The fact that a high proportion of them were directors of banking or 'commercial' undertakings merely reflected the general bias of the British economy itself. Thus 106 of the peers were directors of insurance companies, 66 were directors of banks, and 64 were members of the boards of railway companies.[51] A number held directorships in more than one undertaking. For their part, company promoters were anxious to recruit peers to their enterprises, on the grounds that the appearance of their names on a company prospectus would inspire confidence in the firm's probity and assure prospective investors of its respectability.[52]

But alongside these developments the vibrant atmosphere of the 1920s' 'jazz age' encouraged socialites to move into other fields of employment. That was especially true of younger men who wanted to break the mould of traditional occupations and to meet the needs of the new, more challenging, commercial world in which they found themselves. Some took advantage of the fresh opportunities created in the fields of advertising or the motor trade, or journalism. The latter was particularly affected by the general public's appetite for accounts of the doings of the more famous, or the more notorious, members of High Society. This encouraged the advent of the growing army of gossip columnists, like Lord Castlerosse and Patrick Balfour. In 1930 Paul Cohen-Portheim commented on this trend.

> The interest which the whole nation takes in Society is astonishing. In continental countries for all their *snobisme* and reverence for the nobility, the masses know very little about the 'best people', who remain private individuals; in England people in Society are public characters. Every newspaper tells you about their private lives, every illustrated paper is perpetually publishing photographs of them ... Their parties and their dresses, their weddings, christenings and funerals, their houses and their travels are all described and depicted ... The first duty of Society is to be a show for the masses, particularly during the three months of the London Season.[53]

Some budding entrepreneurs invented new occupations for themselves, so that Cedric Alexander started a 'Social Bureau' to shepherd Americans and other 'socially ambitious people' round Mayfair.[54] The post of social secretary, too, was another alternative whose recruitment might appeal to *nouveau-riche* families, as in the case of the leading High Society hostess, Laura Corrigan. A number of young men were attracted also to the restaurant and night-club business. David Tennant, for example, used some of his substantial income from a family trust to set up a successful night-club, the Gargoyle, which opened in Dean Street in January 1925.[55] Two years later it was praised by *Vogue* for its facilities, with patrons able to 'dance in an oak-beamed parlour surrounded by jolly family parties, or sit by an open hearth eating a scrambled egg and drinking from an enormous cup of coffee'.[56]

Lord Bective, who earned a good deal of publicity and the title of the 'Electric Earl', established an electrical company which provided the electric lighting in the newly refurbished Embassy Club in 1927, among other commissions. *Vogue* was much impressed by the lighting in the Embassy, claiming that 'every one present looked at least four years younger in the becoming light'.[57] More problematic was the career choice of Sir Joseph Tichborne, who became a bookmaker, while Harry Lindsay, a grandson of the Earl of Crawford, earned a modest living by exploiting his skills as a furniture and woodwork restorer and as an adviser on interior decorating at Sindlay's in London, where he was employed on a commission basis.[58]

Patrick Balfour quoted another social commentator who in 1929 drew attention to the large number of men who had

> remained aristocrats by instinct and become democrats by inclination. One young peer I know manufactures margarine. Another bearer of a famous name, sells pills. A third sells underclothes in a large store ... Anthony Vivian ... Lady Weymouth's brother ... is assistant manager of a theatre and ... Ulick Verney, who is a son of Sir Harry and Lady Verney, told me that he sold loose-ledgers.[59]

With some exaggeration, Balfour stated that by the earl

1930s he doubted if there was a single trade or profession which an 'aristocrat' would 'scorn' to take up. There was a particular involvement in retail trade, for instance, so that Lord Victor Paget, a brother of the 6th Marquess of Anglesey, became a partner in a firm of exclusive furriers, while Colonel the Hon. Fred Cripps and his wife owned a hairdressing salon in Bond Street.[60] They, like many other upper-class families, had clearly abandoned the once-almost-universal aristocratic disdain for 'trade' and those engaged in it.

Paul Methuen, heir to hard-pressed Corsham estates in Wiltshire, took another path, becoming a successful artist and a keen naturalist and botanist. After an education at Eton and New College, Oxford, he went as an assistant at the Transvaal Museum, Pretoria for four years. In the late 1920s he studied with the leading British painter, Walter Sickert, and subsequently exhibited his work at a number of leading galleries. His father was forced to sell parts of the estate to boost its financial position in the post-war period and it was only Paul's intervention that prevented Lord Methuen from disposing of the family's valuable picture collection as well.[61]

Henry Weymouth, by contrast, was anxious to equip himself to manage the Longleat estate efficiently, and to that end arranged to be apprenticed to the highly proficient agent for the Lockinge estate, near Wantage, in Berkshire.[62]

However, while some male members of the social elite shared in this diversification process, it should be remembered that many others carried on along traditional class lines. They ran their estates with the aid of bailiffs, took an active part in field sports and politics, and continued to lament their declining A few, like Stephen Tennant, David Tennant's younger brother, could rely on inherited wealth to enable them to live a hedonistic existence and to spend their time seeking beauty and exercising their artistic talents.[63] And for some, as Charles Masterman mischievously suggested in 1923, there was 'still an almost unlimited field of support possible in American marriages'.[64] However, unlike in the Edwardian era, American heiresses do not seem to have been particularly attracted to impoverished British aristocrats in the 1920s; and with the Wall Street stock market crash in the autumn of 1929, even this source became problematic anyway.

For contemporaries, though, it was among the female members of High Society that the biggest change of attitude occurred, as younger women, in particular, rebelled against old-style feminine stereotyping. As Barbara Cartland, herself one of the new generation of 'bright young people', declared, 'We didn't want to be ladylike in 1920. We wanted to be dashing.'[65] Some may have been encouraged in their desire for independence by their experiences during the First World War, and the sense of personal freedom that many of them had then enjoyed. But far more, in Patrick Balfour's opinion, were affected by the extension of the franchise to women at the end of the war and their subsequent involvement in political and community life as magistrates and even, in a very limited way, as Members of Parliament. It became the rule rather than the exception, according to Balfour, 'for Society debutantes to take up some sort of employment. They were not too proud to serve as shop assistants, either among many hundred others in a big store, or else, superior, in the smaller and smarter dress-shops, hat-shops, flower-shops, book-shops and so forth.'[66] In practice this was much too sweeping a generalisation, but it is nonetheless clear that a number of Society women did open shops, whic they often called by their own christian name. Mrs Dudley Coats thus set up 'Audrey,' which specialised in 'scent and wedding-presents', although by 1927 it had become involved in the fashion trade, too.[67] Poppy Baring, a daughter of the banking dynasty and a friend of Prince George, the future Duke of Kent, similarly established a dress shop named 'Poppy', while Jean Norton, Edwina Mountbatten's close friend, ran a cinema called the New Gallery Picture House in Regent Street. The Picture House's proprietors hoped thereby to attract Mrs Norton's well-to-do friends by showing films that she thought would appeal to them. Her husband, a film producer, supported the move, thinking she might catch the eye of a movie mogul and make her fortune as a star of screen and stage.[68] That did not happen. Other women, in more mundane fashion, ran laundries, beauty parlours and hotels, finding their clientele from among their friends.[69]

But there was a growing number for whom the need to earn cash was the main motivation for their commercial activity. At the beginning of the 1920s Nellie Romilly, Clementine Churchill's sister, found herself in difficult financial circumstances, with a 'severely war-wounded husband and two small children'. To help provide for them all, she proposed to open a hat shop. At the end of January 1921 she had found suitable premises for the shop and her brother-in-law, Winston Churchill, agreed to lend her £500, so that she could start her business. A little later, when Nellie s still 'beset by worries' he assured her that he would help   solve them.[70]

   financial pressures affected Barbara Cartland. r was killed in May 1917, leaving his wife and n very poor circumstances. In 1919 Barbara's l mother transferred herself and her family from their Edgbaston home to South Kensington, where she opened a wool shop. At the same time, by carefully limiting their outgoings, she was able to give her daughter a modest London Season. Barbara herself earned a little by drawing menu cards for parties. Later, like some of her contemporaries, she opened a hat shop which she called 'Barbara'. But it soon proved a failure and had to be sold. She then began to write gossip paragraphs for the *Daily Express* and was befriended by its proprietor, Lord Beaverbrook. He in turn introduced her to some of his influential friends and acquaintances. In 1923 she published her first novel, *Jigsaw*, which she claimed enjoyed successful publicity because it was written 'by a socialite who worked'. It earned her the respectable sum of £200, and from that point it was as a writer that she was to earn her living. Eventually she was to publish 723 books, the vast majority of them romantic fiction.[71]

Shortage of cash also encouraged Nancy Mitford to take up journalism. Her first contributions took the form of anonymous paragraphs of gossip in one of the Society magazines. She boasted that she had once managed to pay for her train fare to stay with a friend in Scotland 'by photographing the party for *Tatler*'. Later she had occasional signed articles accepted by *Vogue*, such as 'The Shooting Party: Some Hints for the Woman Guest. By the Hon. Nancy Mitford.' In March 1929 she told a friend how much money she had made from articles, '£22 since Christmas'. Later she claimed to be making £4 4s a week by writing articles and hoped that this would soon enable her to be self-supporting. 'I regard financial independence as almost the sum of human happiness.'[72] In 1930 she was commissioned to write a weekly column for *The Lady*, at five guineas a week. The magazine had been started by her maternal grandfather in the 1880s. 'To celebrate this I went out today & bought myself a divine coral tiara', she reported. As Selina Hastings points out, in her character as 'The Lady' Nancy attended the Chelsea Flower Show, the Fourth of June at Eton, the Aldershot Tattoo, and a number of other events. As she told her friend, Mark Ogilvie-Grant, they were 'sending me to everything free, the Opera, the Shakespeare festival at Stratford, etc. I think I shall get lots of fun out of it.' With the need to earn money, however, 'always before her', and forced to stay in the family home at Swinbrook in Oxfordshire, once the London Season was over, she began to write her first novel. *Highland Fling* was published in March 1931, and although it attracted little press coverage, it enabled Nancy to earn £90.[73] Earlier *The Lady* had also given her the opportunity to make money in a more unusual way, by selling some of her clothes. These, like those of other members of the family, were made by Gladys, Lady Redesdale's lady's maid, and all Nancy had to pay for was the material. She answered an advertisement by a doctor's wife in *The Lady* seeking to purchase suitable second-hand clothes. Nancy was able to sell some of her surplus garments for more than they had cost her, while the doctor's wife, impressed by their superior quality and price, 'kept asking for more'.[74]

Financial motives may have lain behind the many other titled women who ventured into journalism and whose work was castigated by Beverley Nichols. At the time he was himself working in Fleet Street and he wrote critically of the

astonishing array of obscure countesses, viscountesses and, if the worst came to the worst, wives of baronets, all pontificating with monotonous regularity on the problems of the hour. It mattered not at all that these ladies were, in many cases, barely literate, and that the ideas they were supposed to originate had been put into their empty heads by some member of the reporting staff. The public could not be expected to know that. All they knew was that here was the Countess of X proclaiming to nearly a million readers that the 'modern girl' was this, that or the other.[75]

Helen Hardinge was among those who took up her pen, writing an article for *Vogue* on 'The Child at Home', in which she pointed out that in the modern nursery the timetable for 'sleep time' and 'meal hours' was strictly observed. Her correspondence at this time with her mother suggested that in reality she depended heavily on her children's nanny for their daily care and training.[76]

The contents of journals like *The Tatler*, *The Bystander* and *Vogue* confirmed the involvement of many socialites in the fashion trade. In 1927, for example, *Vogue* mentioned that Olga, Lady Egerton, was the English director of design for the House of Paul Caret of Paris. In London there was Lady Bingham's chic shop, 'Rose Bertin', which was 'becoming as smart for dresses as it has always been for hats', while Princess Poutiatine had a 'charming hat shop' called 'Chapka'. But it was Lady Victor Paget's 'intimate shop in an old Georgian house in Grafton Street' that *Vogue* singled out for special praise. Here Lady Victor herself was almost always present and customers were 'apt to find nearly everybody else as well'. It was 'distinguished for its chic and smartness', with the proprietress herself selecting her gowns and often modelling them as well, as photographs in *Vogue* confirmed.[77] Patrick Balfour, too, was impressed by Lady Victor's 'acumen and ... capacity for hard work'. Unlike a number of her less dedicated competitors, she was able to build up a successful business, whereas those who were 'simply playing' at running a shop 'soon grew tired of the game' or found that 'friends, though they might be the best buyers, were not the best payers'.[78] A few women, including the strikingly beautiful Paula Gellibrand, became successful mannequins, and paved the way for other girls, like Nancy Beaton, Cecil Beaton's sister, to model clothes in *Vogue*.[79]

A remunerative option for a small number of women, like Lady Diana Cooper, was the endorsement of cosmetics or similar products. Patrick Balfour noted that, a few years before, the manufacturers of face creams and the like had found it hard to persuade Society women to advertise their wares. They were not tempted even by the offering of 'large sums'. But by the end of the 1920s, debutantes were keenly competing 'for this honour'. The motive was not simply financial. They also revelled in the publicity it brought. 'She who is invited to advertise "Pond's" [face cream] has a definite "score" over her less solicited contemporaries.'[80]

On a broader basis, as Patrick Balfour also pointed out, while the menfolk had separated their business interests from their social life, their wives and daughters had no such scruples. They took advantage of the chance to bring the two together for their own profit. Accordingly, they resolutely brought 'trade into Society'. That included conducting business transactions over the luncheon table, perhaps while working on a commission basis for firms hoping to benefit from their social connections and their skill in identifying potential American customers or 'socially ambitious suburbans'. He then added, rather ruefully,

> Formerly Society was held to be a force in politics; now it is a force only in the retail trade. The two are inextricably intertwined. You can hardly go to a party but what somebody tries to sell you something or to decorate your

house ... Moreover the most enterprising among the ordinary traders, instead of complaining of the blacklegs of Mayfair, now recognise that Mayfair is a business asset. They encourage social celebrities to superintend their various departments and pay commission to others for the introduction of custom.[81]

Another innovation was the adopting of acting as a career by members of the social elite. Lady Diana Cooper had been a pioneer in this when she starred in her first film, *The Great Adventure*, in 1922. Soon after she embarked on a lucrative theatrical career, appearing in Max Reinhardt's spectacle, *The Miracle*. For this she earned a great deal of money, touring not only in Britain and, more particularly, the United States of America but elsewhere in Europe. Then there were the Ruthven twins, who took on various stage roles, including appearing in *Alice in Wonderland* at the Golders Green Hippodrome during January 1927.[82] Other stage-struck girls included Brenda Dean Paul and Elizabeth Ponsonby who were to gain greater notoriety as leading members of the 'Bright Young People' of the 1920s, rather than for their acting abilities. Diana Churchill, Winston and Clementine's eldest daughter, also aspired to go on the stage at one time and even studied at the Royal Academy of Dramatic Art. But she lacked talent and after a time gave up the idea of acting. In the following decade her sister was to nurture similar stage ambitions, to her mother's evident exasperation. She wrote wearily to a friend that in her opinion neither girl had 'the slightest talent or even aptitude' for acting and it was strange that they should have 'this passionate wish to go on the stage'.[83]

Brenda Dean Paul, a baronet's daughter, was only sixteen when in 1923 she took lessons at the Nancy Price School of acting near to her London home, before moving on briefly to the Royal Academy of Dramatic Act.[84] From there she began to tour in repertory during 1924 and 1925, without much success. At that point she formed a relationship with an artist whom she identified only as 'W' in her reminiscences. He was ten years her senior and the affair ended in 1927. Brenda then went to Berlin on a vague belief that she had been promised a screen test; there she stayed for three weeks, sampling the bohemian night life of the German capital, before returning to England. As nothing had come of her prospective film career she decided to go to Paris. There she was introduced to cocaine and soon became addicted. On her return to London she took her place as a leader of the 'bright young things', acquiring a reputation as 'a voluptuous girl' with 'plenty of sex appeal'. She had a series of lovers, before suffering a miscarriage or an abortion in 1931. After this she became very ill and for the rest of the 1930s she experienced years of poor health brought about by her drug addiction and her chaotic lifestyle.[85] As early as November 1931 she received seven summonses for offences against the Dangerous Drugs Act, but managed to escape prison. Instead she was put on probation for three years and went to a nursing home. But the many efforts made to cure her addiction all failed. Even in the 1950s she was still appearing in court for drugs offences and was also making sporadic efforts to revive her stage career. When she was found dead in her Kensington High Street flat in July 1959, it was widely suspected that a drugs overdose was the cause, although the official verdict was that she had died from a heart complaint.[86]

Elizabeth Ponsonby, too, learnt the rudiments of acting at a London drama school when she was in her late teens, at the end of the First World War. She then joined the

Nottingham Repertory, but failed to make a mark. At first she obstinately refused to accept that she had little hope of a stage career and continued instead to hover on the fringes of the professional theatre. She came forward as a leader of the 'Bright Young People' in 1924, when her father became a minister in the first, short-lived, Labour government. His appointment opened up West End opportunities for his daughter and she took various jobs in a revue, as a model, and as a walk-on role in the theatre, for which she was apparently paid £5 a week. But most of all she enjoyed the publicity she gained as a result of the extravagant pranks in which she was involved, to the distress of her highly respectable parents.[87]

At the same time other, more solid, career opportunities were opening up for women in such new spheres as interior decorating and garden design. Three names stand out in this connection, namely Syrie Maugham, the estranged wife of the novelist W. Somerset Maugham, Lady Colefax in interior decorating, and Norah Lindsay, also separated from her husband, in garden design. For both Sibyl Colefax and Norah Lindsay, it was financial necessity that drove them to take up a business career, while for Syrie Maugham her work provided some compensation for her unhappy married life, as well as yielding a useful additional income. Syrie's marriage eventually ended in divorce in 1929.

Prior to 1914 little attention was paid to interior decorating as a career in Britain, unlike the situation in the United States of America. In this country, therefore, Syrie Maugham was to be a pioneer. Already in April 1919, two years into her marriage, *Vogue* was featuring photographs of brightly painted chests and tables she had decorated and which were available at her shop, called 'Syrie', in Baker Street. Other decorated and painted furniture was also available there. She had opened the shop with a capital of £400 raised partly from her own resources and partly with the help of friends. The business flourished and by 1922 had become firmly established.[88] Two years later she moved to larger premises at the corner of Grosvenor Square. Syrie proved an astute businesswoman and was always ready to use her own home to promote sales, to supplement her shop. According to Somerset Maugham himself, she was happy to sell furniture from her drawing room, a policy which he, perhaps not unnaturally, resented.

However, it was in 1927, when she moved to a new house in King's Road, Chelsea, that she made her greatest impact. There some art deco furniture was combined with a concentration on white, including white walls and lambskin carpets. 'With the strength of a typhoon she blew all colour before her,' declared Cecil Beaton. To that end she 'bleached, pickled or scraped every piece of furniture in sight'.[89] She held a house-warming party for friends in the summer of 1927 but, with an eye to commercial possibilities, she also invited a member of *Vogue*'s staff, among others. The latter obligingly commented not only on the party's great success but upon the 'picture of Mrs Maugham's white room – white lilies, white peonies, white-shaded lights, and the lovely pale face of our hostess ... in sharp contrast as she talked to the two dark negroes who sang their spirituals so wonderfully', as part of the entertainment.[90]

Syrie's house in Chelsea, as well as her villa at Le Touquet in France, which was completed in 1926 and where the white theme was also adopted, thus became what one writer has described as 'society showrooms for her wares'. The fact that she was an agreeable hostess as well as a good businesswoman helped her to obtain commissions from clients in Britain and in the United States, most of whom were attracted by her signature theme of white. At the same time she began to open shops in America, the first of them in Chicago in 1926. Others soon followed in New York, Palm Beach and Los Angeles. For much of the 1920s Syrie spent six months of each year in London and the remaining six months in America, interspersed with visits to France.[91]

Mrs Maugham was comfortably off, and she pursued her business career energetically for reasons of personal satisfaction and to support her daughter, Liza, rather than from real financial necessity. That was not true of Lady Colefax. Her home in King's Road, Chelsea, had always been admired for its elegance and impeccable taste, avoiding any appearance of clutter. Even her critics conceded that. For much of her married life, up to the early 1920s, she had always been comfortably off, relying on her husband's income as a patents lawyer to bring in the substantial sum of around £20,000 a year. However, with the downturn in trade in the 1920s this became problematic, and the situation was made worse by the fact that Sir Arthur Colefax's increasing deafness made it impossible for him to continue with his legal practice. In 1928, therefore, Sibyl found herself with a small income and many outgoings. She decided she must turn her amateur talent for interior decorating to commercial use. To this end she took a room on the first floor of a friend's property in Bruton Street where she worked initially in collaboration with the antique dealers, Stair and Andrew.[92] At first she operated on a one-person basis, 'undertaking all the visiting, the measuring ... climbing ladders, supervising plumbing' and carrying out a host of other tasks from nine in the morning until six or seven at night. Then in 1929 came a further severe blow. Her elder son, Peter, who was working in the United States and who had invested the Colefaxes' limited savings on the

American stock market, found it was all lost in the Wall Street Crash of October in that year.[93]

For Sibyl, who had gone into business very reluctantly at the age of fifty-four, the combination of events imposed great stress. She had set herself the target of earning £2,000 a year from her interior decorating and by driving herself and those whom she employed very hard, she was able to do so. But she found the world of commerce dull and unrewarding, compared to her former busy life as a leading Society hostess. Indeed, even in these circumstances she managed to hold some dinner parties and to visit friends. However, throughout there was the pressure to earn money, as she confided to her American friend, Bernard Berenson, in Florence:

> It's quite true we went smash in October and ever since I've been working like a beaver ... Arthur of course is making income ... [but] the Bar is at its worst for 25 years ... somehow we've got to build up capital.[94]

In November 1930 she referred ruefully to her 'Cinderella evenings by which I mean after a bath I forget all the drearies and go out or have people in who talk & translate me to another place'. But she could never forget her financial difficulties. 'It's like walking on a tight rope & suddenly realising that there's *no* net below one – There is none below us,' she told Berenson.[95]

Around this same time Virginia Woolf commented to her sister on the change which had taken place in Sibyl, noting how she had 'transformed herself into a harried, downright woman of business ... and has lost almost all her glitter and suavity ... She is at her office from 9.30 to 7 ... After all, she ... has practised society for 35 years; and now to become a

hardhearted shopkeeper – and she is very successful too …
must be a grind. She too has shrunk and faded.'[96]

As a result of Lady Colefax's determination and commercial
acumen, the venture prospered, so that by the end of the
1930s, in partnership with a gifted young decorator, John
Fowler, her business had become the important Mayfair
interior decorating firm of Colefax and Fowler.[97]

The financial necessity which had driven Sibyl Colefax into
business also turned Norah Lindsay in the same direction.
She had long given informal advice to friends on how they
could improve their garden, and her own garden at Sutton
Courtenay Manor was widely admired. By 1924, however,
she had little income coming in from her estranged husband,
Harry, and her home had been let for several months at a
time to provide extra income. She had then to rely on the
hospitality of her friends to tide her over these spells of
temporary homelessness. In 1924 Norah was aged fifty-one
and it was while she was staying with one of her friends,
Lady Horner, at Mells in Somerset that the latter suggested
she should make a charge for her gardening advice.[98] She
took up the suggestion and it proved to be the start of her
commercial career. In that same year she was paid a retainer
of £100 a year by the Astors, to oversee the plant selection
and planting at Cliveden, and other commissions soon
followed, for example from Sir Philip Sassoon.

Negotiations, however, were not always easy, especially
with her volatile friend, Lady Astor. Nancy Astor quickly
criticised Norah if she thought too much money was being
spent on the Cliveden garden, or if she believed the Astors'
best interests were being neglected. In 1927, for example,
Norah strongly defended herself against a charge that she
had been neglectful and profligate, pointing out that as a
professional gardener she was given the same terms by the

nurserymen 'as all the other landscape gardeners ... My own fees I have never raised since I started ... I know a man like Peto who charges £100 a visit wd. laugh at £5 or £10!! But I have so loved the work at Cliveden ... and I don't think you could have got the result any cheaper.'[99]

The quarrel blew over and Norah's business continued to expand so that by the end of the 1920s she had a client base of at least twenty-six properties, mostly in England but with a few on the Continent, especially in France.[100] Nonetheless she found the work physically demanding, especially as she grew older. In the autumn of 1926 she confessed gloomily to a younger sister, 'I am a tired and cold businesswoman! I used to adore lying in bed in a hot bedroom and having nothing to do.' But except for brief periods when she was staying with friends, such self-indulgence was no longer possible.[101] Yet, like Lady Colefax, she carried on working and also published occasional articles on gardening, for example in *Country Life*. In this way she secured a modest livelihood to the end of the 1930s. But then her age and the effects of the Second World War soon led to a sharp decline in her commissions and consequently in her income. She became increasingly dependent on her younger sister, Madeline, who had married the wealthy Howard Whitbread, heir to the Whitbread brewery business. They lived at Southill Park in Bedfordshire and by 1944 Norah was spending almost six months of the year with them, intermixed with visits to other friends, usually for several weeks at a time.[102] Yet by her skills and determination Norah Lindsay had developed a career for herself and had taken advantage of her Society contacts to gain gardening commissions for a period of at least fifteen years.

Nevertheless, alongside these women who had 'broken the mould' of the stereotypical lady of leisure, however reluctantly, countless others continued to enjoy a comfortable existence along traditional lines and free from financial pressures. Yet even they, to a limited extent, diverted temporarily from the stereotype during the General Strike of 1926. This broke out on 3 May and for nine days there were fears that the country would be brought to a standstill by industrial action. It arose from a demand by the coal miners for a National Mining Board to determine wage levels and to achieve the maintenance of a seven-hour working day. These demands the government and the coal owners refused to accept and so, under the direction of the General Council of the Trades Union Congress, other workers then came out on strike in solidarity with their cause. They included railwaymen, dockers, road transport workers, printers, men in the metal trades and those in the building industry.[103]

The government responded by recruiting thousands of special constables, drawn from volunteers who came forward in large numbers. According to Barbara Cartland, 'The whole of Buck's Club and White's were enrolled as special constables.' In addition there were members of the Territorial Army. Hundreds of undergraduates came up from Oxford and Cambridge to London not only to serve as special constables but to take on a variety of other tasks, such as unloading ships and working on the railways. Lady Howard de Walden put up about 200 of them in her ballroom and also organised a canteen in her garage to feed not only them, but other youths who had been put up in various households in Belgrave Square.[104]

One commentator claimed that during the General Strike many businessmen 'realised a life-time's ambition by driving an engine, acting as a guard, or manning a signal box', in order to keep the railways running.[105] According to *The Bystander* the Earl of Portarlington worked as a porter at Paddington station and Lord William Nevill sat for hours each day at South Kensington station snipping tickets and telling people their platforms. The underground railway was 'portered, conductored and guard-ed by cohorts of bareheaded young men chiefly ... from Oxford and Cambridge, in grey flannel trousers and Fair Isle "pullovers,"' declared the magazine.[106] *The Tatler* published a photograph of the Hon. Mrs Beaumont sweeping out the stable yard at the Great Western Railway yard at Paddington, to make sure the horses were not neglected, as they had allegedly been during the 1919 railway strike.[107]

Food supplies were secured by volunteer lorry drivers, often with police escorts, while Hyde Park was transformed into a 'vast centre for the distribution of milk'.[108] Men and women worked in temporary canteens kept open night and day to provide for the emergency lorry drivers. Even the Mitford sisters set up a canteen near their Oxfordshire home, mainly under the supervision of the second sister, Pamela, who was the practical member of the family.[109]

Among others who became involved were Edwina Mountbatten and her friend, Jean Norton. Edwina had no strong views on the rights and wrongs of the strike but was simply determined that London should not be brought to a standstill. Initially she worked from 11 a.m. to 4 p.m. at the YMCA canteen in Hyde Park, making tea and cooking sausages for volunteer lorry drivers. She and Jean also sold copies of the *Daily Express* and *Evening Standard*, which the Beaverbrook presses were still producing but which the distributors would not deliver. After three days, the printing stopped and Jean and Edwina then stood in for the switchboard operators, who had also joined the strike. Edwina, in particular, had found the canteen work tiring, unused as she was to standing for hours in a hot kitchen.

But the switchboard work proved even more taxing. For five days she remained on duty from 9 a.m. to midnight, while 'the telephone never stopped' and she and Jean 'nearly went mad'. She also did shift work in the *Express* transport canteen, and by the time the strike ended, she was pale and drawn and utterly exhausted. As Janet Morgan notes, 'Doing the same routine job, day after day, was more killing than she had realized; like other volunteers, [she] was learning what it took to keep the wheels turning.'[110] It was a far cry from her usual pleasure-seeking lifestyle.

Barbara Cartland became involved, too, carrying messages to parts of London she had never seen before. But, as she later wrote, 'For the majority of young people in the twenties the strike seemed at the time an adventurous excuse.'[111]

Some violent clashes between strikers and volunteers and the police took place during the nine days the strike lasted, but there was no loss of life. It was eventually called off on 12 May by the General Council of the TUC, ostensibly so that negotiations could take place to settle the miners' grievances. The decision caused rejoicing and much relief among members of the social elite, and particularly among the volunteers. *The Bystander*, for example, sounded a triumphant note of self-congratulation. 'Our young men showed up magnificently. A week before the strike there were Jeremiahs who spoke gloomily of the modern tendency in our Universities ... But the way those youngsters ran our trains and manoeuvred ten-ton lorries ... was a joy to all beholders ... Most of the young women in Mayfair were serving in the canteen in Hyde Park for the lorry drivers, soldiers, and others engaged in milk distribution'.[112]

The miners, not surprisingly, felt they had been betrayed by the General Council's decision. They continued their strike for several more months, before the dispute crumbled away in September 1926. The coal owners had won, and the miners lost their national agreement and had instead to work for longer hours on lower wages.[113]

As one writer has put it, the General Strike showed 'what was known already, that people who dress like gentlemen will instinctively take sides against people who commonly work with their coats off'.[114] In the meantime, the upper classes breathed a sigh of relief and quickly began to take up the customary, if somewhat delayed, social activities associated with the London Season. Lady Mountbatten, for one, neither moralised nor reminisced over her role in the dispute. She simply 'picked up her old life where she had left off'. That included visiting the theatre, going to Mrs Corrigan's annual cabaret party, attending the Duchess of Sutherland's summer fancy dress party, where she went dressed as a gipsy, and joining in Emerald Cunard's party for the Prince of Wales. At the same time she continued her extra-marital affair with the American, Laddie Sanford.[115]

Edwina was not alone in putting the temporary unpleasantness of the strike firmly behind her. As *The Bystander* commented on 9 June,

> What a summer this is going to be! Their Majesties' Courts are to-day and tomorrow and the Ranelagh Horse and Polo Pony Show is even now in progress. The first Test Match opens ... on Saturday and Ascot opens on Tuesday.[116]

A week later it commented on 'all the other gaieties' that were taking place: 'dinners, lunches, and exactly twenty dances of the first-rate importance, and you can imagine what life in London has been this last week. The three dances of the greatest importance all took place on the same night ... which meant a lot of running to and fro to those – as many did – who went to all three.' Earl Winterton, who restricted himself to the Duchess of Sutherland's fancy dress ball, described it in glowing terms. It was 'held in the open air in the tennis court with Ambrose's band; all the beautiful women of ... the most celebrated set of society were there ... a great evening – colour, beauty, good fun'.[117] It was a world far distant from the struggling mining communities who were seeking, without success, to preserve their already precarious standard of living.

But for some, the events of the General Strike and its aftermath gave pause for thought. Among them was Barbara Cartland. 'It was for me, and a great number of my contemporaries, a milestone', she wrote, years later. 'It was a moment when we ceased to be young and carefree and thoughtless, when we began to think ... After the General Strike we ostensibly went on dancing, yet some of the gaiety and spontaneity seemed to have gone out of it.'[118]

6

The 'Bright Young People' and the End of an Era

... the chief characteristic of the Bright Young People was that they made a business of 'pleasure' and hunted the 'good time' until exhaustion overcame them. By the end of the decade the Wild Party was over ... the period with which this book deals came to an end in a confused welter of treachery, fraud and ... despair.

Douglas Goldring, *The Nineteen Twenties. A General Survey and some Personal Memories* (London, 1945), pp. 229 and 251.

Young people and those who do not know the ways of the world are apt sometimes to rebel against custom, convention, etiquette – to rebel ... against any restraint of their wishes, of their display of personality, forgetting that if community life is to be lived at its best the greatest good of the greatest number must be considered before the desires of the few.

Lady Troubridge, *The Book of Etiquette* (London, 1926), p. 2.

There seems to be little private entertaining this autumn,

probably on account of all these crashes ... The new collapses in Wall Street and their reflexion over here are making us all feel rather gloomy about our financial affairs, though we seem to hide our feelings fairly well from the world at large.

The Tatler, 20 November 1929.

The 'Bright Young People'

To the public at large the escapades of the 'Bright Young People' provided a dramatic picture of social life in the 'Roaring Twenties', with their cocktails, jazz, and sometimes flagrantly abandoned behaviour. But at a deeper level they were responding to the uncertainties and the turbulence of the post-war world by engaging in a series of high-profile pranks and parties, at a time when the cult of youth was exerting an important influence upon Society's view of itself. To some extent the 'empty restlessness' of the age was captured in the lyrics of Noel Coward, such as his 'Dance Little Lady' of 1928:

Tho' you're only seventeen
Far too much of life you've seen
Syncopated child.
Maybe if you only knew
Where your path was leading to
You'd become less wild.
But I know it's vain
Trying to explain,
While there's this insane
Music in your brain.[1]

The tensions and the feelings of alienation experienced

by many young people were confirmed by Cyril Connolly when he commented on the difficulty his generation found in accepting the duties associated with adult life in the way their fathers had. The war had undermined the old sense of stability. 'They could not settle down to boring jobs and unprofitable careers with pre-war patience.'[2] Patrick Balfour described the post-war generation of young men, which included himself, as a 'rebel army', resisting 'parental tyranny' and 'the limited conception of life for which it stood', even though they were unable to bring forward any constructive policy of their own as an alternative.[3]

Brenda Dean Paul, herself a member of the bright young set, underlined these views when she claimed that those such as she, who were 'faced with the problems of life far earlier than our parents, had no inclination to conform ... and broke gradually away, forming little groups or "coteries", which came to be known by the papers as "the bright young people"'. A 'camaraderie of youth had arisen', a desire for independence and equality which 'gave birth to a new code of social manners'.[4] For her that could mean that partying went on into the early hours of the morning, so that 'for years I never went to bed before four or five in the morning. Constantly burning the candle at both ends, and in the middle too, I must have had a constitution of iron, for throughout those years I seldom if ever bothered to have a regular meal.' Only later, aggravated by her serious addiction to drugs, did her health finally give way.

Barbara Cartland remembered that these outbursts of youthful exuberance were greeted in conventional circles with disapproval. Modern girls were condemned as 'vulgar, absurd, improper, fast, over-sexed, abominable, shaming, humiliating'. To the novelist Winifred Graham, they were mere 'travesties of womanhood'.[5]

Most of the leaders of this new group, numbering only a few hundred, were well connected and rarely followed any definite career. In a small number of cases, members of the middle class, including Evelyn Waugh and Cecil Beaton, were able to gain entry into this world through their university connections and, later on, through the successful demonstration of their artistic and literary gifts. In Waugh's case, by the end of the decade he had begun to win plaudits for his novels on life among the social elite during the twenties, while Beaton was not only being lionised as a successful photographer and designer, but as a contributor to Society magazines, including *Vogue*, for which he wrote several articles.[6]

Prominent among the activities of the bright young set were the holding of fancy dress parties and the organising of 'treasure hunts', these latter being carried on by motor cars in the middle of the night, amid much noise and excitement. Parents, for the most part, reacted to these outbursts with despair or anger, according to their temperament. Hence the former Labour minister, Arthur Ponsonby, noted in his diary in the middle of the decade how helpless he and his wife felt when they were dealing with their headstrong daughter, Elizabeth, who was one of the leaders of the Bright Young People. 'If I were to do the heavy father and reprove, rebuke, and correct she would simply leave us,' he wrote sadly. 'Slender as it is becoming the link between us and her is still of some value.'[7]

In contrast, the fiery-tempered Lord Redesdale openly displayed his angry contempt for the 'effeminate young men with violet-scented hair' who were invited by his eldest daughter, Nancy, to his Oxfordshire home, and who arrived in 'noisy open sports cars'. 'They lounged about the house dressed in Oxford bags with 28-inch bottoms, loud Fair Isle sweaters and silk ties, making silly jokes and roaring with laughter at everything that [he] and his generation regarded as sacred.'[8] Flippancy about the war was regarded as a particular offence.

The main aim of these young people was seemingly to abandon the restraints their parents sought to impose and to seek in pleasure an antidote to the troubled times in which they were living. Some of them were 'rich and aristocratic' while others were 'downright disreputable', plumbing the depths of 'drink, drugs and disappointment'. The liberty they sought included a rejection of many of the sexual standards which had applied in pre-war society. There was what one writer has called a 'debunking' in regard to questions of sex.[9] So although homosexual relationships between males remained illegal, many of the young aesthete leaders of the day, like Brian Howard and Stephen Tennant, openly pursued them in contrast to the clandestine arrangements which had prevailed before 1914. Indeed, as one of their Oxford University contemporaries put it, even for those who were not homosexually inclined 'it was *chic* to be queer' in the 1920s.[10]

Lesbianism, too, was more widely discussed among the *avant-garde*, although it was still regarded with abhorrence by most members of the general public. In 1921 there was even a proposal put forward in the House of Commons to make it a crime, punishable by imprisonment, as was the case for homosexual contacts between males. One of the sponsoring MPs claimed that the practice had become 'very prevalent' and that the lunatic asylums were 'largely peopled' by women who had indulged in the vice. The fact that the offence was difficult to prove and might encourage blackmail was no reason to prevent its being made a punishable offence. The proposition was approved by a thinly attended House of Commons on 4 August but was rejected in the House of Lords eleven days later. This was partly because it would be difficult to implement, since many women shared a bedroom for companionship or because of shortage of space, and might give rise to blackmail, and partly because any prosecutions that resulted from such cases would make the practice known to thousands of people who had hitherto been unaware that such offences were committed. In the end those views prevailed and 'gross indecency between females' was never subjected to any legal penalty.[11]

Some contemporaries argued that the 'violation of traditional sexual limits and roles' that had occurred during the war and its immediate aftermath, and which had led to females becoming 'assertively boyish', had encouraged a change in attitude among women. However, among the most prominent lesbians in High Society was Vita Sackville-West. She conducted a series of relationships with other women throughout her adult life, including before 1914. Yet at the same time she successfully preserved her family life and her marriage to Harold Nicolson. In the immediate post-war period her most passionate affair was with Violet Keppel, or Violet Trefusis as she became when, under maternal pressure, she married Denys Trefusis in June 1919. With Violet, Vita travelled to Europe, particularly to France, where she often donned male attire and called herself Julian. At around this same time, somewhat ironically, Harold was himself embarking on one of his numerous homosexual relationships, on this occasion with the young Paris dress designer, Edward Molyneux.[12] In the end, the affair between Violet and Vita petered out in 1921, albeit amid bitterness and feelings of betrayal on the part of Violet. Vita then embarked on other affairs, including forming a relationship with the novelist Virginia Woolf, who might in many respects be regarded as the love of her life. Virginia's own feelings were more reserved, and her biographer, Quentin Bell, concludes that while she was prepared to attribute to Vita 'an almost impossible degree of charm and distinction', she felt no 'blind passion' towards her. The fact that Vita was 'in love' with her flattered and pleased her but that was probably as far as it went. 'There may have been – on balance I think that there probably was – some caressing, some bedding together,' writes Bell. 'But whatever may have occurred between them of this nature, I doubt very much whether it was of a kind to excite Virginia or to satisfy Vita.'[13] Interestingly, Michael Bloch has suggested that while Vita, a romantic by nature, generally loved one woman at a time, Harold had a far more pragmatic attitude towards sex, and could be interested in several young male partners at any one time.[14]

In 1928 the publication of Miss Radclyffe Hall's novel, *The Well of Loneliness*, seemed to mark a new acceptance of lesbian relationships, but it was soon banned under the 1857 Obscene Publications Act, and gave rise to harsh comments in many traditional circles.[15] Lady Hamilton, who was lent the book by Lord Esher, read it but confessed to being glad to 'get it out of my room – it gave me nausea. I cannot understand why she is not imprisoned for writing it – it is a book poisoning the very roots of home life ... Apart from what she pleads about, which is abnormal vice, she writes as if sex was the only thing on God's earth, as if there were not happy useful lives to be lived without the trail of the beast.'[16] But the strongest condemnation of the book came from the editor of the *Sunday Express*. Soon after its publication he declared in florid language that he would 'rather give a healthy boy or a healthy girl a phial of prussic acid than this novel. Poison kills the body, but moral poison kills the soul.'[17] After the trial, which led to the book being condemned as an obscene libel, conditions became more difficult for many lesbians, unless they enjoyed high social status like Vita Sackville-West and were careful to maintain a low profile before the wider public, or they mixed in bohemian circles where sexual liberty was the norm.

These aspects of female relationships, however, impinged little on the doings of most of the Bright Young People. Among the most prominent of them in the early days were the Jungman sisters, Zita and Theresa, the wealthy, emancipated daughters of Mrs Richard Guinness by her first marriage. There was, too, Elizabeth Ponsonby, whose thwarted desire for a stage career found some compensation in the publicity she gained from the many pranks with which she was associated. Lady Eleanor Smith, whose father, Lord Birkenhead, had been lord chancellor, was another member of the coterie. Among their various escapades they engaged in a series of hoaxes, including the Jungman sisters pretending to be journalists and interviewing Hollywood stars, who were unaware of the trick being played upon them. In another spoof, Lady Eleanor Smith disguised herself as a Russian princess in exile after the Revolution, and with the help of her friends was able to deceive and ultimately humiliate a pompous young man of her acquaintance.[18] Then there was the time when, under Brian Howard's direction, a group of them played 'Follow my Leader' through Selfridges store. They rushed in and out of the departments, up and down in the lifts, and climbed over the counters, no doubt to the annoyance of customers and the confusion of staff. Selfridges seem to have accepted it in a friendly fashion, but it made headlines in the newspapers.[19]

In an attempt to inject further excitement into their

day-to-day existence, a sophisticated form of paperchase was initiated by the Jungmans, too. It involved travelling all over London to follow the clues. Loelia Ponsonby became involved at an early stage, although the initial experiment seems to have been made by Zita and Theresa Jungman with Lady Eleanor Smith and another friend, Enid Raphael. According to Loelia,

> Zita and Eleanor were the hares with five minutes start and they zig-zagged about London using buses and undergrounds and leaving clues behind them as they went. This turned out to be such an exciting game they asked me and some other girls to join in and we used to amuse ourselves on blank afternoons by chasing each other round London ... The route was thought up beforehand. You arrived with your partner (we always hunted in couples) and were handed a piece of paper on which was written a cryptic message which, when solved sent you to the spot where the next clue on the chain was hidden. Part of the fun was thinking out original places in which to hide the clues ...[20]

So enjoyable was it that the men wanted to join in. This led to the development of the treasure hunts and a change of character. The hunts were held at night, after dinner, and the participants travelled by car rather than on public transport. They were also 'tremendously noisy'. As there were no traffic lights, recalled Loelia Ponsonby, 'we used to race madly through the empty streets, rushing out to suburbs and the East End, regardless of the feelings of the inhabitants who were trying to get to sleep'. She reported how they would assemble about midnight at a given place, where the clues were handed out. 'After that we behaved like Furies.'[21]

Barbara Cartland also joined in and she remembered that in time the clues became more complicated. On one occasion Lord Beaverbrook even had printed fake copies of the *Evening Standard* with a clue hidden in the imaginary news.[22] All of the participants paid ten shillings into a pool and that furnished the prize for the winning pair. 'This meant that sometimes the sum to be won was nearly £100,' Barbara noted, 'and there was not only a lot of tense competition but a lot of cheating.'

Soon the press got hold of the story, especially when the Prince of Wales became involved, as happened in late July 1924. On 26 July, the day after the meeting, the *Daily Mail* published a detailed account of it all, under the heading

THE PRINCE IN A TREASURE HUNT
MIDNIGHT CHASE IN LONDON
50 MOTOR CARS
THE BRIGHT YOUNG PEOPLE

Those joining in met at around 2 a.m. and after receiving their first clues, they leapt into their motor cars and 'with barking exhausts that echoed through the stillness of the streets, were on their way to the Adelphi Arches'. By 3.30 a.m. 'slow cars had given place to high-powered ones, and slow wits to faster wits, so that the field, which had started some 50 cars strong, all closely packed ... was straggled out'. Carefully arranged *coiffures* and expensive dresses were disarranged, and according to the *Daily Mail* reporter, that ought to please the dressmakers since few of the frocks the girls were wearing as they crawled on all fours on the not-too-clean streets of Seven Dials, searching for a clue chalked on one of the pavements, would 'ever see the lights of a ball-room again'. The prince headed this search, pursued 'by Mrs Viola Parsons'.

The treasure hunters discovered their final clue in the more salubrious surroundings of Norfolk House, St James's, where 'a splendid breakfast had been prepared and a string band to cheer them after their strenuous adventures'. Somewhat incongruously the Prince of Wales seems to have taken part wearing a blue serge suit and a bowler hat, though whether he was still wearing the latter at the end of the chase, the newspaper did not say.

Eventually, though, as 'every sort of person began to have treasure hunts', Loelia Ponsonby and some of her friends lost interest in them, though others carried on. 'I don't think I went to one after nineteen twenty-four or five,' wrote Loelia. 'Nor had I anything to do with the scavenging parties which succeeded the treasure hunts as an after-dark amusement. The competitors were given a list of objects which they had to obtain somehow and the embarrassment of trying to borrow them in the middle of the night can only have been equalled by the boredom of taking them back next day.'[23] She also came to resent the way in which any 'Bohemian rag or large-scale practical joke' which took place in the West End of London between 1924 and 1930 was attributed 'to these Bright Young People. They did not distinguish between us, the original Treasure Hunters, and the friends of my cousin Elizabeth [Ponsonby]. She organized parties which we thought exhibitionist – they always seemed to be held where there were photographers and where they would create the maximum disturbance.'[24]

Barbara Cartland, too, avoided the scavenging parties. She remembered meeting one girl who had dropped out of a scavenger competition when she and her partner were asked to collect 'the most impossible things'. They included 'a policeman's helmet – and if we took that we're sure to be arrested. A red hair from an actress' and a pipe smoked by Stanley Baldwin, the then Prime Minister.[25]

However, it was for their parties, particularly their fancy dress parties that the Bright Young People became notorious. Associated with these was the jazz music to which they danced, especially the Charleston in 1925. Evelyn Waugh noted in his diary in December of that year how one of his friends, Olivia Plunket Greene, had become 'literally "Charleston crazy"' and was miserable 'until in an interval after supper she found a fairly empty room to dance it in'.[26]

The frenetic atmosphere all this created was described by Patrick Balfour when he noted how each year the London Season became more feverish, with people rushing from one party or restaurant to another, and then on to a third or fourth in the course of a single evening. They would

> finish up with an early morning bathing-party, transported at 60 mph to the swimming-pools of Eton through the dawn. On the river, a languid evening in a punt is not enough. There must be dancing as well, at Datchet or at Bray, and a breakneck race down the Great West Road afterwards.[27]

Society was also leavened by the admission of people from the theatre and the arts, and with some actresses marrying into the peerage. Beatrice Lillie, for instance, became Lady Peel, the dancer June became Lady Inverclyde, and Gertie Millar ended up as the Countess of Dudley.[28] Not to be outdone the young Earl of Northesk married an American-born former member of the Ziegfeld Follies.

The bright young set became particularly newsworthy, however, when they began to hold 'themed' or 'freak' fancy dress parties, having become dissatisfied with the organising of ordinary fancy dress events. Brenda Dean Paul claimed that it was in 1926 that she attended her first 'freak' party. It was held by David Tennant at his Gargoyle club, and though intended as an Edwardian party, it was accompanied on the invitation by instructions to 'Come as you were twenty years ago'.[29] The result was 'a crazy children's party', when even the band wore Eton suits and collars and school caps. 'Baby "pens", high chairs and prams lined the walls.'

Other freak parties followed, and Brenda listed a number of them. They included 'pyjama parties, Greek parties, Russian parties, sailor parties, American parties, murder parties, bathing parties and so on'.[30]

Some of these events proved more controversial than others. David Tennant's pyjama party, to which guests were instructed to bring their own drink, was one such. The *Daily Mail*, reporting on it and on another Tennant party in 1928, wondered how Lord Grey of Falloden, David's stepfather and a former Foreign Secretary, viewed such unconventional affairs, since he was 'very much a fine old diplomat on his dignity'. Lady Grey, David's mother, was also 'of the older school'.[31]

However, one of the most widely publicised of these gatherings was the midnight bath party arranged during a heat wave in July 1928 at St George's Baths in Buckingham Palace Road. It was given by Mrs Plunket Greene, Elizabeth Ponsonby, Edward Gathorne-Hardy and Brian Howard, with the guests requested to bring with them bathing costumes, a towel, and a bottle of alcohol. They arrived in taxi-cabs and motor cars, with some still in evening dress, others in pyjamas and dressing gowns, and a few in bathing costumes covered by coats. Each guest had to produce an invitation card, to prevent gatecrashers, and while some quickly entered the water, where a series of informal games were played, others danced in the entrance hall to the music of a black jazz band. Large rubber horses supported some of the bathers in the water, while changing beams of coloured light played on the water, the surface of which was strewn with flowers. 'One man', according to the *Daily Mail*, 'dived from the high dive', bizarrely clad in a dressing gown and a soft felt hat.[32] The shouts and cries of the revellers could be heard 'many hundred yards away from the swimming baths', the newspaper reported. According to Tom Driberg, now working for the *Daily Express*, the bathing costumes worn were of the 'most dazzling kinds and colours', while a special 'Bathwater Cocktail' was produced specially for the occasion.[33]

However, it was not the rowdiness of the scene but its nature that aroused critical attention. 'Great astonishment and not a little indignation,' declared the *Sunday Chronicle*,

> is being expressed in London over the revelation that in the early hours of yesterday morning a large number of Society women danced in bathing dresses to the music of a negro band at a 'swim and dance' gathering organized by some of Mayfair's Bright Young People.[34]

The principal objection raised by a 'well-known Society hostess' was that the youthful guests had behaved with such a lack of decorum before a black dance band. Even Barbara Cartland's mother shared these reservations. 'Fancy dancing in bathing dresses!' she declared. 'I've never heard of anything so improper! – and watched by black men!' She expressed relief that Barbara herself had not taken part in such a decadent event.[35]

Another almost equally controversial party mentioned by Barbara Cartland was a 'Baby Party' held in Rutland

Gate, Kensington, in July 1929, with the guests invited to have 'Romps from ten o'clock to bedtime ... and we'll love to have Nanny too. Pram park provided. Dress: anything from birth to school age.' The *Daily Express* gave it a good deal of publicity, with the guests apparently arriving in perambulators in some cases and riding rocking horses in the gardens. They 'chased each other on donkeys and scooters, and bowled hoops'. The result was that

> screams resounded in the brilliantly lighted square ... The guests were dressed as babies in long clothes, Girl Guides, Boy Scouts, nurses. They had comforters in their mouths and carried toy boats, dolls, pails and spades. An attempt was made to take the donkeys into the house. They were led up the steps, a butler pushing them from behind. Late in the evening the crowd was scattered by the violent ringing of a fire-bell. It was only some of the Bright Young People arriving in a taxi-cab. Cocktails were served in nursery mugs, and the 'bar' was a babies' pen.[36]

By this time, however, people were growing tired of such 'immature, vulgar' behaviour, as one newspaper critic put it, while another declared it was the type of conduct which 'leads to Communism'.[37] *The Bystander*'s correspondent also expressed irritation, declaring that when she discovered that she was expected to attend in 'a short dress and socks', she had jibbed, 'because I am rather tired of "freak" parties'. She also condemned the Circus Party, which had been organised by the dress designer Norman Hartnell shortly beforehand, and which had involved live animals, as well as various sideshows and dancing to a circus orchestra: 'the wolves looked so unhappy ... I don't think you should have live animals at parties, because animals hate being made fools of.'[38] Brian Howard, meanwhile, had perpetrated what his biographer described as one of his 'less admirable jokes' by having several invitations 'professionally "forged" so that he and his uninvited friends could go' to the Circus Party.[39] But once they had arrived they found it little to their liking and soon departed.

One of the last of these wild parties, held in 1931, ended in disaster. It was called a White Party because the host, a man named Sandy Baird, who held it in a big barn attached to his mother's country house in Kent, insisted 'on an all-white theme. A band came down from London' and everyone attending duly wore white. However, there was a quarrel towards the end of the party involving some of the guests, and one young man drove off recklessly, with the former Elizabeth Ponsonby, now Elizabeth Pelly, as a passenger. He crashed the car and was killed, although the badly shaken Elizabeth was unhurt. It made headlines in all the newspapers, and the accident helped to 'sober up the Bright Young People more than any amount of adult disapproval'.[40]

Meanwhile, Elizabeth, who had only married in 1929, was already contemplating separation from her weak and ineffectual husband, Denis Pelly. In the event she divorced him soon after, on the grounds of his adultery, with the decree nisi granted in 1933. By this time she was already drinking heavily, to her father's despair. Indeed, as early as December 1929 Arthur Ponsonby noted in his diary, 'Elizabeth and Denis's affairs must necessarily darken everything and oppress us ... I cannot see any way out at the moment.'[41]

As Patrick Balfour sourly pointed out, by the late 1920s every 'ill-bred escapade of the younger generation' was being attributed to the Bright Young People, even when it was carried out by some of their hangers-on. They were being judged by the 'later and viler manifestations' of their unorthodox behaviour rather than by their earlier displays of romantic independence.[42] But by 1929 the mood within Society generally was darkening, as economic problems mounted and as the feckless conduct and rowdy drunkenness displayed by some members of the bright young set increasingly jarred with the prevailing public mood.

The End of an Era

The growing unemployment in the 1920s, while not directly affecting most members of the social elite did, nevertheless, cast a blight over their activities. Loelia Ponsonby for one found some of the extravagant events being organised increasingly unpalatable, although, as she confessed, it was she and her brother who in November 1926 had initiated the 'bottle-party'. It was at a time when their parents were away, and the large family drawing room with its parquet floor seemed a perfect venue for a dance. But, as usual, the Ponsonbys were short of cash, so they decided to ask 'the girls to bring the food and the men the drink'. It all worked out very well. 'On arrival each guest was relieved of a discreet parcel which was unpacked and laid out in the dining-room.' The novelist Michael Arlen even arrived with a dozen bottles of pink champagne. The music for dancing was provided, rather amateurishly, by the guests themselves strumming on the piano. Later there was an impromptu one-man cabaret show.[43] The idea proved so successful, especially at a time of increasing austerity, that it was taken up by other hosts and hostesses. Unfortunately, as the years went by the 'bottle parties' became rowdier until they degenerated in some cases into drunken, drug-driven orgies. Gatecrashing became increasingly common at the larger parties, while some events ended in fights. Allanah Harper, one of the Bright Young People, who had been to school with Zita Jungman and was a close friend of Cecil Beaton, became a victim of this. She described finding herself at one of David Tennant's parties 'in the middle of a jealous fracas ... which ... resulted in my dress being practically torn off and tufts of my hair held up as trophies.'[44] After that, she 'never went to parties of this kind again'.

Beaton himself also commented on the bad manners and arrogance of some of the girls. 'If an unfavoured young man came up to talk to them, they would sit silently staring at their baffled victim and then suddenly burst into derisive laughter.' At country house parties, 'their highly powered motor cars were not infrequently driven through imposing gateways, breaking stone piers and filigree of wrought iron'.[45] One 'high-spirited young lady even managed to crack the bottom of an ornamental lake'.

Against this background, the activities of the bright young set were increasingly condemned. They seemed callow, insincere, flippant and lacking a sense of moral equilibrium, at a time of mounting social distress. Loelia Ponsonby wrote of the 'pathetic bands of hunger marchers on the streets of London' and of rising unemployment. 'At every lunch-party the topic cropped up and ... I could not help being struck unpleasantly by the bejewelled, orchidaceous ladies and their affluent consorts smugly declaring over the caviare that there was no solution to the problem.' She then added sharply, 'one feels that a nobler community would have voluntarily submitted to higher taxation in order to lighten the soul-destroying poverty of more than one-and-a-half millions of their fellow countrymen.'[46]

Of course some elegant fancy dress parties continued to be held, such as the Mozart party arranged by David Tennant and his then wife, the actress Hermione Baddeley, on 29 April 1930. The guests wore eighteenth-century costumes and proceedings began with a recital of Mozart's music. David Tennant himself appeared as Don Giovanni. There was dancing and Barbara Cartland considered it was 'all highly respectable, and no one could say a word against it'.[47] However, she did not mention that even this had a bizarre twist in that some of the revellers went out into Piccadilly in the early hours of the morning and came upon workmen digging up a gas pipe in the street. Cecil Beaton seized the pneumatic drill and a photograph shows the tall figure of Patrick Balfour standing on a pile of rubble beside a bemused workman. The former Elizabeth Ponsonby, now Elizabeth Pelly, was standing beside Cecil Beaton's right arm.

Diana Mitford, the third daughter of Lord and Lady Redesdale, who had married the wealthy Bryan Guinness in January 1929, claimed to have taken little part in the doings of the bright young set at this time. However, in fact the Guinnesses' London home became the venue for one of the most notorious hoaxes perpetrated by them when, in July 1929, the notorious 'Bruno Hat' art exhibition was organised at a cocktail party they arranged. The idea was the brainchild of Brian Howard and had its origins in the scepticism with which many of the social elite regarded the new trend in French abstract art led by Picasso and his fellow pioneers. The 'Hat' works were painted by Howard on bath mats and had rope picture frames. Tom Mitford, in disguise, masqueraded as the 'artist', Bruno Hat. He was in a wheelchair, wearing a black suit, and sporting a black wig, drooping false moustache and dark glasses. He claimed to be of German origin and to have a poor command of English, having only arrived in England in 1919. A catalogue of the exhibition, which was part of the spoof, was written in pretentious language by Evelyn Waugh and claimed great things for Hat's artistic abilities. There was even a female attendant with a price list for the paintings. Howard had given them impressive titles, such as *The Adoration of the Magi* for a picture comprising 'cubes, lines and splodges'.[48] Some of those attending were 'in the know', but many were not, and it seems that one or two of the pictures were sold to people who were not in on the secret. The hoax was, however, revealed the next day by Bryan Guinness himself, who thought the joke was getting out of control. According to Bryan and Diana's son, Jonathan, the newspapers reported it in a big way, and while most comments were friendly, at least one review 'was rather sour and pompous'. He then added, 'Perhaps Bryan had been wise to bring the deception to an end when he did; journalists, like the rest of us, dislike being made fools of.'[49] Diana herself thought that for Brian Howard 'the joke was not altogether a joke, and that he was inwardly disappointed not to have been discovered as an unknown master'.[50]

Meanwhile on the national stage events were becoming still more gloomy. The economic crisis which was to engulf the country in the 1930s began to manifest itself in the autumn of 1929. There was first of all a blow to the standing of the City of London caused by the collapse of an intricate web of companies, some fraudulent, built up by the financier Clarence Hatry and his fellow directors of the Austin Friary Trust. As a result of this, it was estimated that investors lost around £15 million and Hatry himself was subsequently sent to prison along with three fellow directors.[51] According to 'Mr. Gossip' in the *Daily Sketch*, soon after Clarence Hatry's arrest, his brother Eric was seen in the Embassy Club smoking a cigar and with a 'procession of friends' stopping at his table to greet him: 'I hear that Eric Hatry during the past week has offered to make good out of his own pocket the losses of those friends of his whom he advised to invest in his brother's companies,' reported 'Mr. Gossip'.[52] Whether this actually happened is another matter.

Still worse was to follow, with the Wall Street Crash of late October 1929 signalling the general collapse of the American stock market. This affected not only leading socialites like Sir Arthur and Lady Colefax, who lost their life's savings, but many others. Among them were Winston and Clementine Churchill. Winston was in the United States to secure further contracts for his writing when the collapse occurred. On his return to England early in November he told a shocked Clementine that he had lost a small fortune in the crash. As partial compensation, however, he had signed contracts for magazine articles which would earn him £40,000. As his daughter Mary wrote:

> He could ... keep them all by his pen and his prodigious industry, but the loss of such a capital sum was a body blow. They retreated to lick their wounds at Chartwell, where a regime of stringent economies was promulgated. As for their London life, for a year or two they either took furnished houses for a few months at a time, or, with more economy and convenience, stayed at the Goring Hotel near Victoria Station.[53]

To meet the crisis, Chartwell was run down to a low ebb during that winter, so that Winston's study was the only room left open in the house, to enable him to work there at weekends. Clementine mostly stayed in London.

Beverley Nichols, too, remembered opening a newspaper and reading with horror the headline 'Wall Street Crashes. Stocks Stumble in Frenzied Selling'. He checked his own share holdings and discovered that he had lost the equivalent of £2,000, which was about a third of his worldly wealth. 'I had a moment of sheer panic ... And then so great is the resilience of youth, that I threw the paper on the floor, said, "That's that," and dismissed the matter from my mind.'[54]

Most of those affected were unable to accept their changed fortunes so philosophically. Lady Cunard's income was sharply reduced and although she still resolutely continued to entertain, she seems to have sold some of her high-quality pictures, partly to help finance her adored Sir Thomas Beecham's musical ventures. She also made frequent visits to the jewellers to exchange some of the pieces she owned for stones of lesser value. Indeed the valet and later butler, Ernest King, apparently learnt through the servant grapevine that when she died in July 1948, she left an ostensibly valuable emerald necklace to her lady's maid. Unfortunately the maid discovered that the original necklace had been substituted with mere coloured glass.[55] Her clothes, too, were no longer expensive models purchased from the leading couturiers. Instead she bought ready-made garments in Shaftesbury Avenue. They were then adapted as necessary, probably by her loyal lady's maid, Mary Gordon. When she died, her estate in Britain was valued at just under £47,000. Her friend, Loel Guinness, was appointed the sole executor, and she left her maid her wardrobe, all her silver plate 'free of all duties', and the sum of £1,500, again free of all death duties. The residue of the estate was to be divided equally between her daughter, Nancy, from whom she had long been estranged, and her friends Lady Diana Cooper and Robert Abdy.[56]

Another victim of the Wall Street Crash was the wealthy Mrs de Wichfeld, who had once employed Ernest King as her husband's valet. She, too, was reduced to comparative poverty. According to King, when she died soon after, she was so short of cash that her funeral at the Savoy Chapel was paid for by friends, although they were later reimbursed from her estate.[57]

Nancy Mitford, too, was affected in that she began to take her writing career more seriously when Lord Redesdale's shaky finances were put under greater pressure. He consequently reduced her already small allowance still further.[58] Even the wealthy Edwina Mountbatten was warned that from late 1929 to mid-1931, her expenses were mounting while her investment income fell and her tax burden was also increasing. In these circumstances she was advised to sell her large London mansion, Brook House. It was to be demolished and replaced by flats, with Edwina reserving for herself a large penthouse flat overlooking Hyde Park and fitted out to the highest degree of luxury.[59]

Probably Noel Coward best caught the mood of the times with his lyric:

Children of the Ritz
Children of the Ritz
Sleek and civilised
Fretfully surprised
Though Mr. Molyneux has gowned us
The world is tumbling around us
Without a sou
What can we do?
We'll soon be begging for a crust ...[60]

In June 1932, in ironic vein, *The Bystander* also observed:

'Everybody's broke, but that depressing little fact won't stop us going to Ascot. In clothes they see no prospect of paying for, our "lovelies" will parade each day, while we shall all eat too much, drink too much, bet too much, and talk too much.'[61]

In September 1931 Britain devalued its currency when it left the gold standard. This led to the value of the pound falling by a quarter, while shortly beforehand income tax had been raised from 4s 6d to 5s in the pound; there was a cut in the dole paid to the unemployed, and a reduction in the salaries of many workers in the public sector, including a cut in the pay and pensions of members of the armed forces.[62] This latter led to a brief 'mutiny' among sailors of the North Atlantic Fleet at Invergordon. Three days later the government 'decided to abandon parity between the pound and its existing gold reserves', in other words, to leave the gold standard.[63]

In these turbulent times the once-accepted excesses of the Bright Young People seemed to have little place. Indeed, as early as July 1929 *The Bystander* had expressed irritation at the reckless conduct associated with their 'freak parties'. That included the 'Second Childhood' event held in Rutland Gate and described by Barbara Cartland. According to *The Bystander* it had much annoyed the neighbours.

There is nothing very terrible in young people dressing up as infants ... after all it is their own affair if they choose to don the garb of the nursery which they have left not so very long ago. What seems to have occasioned a quite understandable irritation in the hearts of the inhabitants of Rutland Gate was the fact that instead of restricting their activities to the house in which the party was held the guests staged a sort of motor racing carnival round and round the square ... to the accompaniment of shouts, yells, cat-calls and the hooting of motor horns ... No one wants to be a 'kill-joy', but surely there is nothing funny in unseemly and untimely noise.[64]

However, one of the harshest condemnations of their way of life came in *The People* in July 1932, when Richard Norton wrote a lengthy article on 'Those Bright Young Rotters. They Toil not but they Sin.' Behind 'many of the scandals of recent times', he declared,

lurks the shadow of that futile tribe of idlers – the so-called 'Bright Young Things'. Dominated by sex, by drink – in many cases by drugs – they toil not, but sin. They fritter away the money for which others have laboured. They talk and think drivel. Their parties are idiotic and nauseating. They burn up their youth in the flame of night clubs and cocktail parties. They break the law with impunity and expect applause for their imbecilities.[65]

He then went on to itemise the faults and failings he had particularly identified before concluding that 'stupidity' was 'one of their greatest sins ... If they had a spark of insight they would weigh up frankly the worthlessness of themselves. They are no use to anyone. The country would be much better off without them.'

A year later Patrick Balfour, who had himself once been part of the world of the Bright Young People, came to a similar, if less hard-hitting, conclusion. He acknowledged the twenties had been 'a turbulent epoch, but vital' when he and his fellows 'ate ... drank ... were merry, for we knew that today we should die. We counted not the cost ... It was our final fling ... How otherwise can I recapture

274

the recklessness, the lavishness, the carefree hospitality of the Roaring 'Twenties? ... There was no particular object in anything that we did, but we were sensible of its full flavour as we did it ... That irresponsible effortless zest is gone from us all.'[66] Douglas Goldring, writing in 1935, took a more clinical view, arguing that the 'Bright Young People' had been 'played off the stage by a new and tougher gang, who [had] found better things to do than advertising face creams'.[67] In the 1930s, pleasure-seeking and party-going did, of course, continue among the social elite but it was against an increasingly sombre and threatening backdrop, both nationally and internationally. It was a way of life that was to come to an end in 1939 with the outbreak of the Second World War.

Notes

Museum of English Rural Life, University of Reading, is abbreviated to MERL.

1 The Impact of War: 1914–1918

1. J. M. Winter, *The Great War and the British People*, 2nd edn (Basingstoke, 2003), p. 71. Winter suggests that 722,785 British servicemen died in the war, and there were also 15,000 deaths among the crews and passengers of merchant or fishing vessels. He estimates there were 1,266 civilian fatalities from air and sea bombardment. Of 5,215,162 men who served in the Army, 670,375 died or were killed, and a further 1,643,469 were wounded. That meant that 12.91 per cent of those who served died or were killed in the war and 31.51 per cent were wounded.
2. Madeleine Beard, *English Landed Society in the Twentieth Century* (London, 1989), p. 26.
3. Jennifer Ellis, ed., *Thatched with Gold. The Memoirs of Mabell, Countess of Airlie* (London, 1962), p. 129.
4. Richard Davenport-Hines, *Ettie. The Intimate Life and Dauntless Spirit of Lady Desborough* (London, 2008), p. 166.

5. Philip Ziegler, *Diana Cooper. The Biography of Lady Diana Cooper* (Harmondsworth, 1983 edn), p. 57.

6. Arthur Marwick, *The Deluge. British Society and The First World War* (London, 1965), p. 143.

7. John Charmley, *Duff Cooper. The Authorised Biography* (London, 1997 edn), p. 14.

8. Anne Chisholm, *Nancy Cunard* (Harmondsworth, 1981 edn), p. 55.

9. Hugh Ford, ed., *Nancy Cunard: Brave Poet Indomitable Rebel 1896–1965* (Philadelphia, New York, London, 1968), p. 12. Chisholm, *Nancy Cunard*, p. 52.

10. Ford, ed., *Nancy Cunard*, pp. 18–19.

11. Chisholm, *Nancy Cunard*, p. 55.

12. *The Bystander*, 29 July 1914.

13. The Countess of Carnarvon, *Lady Almina and the Real Downton Abbey. The Lost Legacy of Highclere Castle* (London, 2011), p. 125.

14. Margot Asquith, *Autobiography* (Vol. 2) (Harmondsworth, 1937 edn), pp. 117–119.

15. John Vincent, ed., *The Crawford Papers* (Manchester, 1984), p. 340.

16. The Countess of Carnarvon, *Lady Almina*, p. 126.

17. The Countess of Carnarvon, *Lady Almina*, pp. 121–124.

18. W. J. Reader, *At Duty's Call. A Study in Obsolete Patriotism* (Manchester, 1988), p. 104.

19. *The Bystander*, 22 July 1914. 'To the London newspapers,' it declared, 'there seem to be no European problems at all ... To London ... there is Ulster, Ulster, and only Ulster.'

20. 'English History' in the *Annual Register for 1914* (London, 1915), p. 175.

21. Vincent, ed., *The Crawford Papers*, p. 341.

22. Beard, *English Landed Society*, p. 29.

23. Randolph S. Churchill, *Lord Derby. 'King of Lancashire'* (London, 1959) p. 184. According to *Country Life*, 24 July 1915, when the war broke out, Lord Derby set himself the

target of raising recruits 'not by the thousand, but by the tens of thousand'.

24. Reader, *At Duty's Call*, p. 118.

25. Pamela Horn, *Rural Life in England in The First World War* (New York, 1984 edn), p. 28.

26. Mark Pottle, ed., *Champion Redoubtable. The Diaries and Letters of Violet Bonham Carter. 1914–1945* (London, 1998), pp. 7–8.

27. Horn, *Rural Life*, p. 28.

28. *Country Life*, 29 August 1914.

29. *The Bystander*, 12 August 1914.

30. Davenport-Hines, *Ettie*, p. 185.

31. Beard, *English Landed Society*, pp. 28–29.

32. Horn, *Rural Life*, p. 25.

33. Winter, *The Great War*, p. 93.

34. Lady Cynthia Asquith, *Diaries 1915–1918* (London, 1968), pp. 20, 85 and 90.

35. Asquith, *Diaries*, p. 97. On 1 July 1916, she heard of the death of her eldest brother: 'my Beautiful brother that I have loved so since I was a baby'.

36. Pamela Horn, *Ladies of the Manor: Wives and Daughters in Country House Society, 1830–1918* (Stroud, 1997 edn), p. 201.

37. The Countess of Carnarvon, *Lady Almina*, pp. 143–144.

38. Horn, *Ladies of the Manor*, p. 198–199.

39. Davenport-Hines, *Ettie*, pp. 183 and 187.

40. Davenport-Hines, *Ettie*, p. 187.

41. Vincent ed., *The Crawford Papers*, p. 349.

42. Vincent ed., *The Crawford Papers*, p. 341.

43. Vincent ed., *The Crawford Papers*, pp. 349 and 351.

44. *Country Life*, 22 August 1914. It was suggested that some of the houses might serve as convalescent homes, rather than as base hospitals with their demand for scarce nursing staff.

45. Ziegler, *Diana Cooper*, pp. 64–66.

46. Ziegler, *Diana Cooper*, pp. 70–71.

47. Ziegler, *Diana Cooper*, p. 71.

48. Diana Cooper, *Autobiography* (Wilton, Salisbury, 1979 edn), 129–130.

49. Cooper, *Autobiography*, p. 142.

50. Ziegler, *Diana Cooper*, pp. 66–67. Cooper, *Autobiography*, pp. 135–136.

51. Lois Gordon, *Nancy Cunard. Heiress, Muse, Political Idealist* (New York, 2007), pp. 52, 55, 59 and 62.

52. Stanley Jackson, *The Savoy. The Romance of a Great Hotel* (London, 1964), pp. 60–61. Andrew Cook, *Cash for Honours. The Story of Maundy Gregory* (Stroud, 2008) p. 36.

53. Gordon, *Nancy Cunard*, pp. 63–64.

54. Chisholm, *Nancy Cunard*, p. 68. Gordon, *Nancy Cunard*, p. 64.

55. Horn, *Ladies of the Manor*, p. 203.

56. Rosina Harrison, *Rose: My Life in Service* (London, 1975), 22.

57. Asquith, *Diaries 1915–1918*, p. 156, entry for 19 April 1916.

58. Horn, *Ladies of the Manor*, p. 203. For an index of retail prices during the war years see, for example, *The British Economy Key Statistics 1900–1970* (London and Cambridge Economic Service, n.d. *c.* 1971), p. 12.

59. Horn, *Rural Life*, p. 29. Horn, *Ladies of the Manor*, p. 203.

60. *Country Life*, 4 September 1915.

61. Pamela Horn, *Behind the Counter. Shop Lives from Market Stall to Supermarket* (Stroud, 2006), p. 177. By 1918 there was rationing of meat, tea, butter and margarine.

62. Asquith, *Diaries, 1915–1918*, p. 269, entries for 6 and 7 February 1917.

63. Asquith, *Diaries 1915–1918*, p. 269, entry for 8 February 1917.

64. Marion Fowler, *Blenheim. Biography of a Palace* (London, 1989), p. 217.

65. Ellis, ed., *Thatched with Gold*, pp. 131–133.

66. F. M. L. Thompson, *English Landed Society in the Nineteenth Century* (London, 1963), p. 328.

67. *Country Life*, 16 November 1918. Thompson, *English Landed Society*, p. 329.

68. *Country Life*, 14 and 28 December 1918.

69. The Countess of Carnarvon, *Lady Almina*, p. 236.

70. Horn, *Ladies of the Manor*, pp. 203–204.

71. William Shawcross, *Queen Elizabeth. The Queen Mother* (London, 2009), pp. 52–53, 56 and 59.

72. Airlie MSS. in the British Library, Add.MSS.82761, f.66, 8 October 1917.

73. Airlie MSS. Add.MSS.82761, f.78, 19 February 1918.

74. Anne de Courcy, *Circe. The Life of Edith, Marchioness of Londonderry* (London, 1992), pp. 107–110.

75. de Courcy, *Circe*, p. 133. Pamela Horn, *Women in the 1920s* (Stroud, 2010 edn), p. 29.

76. Diaries of Margot Asquith 1917–1923 cm Microfilm X 15/7 in the Bodleian Library, Oxford, entry for 28 December 1918, reverse f.56.

77. de Courcy, *Circe*, pp. 134–135.

78. de Courcy, *Circe*, pp. 115–116.

79. de Courcy, *Circe*, pp. 116–118.

80. Horn, *Rural Life*, pp. 39–40.

81. Winter, *The Great War*, pp. 97–98.

82. The will was written on Garrick Club notepaper, dated 11 August 1914, f.195 in Violet Milner MSS, VM27 at the Bodleian Library, Oxford. Lady Cecil married Lord Milner after the death of her first husband. She copied out correspondence and all the information she could glean about her son's death in VM.27. Fragment from the diary of Helen Cecil, 12 August 1914, also in VM.27.

83. George Cecil to his mother, 27 August 1914 in VM.27, f.5.

84. See correspondence in VM.27. On 6 November 1914, Brigadier General Robert Scott Kerr wrote to Lady Cecil, noting optimistically that 'it is encouraging that there is still some hope that all may be well with him, so many are being heard of as safe about whom we had given up all hope'.

Account of George's death from Private J. Snowden, 24 November 1914. He was wounded in the same action and witnessed George being shot. Snowden himself was taken prisoner, but rescued when the French reoccupied the land where his German field hospital was sited.

85. Helen Hardinge, *Loyal to Three Kings. A Memoir of Alec Hardinge, Private Secretary to the Sovereign 1920–1943* (London, 1967), p. 19.
86. The Hon. Julian Grenfell to Mrs Astor, 21 November 1914 in Astor MSS. MS.1416/1/2/14 at MERL.
87. Davenport-Hines, *Ettie*, pp. 190–194.
88. Asquith, *Diaries 1915–1918*, entry for 27 May 1915, p. 31.
89. Asquith, *Diaries 1915–1918*, entry for 12 June 1915, p. 41.
90. Billy Grenfell to Nancy Astor, postmarked 2 July 1915, in Astor MSS. MS.1416/1/4/42 at MERL.
91. Billy Grenfell to Nancy Astor, postmarked 14 July 1915, in Astor MSS. MS.1416/1/4/42 at MERL.
92. Billy Grenfell to Nancy Astor, undated, in Astor MSS. MS.1416/1/4/42 at MERL.
93. Davenport-Hines, *Ettie*, pp. 199–200. The attack ended 'as it was bound to end in the loss of very nearly the whole of a battalion'.
94. John Julius Norwich, ed., *The Duff Cooper Diaries* (London 2006 edn), p. 14, entry for 3 August 1915.
95. Asquith, *Diaries 1915–1918*, p. 103, entry for 21 November 1915.
96. Horn, *Ladies of the Manor*, pp. 195–196.
97. Ziegler, *Diana Cooper*, p. 96.
98. Asquith, *Diaries 1915–1918*, p. 323, entry for 30 July 1917.
99. Norwich, ed., *The Duff Cooper Diaries*, p. 46, entry for 14 January 1917.
100. Norwich, ed., *The Duff Cooper Diaries*, p. 41, entry for 6 December 1916.
101. Ziegler, *Diana Cooper*, p. 101. Norwich, ed., *The Duff Cooper Diaries*, p. 53, entry for 17 May 1917.

102. Norwich, ed., *The Duff Cooper Diaries*, pp. 53–54, entries for 19 and 21 May, 18 June and 5 and 6 July 1917. On 22 June, he noted: 'Today I left the Foreign Office without a single regret.'

103. Norwich, ed., *The Duff Cooper Diaries*, 22 November 1917 and 27 February 1918, pp. 60 and 65–66. On 23 November 1917, he received news of the death of Edward Horner, almost the last of his pre-war circle to have survived so far: 'By his death,' he wrote in his diary, 'our little society loses one of the last assets that gave it distinction. And I think we have paid more than our share.'

104. Norwich, ed., *The Duff Cooper Diaries*, p. 66, entry for 1 March 1918.

105. Norwich, ed., *The Duff Cooper Diaries*, pp. 71–72, entry for 11 June 1918.

106. Norwich ed., *The Duff Cooper Diaries*, pp. 70–71, entry for 21 May 1918.

107. Ziegler, *Diana Cooper*, p. 121. Charmley, *Duff Cooper*, pp. 23–25.

108. Horn, *Ladies of the Manor*, pp. 215–216. Horn, *Rural Life*, p. 40.

109. Horn, *Rural Life*, pp. 204–205.

110. *Country Life*, 16 November 1918.

111. Helen Cecil to Lady Violet Cecil, 12 November 1918 in Violet Milner MSS, VM.28 at the Bodleian Library, Oxford.

112. Robert Graves and Alan Hodge, *The Long Weekend. A Social History of Great Britain 1918–1939* (London, 1991 edn), pp. 17–18.

113. Norwich, ed., *The Duff Cooper Diaries*, 11 November 1918, p. 85.

114. Davenport-Hines, *Ettie*, pp. 228–229. Other bereaved mothers wrote to comfort one another, like Elizabeth Kenmare, whose son Dermot had been killed. She told Ettie: 'PEACE DAY: I know, darling, that your agony was doubled.'

115. Norwich, ed., *The Duff Cooper Diaries*, pp. 86 and 89 entries for 12 November 1918 and 9 and 12 December 1918.

116. Graves and Hodge, *The Long Weekend*, p. 22. Chisholm, *Nancy Cunard*, p. 70.
117. Loelia, Duchess of Westminster, *Grace and Favour* (London, 1961), pp. 83–84.

2 Adjusting to Peace: 1919–1921

1. Helen Hardinge, *Loyal to Three Kings. A Memoir of Alec Hardinge, Private Secretary to the Sovereign 1920–1943* (London, 1967), pp. 22–23.
2. Colin Clifford, *The Asquiths* (London, 2002), pp. 471 and 477.
3. Clifford, *The Asquiths*, pp. 432 and 471.
4. See entry for Edward Turnour, 6th Earl Winterton in the *Oxford Dictionary of National Biography* (Oxford, 2004).
5. Winterton Diary No. 24, entry for 23 March 1920, at the Bodleian Library, Oxford. Alan Houghton Brodrick, *Near to Greatness. A Life of the Sixth Earl Winterton* (London, 1965), p. 187, dates the quotation wrongly and reproduces it inaccurately.
6. Winterton Diary No. 22, entry for 19 February 1919, at the Bodleian Library. For Sir Philip Sassoon's military appointment see Peter Stansky, *Sassoon. The Worlds of Philip and Sybil* (New Haven and London, 2003), p. 56.
7. *The Bystander*, 2 March 1921.
8. Patrick Balfour, *Society Racket. A Critical Survey of Modern Social Life* (London, 1933), pp. 73 and 77.
9. Winterton Diary No. 22, entry for 1 April 1919.
10. Winterton Diary No. 22, entry for 29 May 1919.
11. *The Field*, 15 March 1919.
12. Loelia, Duchess of Westminster, *Grace and Favour* (London, 1961), p. 84.
13. *The Bystander*, 14 April 1920.
14. *The Tatler*, 9 April 1919.

15. Janet Morgan, *Edwina Mountbatten. A Life of Her Own* (London, 1992 edn), p. 87.

16. Stanley Jackson, *The Savoy. The Romance of a Great Hotel* (London, 1964), p. 64.

17. Frances Donaldson, *Child of the Twenties* (London, 1986 edn), pp. 68–71.

18. Rupert Godfrey, ed., *Letters from a Prince. March 1918–January 1921* (London, 1999 edn), p. ix. Stella Margetson, *The Long Party. High Society in the Twenties and Thirties* (London, 1976 edn), pp. 36–37.

19. John Julius Norwich, ed., *The Duff Cooper Diaries* (London, 2006 edn), p. 137, entry for 12 December 1920.

20. Robert Graves and Alan Hodge, *The Long Weekend. A Social History of Great Britain* (London, 1991 edn), 119–120. Balfour, *Society Racket*, p. 118.

21. Mrs Kate Meyrick, *Secrets of the 43 Club* (London, 1994 edn), pp. 12–22.

22. Meyrick, *Secrets of the 43 Club*, p. 104.

23. Meyrick, *Secrets of the 43 Club*, p. 33.

24. Meyrick, *Secrets of the 43 Club*, p. 52.

25. Barbara Cartland, *We Danced All Night* (London, 1994 edn), p. 113.

26. *Hansard*, 5th Series, Vol. 176 (14 July – 7 August 1924), pp. 1541–1542, 24 July 1924.

27. Quoted in Margetson, *The Long Party*, p. 105.

28. Winterton Diary No. 23.

29. Winterton Diary No. 23, entry for 19 November 1919.

30. Philip Ziegler, *Diana Cooper* (Harmondsworth, 1983 edn), p. 149.

31. Norwich, *The Duff Cooper Diaries*, p. 110. On the previous 29 October, he had taken a taxi with Diana Capel in Piccadilly and had driven with her to her home. 'I made love to her and kissed her and promised to meet her next day. I felt rather guilty when I got home.'

32. Ziegler, *Diana Cooper*, p. 132.

33. Ziegler, *Diana Cooper*, p. 151.

34. Cartland, *We Danced All Night*, p. 43.

35. Norwich, *The Duff Cooper Diaries*, p. 125, entry for 16 June 1920.

36. Norwich, *The Duff Cooper Diaries*, p. 95, entry for 11 March 1919.

37. Norwich, *The Duff Cooper Diaries*, p. 90, entry for 20 December 1918.

38. *The Tatler*, 15 June 1921. Norwich, *The Duff Cooper Diaries*, p. 140, entry for 15 March 1921. It was a tribute to Lady Diana's celebrity that when the Coopers went to the theatre on 9 September 1920, she was recognised and asked for 'her autograph' by some 'working girls ... She had to sign about a dozen. She is wonderfully popular. When we walked into the theatre ... there was loud applause from the pit.'

39. Lady Marjorie Dalrymple to Lady Airlie, 23 October 1920, in Airlie MSS, at the British Library, Add.MSS 82762, ff.44–45 and Lady Mary Trefusis to Lady Airlie, 29 October 1920, writing from Sandringham on behalf of Queen Mary, 29 October 1920, f.46.

40. D. J.Taylor, *Bright Young People. The Lost Generation of London's Jazz Age* (New York, 2007), pp. 226–227.

41. Norwich, *The Duff Cooper Diaries*, p. 104, entry for 10 June 1919.

42. *The Bystander*, 12 March 1919.

43. Richard Davenport-Hines, *Ettie. The Intimate Life and Dauntless Spirit of Lady Desborough* (London, 2008), p. 232.

44. Davenport-Hines, *Ettie*, p. 232.

45. Davenport-Hines, *Ettie*, pp. 239–240.

46. Cartland, *We Danced All Night*, p. 68.

47. Marion Fowler, *Blenheim. Biography of a Palace* (London, 1989), p. 218.

48. Leslie Field, *Bendor. The Golden Duke of Westminster* (London, 1986 edn), pp. 149–150.

49. Graves and Hodge, *The Long Weekend*, p. 109.

50. Field, *Bendor*, pp. 151 and 160–161.
51. Graves and Hodge, *The Long Weekend*, p. 47.
52. Martin Pugh, *Lloyd George* (London, 1988) pp. 149–150.
53. *Hansard (House of Lords)*, Vol. 51 (June 27 – August 4 1922), p. 509, 17 July 1922. Pugh, *Lloyd George*, p. 150.
54. *Hansard (House of Lords)*, Vol. 51, 495. Andrew Cook, *Cash for Honours. The Story of Maundy Gregory* (Stroud, 2008), p. 99.
55. Ross McKibbin, *Classes and Cultures. England 1918–1951* (Oxford, 2000), p. 16
56. Douglas Goldring, *The Nineteen Twenties. A General Survey and some Personal Memories* (London, 1945), pp. 3–4.
57. Pugh, *Lloyd George*, p. 150. Goldring, *The Nineteen Twenties*, p. 4.
58. Pugh, *Lloyd George*, p. 151. Cook, *Cash for Honours*, pp. 108–109.
59. Winterton Diary No. 23, entry for 10 July 1919.
60. Winterton Diary No. 22, entry for 3 March 1919. Graves and Hodge, *The Long Weekend*, p. 152, note that anyone in the upper classes who visited Russia, 'such as Claire Sheridan the sculptor' was 'socially ruined', even if no pro-Bolshevist view was expressed, so great was the alarm at Bolshevism.
61. Charles Loch Mowat, *Britain Between the Wars 1918–1940* (London, 1983 edn), pp. 39–40.
62. Norwich, *The Duff Cooper Diaries*, p. 109, entry for 27 September 1919.
63. *Beaulieu Abbey, Palace House, National Motor Museum* (Beaulieu, n.d. *c*. 2010), entry for John, 2nd Lord Montagu of Beaulieu. After going up to Oxford, his passion for engineering led him to sign up as an apprentice at the London & South Western Railway's Nine Elms locomotive depot, where he learned about the working of steam locomotives.
64. Winterton Diary No. 23, entry for 29 September 1919.
65. Mowat, *Britain Between the Wars*, p. 40.
66. Mowat, *Britain Between the Wars*, pp. 120–123.

67. Anne de Courcy, *Circe. The Life of Edith, Marchioness of Londonderry* (London, 1992), p. 162.
68. de Courcy, *Circe*, p. 162
69. de Courcy, *Circe*, p. 163
70. de Courcy, *Circe*, pp. 165–167.
71. David Cannadine, *The Decline and Fall of the British Aristocracy* (New Haven and London, 1990), p. 105.
72. Cannadine, *The Decline and Fall of the British Aristocracy*, p. 93.
73. *A Century of Agricultural Statistics. Great Britain 1866–1966* (London, HMSO, 1966), p. 82.
74. Cannadine, *The Decline and Fall of the British Aristocracy*, p. 97.
75. Cannadine, *The Decline and Fall of the British Aristocracy*, p. 97.
76. Field, *Bendor*, p. 146.
77. Field, *Bendor*, pp. 152–155. Cannadine, *The Decline and Fall of the British Aristocracy*, p. 115.
78. Cannadine, *The Decline and Fall of the British Aristocracy*, pp. 97–98.
79. Peter Mandler, *The Fall and Rise of the Stately Home* (New Haven and London, 1997), p. 243.
80. Leader in *Country Life*, 30 July 1921.
81. *Country Life*, 30 July 1921.
82. Cannadine, *The Decline and Fall of the British Aristocracy*, p. 98.
83. Cannadine, *The Decline and Fall of the British Aristocracy*, pp. 98–99.
84. *Country Life*, 13 August 1921. Lord and Lady Breadalbane had sold 40,000 acres of their Perthshire estate as well as Taymouth Castle itself, which had been their ancestral home.
85. Mandler, *The Fall and Rise of the Stately Home*, p. 246.
86. F. M. L. Thompson, *English Landed Society in the Nineteenth Century* (London, 1963), p. 335.

87. Thompson, *English Landed Society*, p. 329.

88. Madeleine Beard, *English Landed Society in the Twentieth Century* (London, 1989), p. 41.

89. Beard, *English Landed Society*, pp. 41–42.

90. *Country Life*, 15 March 1919.

91. Cannadine, *The Decline and Fall of the British Aristocracy*, p. 108.

92. *Country Life*, 22 March 1919.

93. Thompson, *English Landed Society*, p. 332.

94. Beard, *English Landed Society*, p. 42

95. *The Tatler*, 16 April 1919.

96. Thompson, *English Landed Society*, p. 333.

97. *A Century of Agricultural Statistics*, p. 25.

98. Quoted in Thompson, *English Landed Society*, p. 331.

99. *Country Life*, 7 June 1919.

100. Quoted in Thompson, *English Landed Society*, p. 332.

101. *Country Life*, 1 January 1921.

102. Beard, *English Landed Society*, pp. 51–52. Thompson, *English Landed Society*, p. 336.

103. Cannadine, *The Decline and Fall of the British Aristocracy*, p. 116.

104. *The Tatler*, 21 April 1920. *The Bystander*, 7 April 1920. In 1925 *The Bystander* called the house-breakers who were demolishing Devonshire House 'vandals'.

105. *The Tatler*, 23 June 1920.

106. *The Tatler*, 6 April 1921.

107. Field, *Bendor*, pp. 148–149, 155 and 191. Bendor apparently often anchored his yacht at Bosskop in Norway on his fishing trips.

3 Community Responsibilities and Sporting Pursuits

1. Richard Greville Verney, Lord Willoughby de Broke, *The Passing Years* (London, 1924), p. 56. He also added, perhaps

thinking of himself and his friends: 'there are plenty of people left who are still proud of the traditions and associations of their own shire'.

2. Pamela Horn, *Women in the 1920s* (Stroud, 2010 edn), p. 57.

3. Anne de Courcy, *Circe. The Life of Edith, Marchioness of Londonderry* (London, 1992), pp. 134–135.

4. John Grigg, *Nancy Astor. Portrait of a Pioneer* (London, 1980), p. 85.

5. Diary of Earl Winterton No. 24 in the Bodleian Library, Oxford, entry for 14 April 1920.

6. Horn, *Women in the 1920s*, pp. 147–149. Nicholas Mosley, *Rules of The Game. Sir Oswald and Lady Cynthia Mosley 1896–1933* (London, 1982), p. 118.

7. Nicholas Mansfield, 'Foxhunting and the Yeomanry: County Identity and Military Culture' in R. W. Hoyle ed., *Our Hunting Fathers. Field Sports in England after 1850* (Lancaster, 2007), p. 253.

8. David Cannadine, *The Decline and Fall of the British Aristocracy* (New Haven and London, 1990), p. 162.

9. Cannadine, *The Decline and Fall*, p. 163.

10. John Vincent, ed., *The Crawford Papers* (Manchester, 1984), p. 472.

11. Vincent, ed., *The Crawford Papers*, p. 535, entry for 12 December 1930.

12. Vincent, ed., The Crawford Papers, p. 423, entry for 6 June 1922.

13. William Scarth Dixon, *Fox-hunting in the Twentieth Century* (London, 1925), pp. 223–224.

14. Merlin Waterson, *The Country House Remembered. Recollections of Life Between the Wars (London, 1985)*, p. 34.

15. Waterson, *The Country House Remembered*, pp. 46–48.

16. Raymond Carr, *English Fox Hunting. A History* (London, 1976), p. 234.

17. Diary of Earl Winterton No. 28, entry for 14 January 1921.

18. Hugo Vickers, *Gladys Duchess of Marlborough* (London, 1987 edn), p. 185.

19. Vickers, *Gladys*, p. 219.

20. Quoted in F. M. L. Thompson, *English Landed Society in the Nineteenth Century* (London, 1963), p. 330.

21. Waterson, *The Country House Remembered*, p. 22.

22. Kedrun Laurie, *Cricketer Preferred. Estate Workers at Lyme Park 1898–1946* (Lyme Park Joint Committee, n.d. *c.*1979), p. 32.

23. Peter Mandler, *The Fall and Rise of the Stately Home* (New Haven & London, 1997), p. 243.

24. Mandler, *The Fall and Rise of the Stately Home*, p. 233.

25. Mandler, *The Fall and Rise of the Stately Home*, p. 248–249.

26. Mandler, *The Fall and Rise of the Stately Home*, p. 252.

27. Janet Morgan, *Edwina Mountbatten. A Life of Her Own* (London, 1992 edn), pp. 88–93.

28. Mary Soames, *Clementine Churchill* (London, 1979), p. 247.

29. Randolph S. Churchill, *Lord Derby. 'King of Lancashire'* (London, Melbourne and Toronto, 1959), pp. 393–395.

30. Loelia, Duchess of Westminster, *Grace and Favour* (London, 1961), pp. 207–209.

31. *The Bystander*, 10 June 1925.

32. Rosina Harrison, *Rose: My Life in Service* (London, 1975), p. 140.

33. Harrison, *Rose: My Life in Service*, p. 141.

34. Earl Winterton Diary No. 25, entry for 14 June 1920.

35. Earl Winterton Diary No. 23.

36. Earl Winterton Diary No. 23, entries for 27 August and 4 September 1919, for example.

37. 'Introduction' to Hoyle ed., *Our Hunting Fathers*, p. 13.

38. Selina Hastings, *Nancy Mitford* (London, 2002 edn), p. 27.

39. Earl Winterton Diary No. 23, entries for 23 and 25 September 1919.

40. Rt Hon. Earl Winterton, *Fifty Tumultuous Years* (London, 1955), p. 142.

41. *Country Life*, 3 November 1928.

42. Willoughby de Broke, *The Passing Years*, p. 231 and 'Introduction' to Hoyle ed., *Our Hunting Fathers*, p. 5.

43. Willoughby de Broke, *The Passing Years*, pp. 75–76.

44. *The Bystander*, 5 October 1927.

45. See, for example, entry in Earl Winterton's Diary No. 24 for 10 January 1920. The hunt had already killed one fox when they 'found again in Chalkhurst Rough, and ran hard by Sidney Wood, Knightons,' and so on, but eventually they had to leave off 'at dark pointing for Minstead. Rare good day. Rode Monson and Chestnut, laming the former in a fall.'

46. *The Bystander*, 5 October 1927.

47. *The Field*, 7 December 1918.

48. *Country Life*, 3 November 1928.

49. Waterson, *The Country House Remembered*, p. 86.

50. *The Bystander*, 28 September 1927.

51. Jane Ridley, *Fox Hunting* (London, 1990), pp. 159–160.

52. *The Bystander*, 26 October 1927.

53. Rupert Godfrey ed., *Letters from a Prince* (London, 1999 edn), p. 459, entry for 12 August 1920. On 9 July 1920 (pp. 431–2) he had confided, 'I'm more crazy about riding than ever I was & I just long to make somewhat of a name for myself as a horseman & own & ride the winner of a race … I'm lucky enough to have the dollars & light weight & certainly the keenness!!'

54. *The Bystander*, 28 September 1927.

55. Patrick Balfour, *Society Racket. A Critical Survey of Modern Social Life* (London, 1933), p. 264.

56. Ridley, *Fox Hunting*, pp. 153–54.

57. Waterson, *The Country House Remembered*, p. 16.

58. Ridley, *Fox Hunting*, p. 155.

59. Churchill, *Lord Derby*, pp. 578–79.

60. 'The Fortunes of English Foxhunting in the Twentieth Century: The Case of the Oakley Hunt' in Hoyle, ed., *Our Hunting Fathers*, p. 257.

61. 'Introduction' in Hoyle, ed., *Our Hunting Fathers*, pp. 11–12.
62. Waterson, *The Country House Remembered*, pp. 91–92.
63. Waterson, *The Country House Remembered*, p. 92. For a woman taking part in a shoot at Murthly Castle, Murthly, Scotland, see, for example, *The Bystander*, 21 September 1927, when Miss Colleen Byrne was shown among the 'guns'.
64. Steve Humphries and Beverley Hopwood ed., *Green and Pleasant Land* (London, 1999), pp. 69–70.
65. Humphries and Hopwood ed., *Green and Pleasant Land*, p. 70. Leslie Field, *Bendor. The Golden Duke of Westminster* (London, 1986 edn), p. 172.
66. Humphries and Hopwood ed., *Green and Pleasant Land*, p. 73.
67. *Country Life*, 17 January 1920 and 21 April 1923.
68. *Country Life*, 15 July 1922.
69. *Country Life*, 3 September 1921.
70. Cannadine, *The Decline and Fall*, p. 369.
71. Kenneth Rose, *King George V* (London, 1983), p.293.
72. T. W. Turner, *Memoirs of a Gamekeeper. Elveden 1868–1953* (London, 1954), p. 40.
73. Godfrey ed., *Letters from a Prince*, p. 305, letter dated 14 January 1920. In an earlier letter, dated 24 December 1920, he had expressed himself forcefully, declaring, 'Christ it's bloody here & I'm so depressed … I've absolutely nothing in common with the rest of my family'.
74. Willoughby de Broke, *The Passing Years*, p. 231.
75. *Country Life*, 31 July 1926.
76. Rose, *King George V*, p. 288.
77. Helen Hardinge to her mother, Viscountess Milner, 29 September 1921, in Violet Milner MSS. VM.28. Helen was staying at Braemar at the time.
78. Rose, *King George V*, p. 288.
79. Rose, *King George V*, p. 288.

80. Letters to Lady Airlie from Lady Joan Verney, 23 August 1921, and from Bessie Dawson, 1 September 1921, in Airlie MSS.82762, ff. 63 and 70 at the British Library.

81. Balfour, *Society Racket*, pp. 66–67.

82. Brian P. Martin, *The Glorious Grouse. A Natural and Unnatural History* (Newton Abbot, 1990), p. 81.

83. Martin, *The Glorious Grouse*, p. 81.

84. Waterson, *The Country House Remembered*, p. 100.

85. Justine Picardie, *Coco Chanel. The Legend and the Life* (London, n.d.), pp. 165–69 and 186.

86. Field, *Bendor*, p. 191.

87. *The Field*, 20 September and 11 October 1928.

88. *The Tatler*, 7 January 1920. Robert Graves and Alan Hodge, *The Long Weekend. A Social History of Great Britain* (London, 1991 edn), pp. 34–35, note that during the winter of 1919/20 the Riviera was packed, with sleeping berths on the trains to Cannes and Nice booked up months ahead of time.

89. *The Tatler*, 25 February 1920. See also a contribution by 'Christopher' in *The Tatler*, 21 January 1920, pointing out that a lot of 'well-known people are wintering at Algiers, which threatens to be a serious rival to the Riviera as a fashionable resort.'

90. Field, *Bendor*, pp. 192–93.

91. *The Tatler*, 7 January 1920.

92. *The Tatler*, 5 January 1921. For the Prince of Wales see Sarah Bradford, *George VI* (London, 1991 edn), p. 147.

93. *The Field*, 20 December 1928.

94. *The Bystander*, 7 November 1928.

95. *The Field*, 27 December 1928.

96. C. S. Nicholls, *Red Strangers. The White Tribe of Kenya* (London, 2005), p. 153.

97. Gloria Vanderbilt and Thelma Lady Furness, *Double Exposure* (London, 1959 edn), pp. 216–21. Philip Ziegler, *King Edward VIII* (Stroud, 2001 edn), p. 196.

98. Nicholls, *Red Strangers*, p. 152.

99. *The Field*, 13 September 1928.

100. Nicholls, *Red Strangers*, p. 153. Karen Blixen, *Out of Africa* (London, 2001 edn), pp. 193, 195–96, 305 and 307. Edward L. Steinhart, *Black Poachers, White Hunters* (Oxford, Nairobi and Athens, USA, 2006), p. 127.

101. Steinhart, *Black Poachers*, p. 133.

102. *The Field*, 7 July 1927.

103. Steinhart, *Black Poachers*, pp. 114 and 161.

104. 'Introduction' in Hoyle ed., *Our Hunting Fathers*, p. 23.

105. *Country Life*, 1 January 1921.

106. *Country Life*, 16 July 1921. *The Field*, 27 December 1928.

107. *Country Life*, 16 and 23 July 1921.

108. William Shawcross, *Queen Elizabeth The Queen Mother* (Basingstoke and London, 2009), p. 220.

109. Shawcross, *Queen Elizabeth*, p. 241.

110. Shawcross, *Queen Elizabeth*, p. 225.

111. Shawcross, *Queen Elisabeth*, pp. 226–27.

112. Shawcross, *Queen Elizabeth*, p. 231.

113. Shawcross, *Queen Elizabeth*, pp. 234–35.

114. Shawcross, *Queen Elizabeth*, p. 242.

115. R. W. Hoyle, 'Royalty and the diversity of Field Sports, *c.* 1840–*c.* 1981' in Hoyle ed., *Our Hunting Fathers*, pp. 56 and 58.

116. Steinhart, *Black Poachers*, p. 126. Ziegler, *King Edward VIII*, p. 191.

117. Letter from C. W. Paine in *The Field*, 13 September 1928.

118. Steinhart, *Black Poachers*, pp. 126–27. Ziegler, *King Edward VIII*, pp. 190–91.

4 Social Rituals

1. Patrick Balfour, *Society Racket. A Critical Survey of Modern Social Life* (London, 1933), pp. 59–60.

2. Angela Lambert, *1939: The Last Season of Peace* (London, 1989), p. 6.

3. Jonathan Gathorne-Hardy, *The Rise and Fall of the British Nanny* (London, 1972), p. 237.

4. Mary Soames, *Clementine Churchill* (London, 1979), p. 237.

5. Daphne Fielding, *Mercury Presides* (London, 1954), p. 133.

6. Gathorne-Hardy, *The Rise and Fall of the British Nanny*, p. 207.

7. Janet Morgan, *Edwina Mountbatten. A Life of Her Own* (London, 1992 edn), pp. 161, 165–69 and 185–86.

8. Morgan, *Edwina Mountbatten*, pp. 209 and 213.

9. John Grigg, *Nancy Astor. Portrait of a Pioneer* (London, 1980), p. 69.

10. Rosina Harrison, *Gentlemen's Gentlemen. My Friends in Service* (London, 1976), p. 114.

11. Merlin Waterson ed., *The Country House Remembered. Recollections of Life Between the Wars* (London, 1985), p. 205. Soames, *Clementine Churchill*, pp. 236 and 238.

12. Waterson ed., *The Country House Remembered*, p. 208.

13. Selina Hastings, *Nancy Mitford* (London, 2002 edn), pp. 21–22.

14. Hastings, *Nancy Mitford*, p. 21.

15. Hastings, *Nancy Mitford*, p. 21. Jonathan Guinness with Catherine Guinness, *The House of Mitford* (London, 2004 edn), pp. 236 and 239–40. Unlike many other nurses, 'Blor', the Mitford nanny always supported the governesses and encouraged the children to do their work.

16. Lambert, *1939*, pp. 37–38.

17. Loelia Duchess of Westminster, *Grace and Favour* (London, 1961), pp. 74–76.

18. Loelia Duchess of Westminster, *Grace and Favour*, p. 79.

19. Prospectus of North Foreland School for Girls in the Astor MSS. at MERL 1416/1/2/33.

20. Lady Astor to Miss Mary Wolseley-Lewis, 16 August 1922, in Astor MSS.1416/1/2/33.

21. Phyllis Astor's School Report from North Foreland School, St Peter's-in-Thanet, Summer Term 1924 in Astor MSS. at MERL, 1416/1/3/25. Mary Wolseley-Lewis to Lady Astor, 14 August 1922 in Astor MSS.1416/1/2/33.

22. Hastings, *Nancy Mitford*, pp. 35–36.

23. Hastings, *Nancy Mitford*, pp. 35–36. Guinness with Guinness, *The House of Mitford*, pp. 257–58.

24. Hastings, *Nancy Mitford*, pp. 37–38.

25. Hastings, *Nancy Mitford*, pp. 38–39.

26. Lambert, *1939*, p. 43.

27. Hastings, *Nancy Mitford*, p. 39.

28. Morgan, *Edwina Mountbatten*, pp. 73–74.

29. Morgan, *Edwina Mountbatten*, pp. 74–82.

30. Balfour, *Society Racket*, p. 199. In a letter to *Country Life*, 22 March 1930, the Marquess of Tavistock also condemned 'fagging', not so much for its effect on the young fag, but because it taught a youth of seventeen or so, 'already, perhaps, inclined to suffer from swelled head by reason of his athletic prowess,' to regard privilege and power over younger and weaker people as a way of increasing his personal comfort and convenience, rather than 'as a challenge to service and usefulness'.

31. Selina Hastings, *Evelyn Waugh* (London, 1995 edn), pp. 69–71.

32. Hastings, *Evelyn Waugh*, p. 81.

33. Hastings, *Evelyn Waugh*, p. 88.

34. Fielding, *Mercury Presides*, pp. 105–106.

35. John Fothergill, *An Innkeeper's Diary* (London, 1987 edn), pp. 49–51.

36. Waterson, ed., *The Country House Remembered*, p. 213.

37. Loelia, Duchess of Westminster, *Grace and Favour*, pp. 96–97.

38. Frances Donaldson, *Child of the Twenties* (London, 1986 edn), pp. 79–80.

39. Balfour, *Society Racket*, p. 60.

40. Loelia, Duchess of Westminster, *Grace and Favour*, p. 98.

41. Fielding, *Mercury Presides*, pp. 99–100. Hastings, *Nancy Mitford*, pp. 46 and 51–52.

42. Morgan, *Edwina Mountbatten*, p. 173.

43. Donaldson, *Child of the Twenties*, p. 80.

44. Waterson, ed., *The Country House Remembered*, pp. 58–59.

45. Loelia, Duchess of Westminster, *Grace and Favour*, pp. 82 and 87.

46. Angela Lambert, *1939*, pp. 159 and 203.

47. Fielding, *Mercury Presides*, pp. 92–93 and 96.

48. Lambert, *1939*, p. 154.

49. Anne de Courcy, *1939. The Last Season* (London, 2003 edn), p. 25.

50. William Shawcross, *Queen Elizabeth: The Queen Mother* (London, 2009). The duke had first proposed in February 1921. He did so again in March 1922. He was finally accepted in January 1923.

51. Lady Joan Verney to Lady Airlie, 18 January 1923 in Airlie MSS. at the British Library, Add.MSS.82763, f.42.

52. Lady Joan Verney to Lady Airlie, 24 January 1923 in Airlie MSS. Add.MSS.82763, f.50.

53. Helen Hardinge, *Loyal to Three Kings. A Memoir of Alec Hardinge, Private Secretary to the Sovereign 1920–1943* (London, 1967), p. 30.

54. Hardinge, *Loyal to Three Kings*, pp. 32–33.

55. Hardinge, *Loyal to Three Kings*, pp. 39–40.

56. Helen Hardinge to her mother, Lady Milner, 5 September 1923 in Violet Milner MSS. VM.28 at the Bodleian Library, Oxford.

57. Lesley Lewis, *The Private Life of a Country House 1912–39* (London & Sydney, 1982 edn), p. 12.

58. Lewis, *The Private Life of a Country House*, pp. 111–112.

59. Lewis, *The Private Life of a Country House*, pp. 114–115.

60. *The Bystander*, 24 April 1929.

61. Balfour, *Society Racket*, pp. 127–128.

62. Lambert, 1939, p. 203.

63. Fielding, *Mercury Presides*, pp. 84–85.

64. Fielding, *Mercury Presides*, p. 86.

65. Fielding, *Mercury Presides*, pp. 87–89.

66. Fielding, *Mercury Presides*, pp. 109 and 113–115.

67. Shawcross, *Queen Elizabeth: The Queen Mother*, p. 101.

68. *The Bystander*, 28 May 1919. See also *The Tatler*, 4 June 1919.

69. *The Bystander*, 2 June 1926.

70. *The Bystander*, 29 May 1929.

71. Balfour, *Society Racket*, p. 89. Humphrey Carpenter, *The Brideshead Generation. Evelyn Waugh and His Friends* (London and Boston, 1990 edn), p. 200.

72. Balfour, *Society Racket*, p. 98.

73. Shawcross, *Queen Elizabeth: The Queen Mother*, p. 101. *The Bystander*, 28 April 1920.

74. Loelia, Duchess of Westminster, *Grace and Favour*, pp. 105–106.

75. Hugo Vickers, *Gladys Duchess of Marlborough* (London, 1987 edn), pp. 187–188.

76. Astor MSS, 1416/1/2/42 at MERL, concerning the presentation of Lady Astor's own daughter, Phyllis, and also that of a Miss D. Hart Davies and a Mrs Mitchell Graham.

77. Letters from Lady Astor's private secretary to Molyneux, 29 and 30 March 1928, and from Molyneux to Lady Astor, 27 March and 5 April 1928. Also details of the expenditure with P. Louiseboulanger S. A., 18 April and 21 April 1928 in Astor MSS. 1416/1/2/43.

78. Lady Astor to Lord Irwin, 3 April 1928, in Astor MSS. 1416/1/2/46.

79. Soames, *Clementine Churchill*, p. 244.

80. Richard Hough, *Edwina Countess Mountbatten of Burma* (London, 1985 edn), p. 106.

81. Morgan, *Edwina Mountbatten*, pp. 190, 196–7, 200 and 204.

82. Hough, *Edwina Countess Mountbatten*, p. 107.

83. Margerita Lady Howard de Walden, *Pages from My Life* (London, 1965), 208–211. Lambert, *1939*, pp. 88–89.

84. Lambert, *1939*, p. 89.

85. Balfour, *Society Racket*, pp. 57 and 134.

86. Anne de Courcy, *Circe. The Life of Edith, Marchioness of Londonderry* (London, 1992), pp. 143 and 146.

87. Susan Williams, *Ladies of Influence. Women of the Elite in Interwar Britain* (London, 2000), pp. 18–19.

88. Brian Masters, *Great Hostesses* (London, 1982), p. 50.

89. Masters, *Great Hostesses*, p. 49.

90. Williams, *Ladies of Influence*, p. 20.

91. de Courcy, *Circe*, pp. 200 and 209–210.

92. Hamilton Diaries, Microfilm 20/1/5, entry for 23 February 1927, f.7, Liddell Hart Centre for Military Studies, King's College Archives, London.

93. Masters, *Great Hostesses*, p. 1.

94. Daphne Fielding, *Emerald and Nancy. Lady Cunard and Her Daughter* (London, 1968), p. 70.

95. Cecil Beaton, *The Glass of Fashion* (London, 1954), p. 317.

96. Masters, *Great Hostesses*, p. 127.

97. Masters, *Great Hostesses*, pp. 119, 120–121 and 122. Balfour, *Society Racket*, p. 138.

98. Kenneth Clark, *Another Part of the Wood* (London, 1976 edn), p. 193.

99. Diary of Margot Asquith 1917–1923, Microfilm X 15/7, entry for 11 November 1918, f.247 at the Bodleian Library, Oxford. Clark, *Another Part*, p. 193. Masters, *Great Hostesses*, p. 125.

100. Masters, *Great Hostesses*, pp. 144–146.

101. Nancy Cunard, *Black Man and White Ladyship, an Anniversary* (privately published, 1931; a copy is in the British Library K.520.220), pp. 1–6.

102. Fielding, *Emerald and Nancy*, p. 108. According to Daphne Fielding, Emerald behaved 'with the greatest dignity. "One

can always forgive anyone who is ill," was all she said.' But she was naturally deeply wounded.

103. Fielding, *Emerald and Nancy*, pp. 85–86.

104. Beaton, *The Glass of Fashion*, p. 300. See also Georgina Howell, *Vogue. Six Decades of Fashion* (London, 1975), p. 66.

105. Beaton, *The Glass of Fashion*, p. 300 and Howell, *Vogue*, p. 66.

106. Fielding, *Emerald and Nancy*, p. 101.

107. Loelia, Duchess of Westminster, *Grace and Favour*, p. 115.

108. Masters, *Great Hostesses*, pp. 201–204 and 212.

109. Balfour, *Society Racket*, p. 136.

110. Masters, *Great Hostesses*, p. 241.

111. Kirsty McLeod, *A Passion for Friendship. Sibyl Colefax and Her Circle* (London, 1991), p. 85.

112. Masters, *Great Hostesses*, pp. 86–87.

113. Masters, *Great Hostesses*, p. 87.

114. Masters, *Great Hostesses*, pp. 95 and 97. Apparently the Countess of Pembroke disliked Maggie Greville so much and with such passion that she refused to have her at Wilton.

115. Masters, *Great Hostesses*, p. 88.

116. Clark, *Another Part of the Wood*, p. 236.

117. Clark, *Another Part of the Wood*, p. 188. Loelia, Duchess of Westminster, *Grace and Favour*, p. 113.

118. See Michael Colefax's account of his mother's life, 'Sibyl Colefax, 1874–1950' in MS.Eng.c.3188, f. 2, in the Bodleian Library, Oxford.

119. Masters, *Great Hostesses*, p. 153.

120. Fielding, *Emerald and Nancy*, pp. 101–102.

121. Masters, *Great Hostesses*, pp. 154 and 156.

122. McLeod, *A Passion for Friendship*, p. 27.

123. Michael Colefax, 'Sibyl Colefax. A Human Catalyst' in MS.Eng.c.3188, f.15 at the Bodleian Library, Oxford.

124. Lady Colefax to Bernard Berenson, 1918–45, letter undated, *c*. 1920 in Colefax MSS., MS.Eng.c.3176, f.7 at the Bodleian Library, Oxford.

125. Virginia Woolf to Grace Raverat, 1 May 1925 in Nigel Nicolson ed., *A Change of Perspective. The Letters of Virginia Woolf, Vol. III 1923–1928* (London, 1977), p. 181.
126. Virginia Woolf to Vita Sackville-West, 7 June 1926 in Nicolson ed., *A Change of Perspective*, p. 272.
127. McLeod, *A Passion for Friendship*, p. 93.
128. McLeod, *A Passion for Friendship*, p. 93.
129. Masters, *Great Hostesses*, p. 166.
130. Masters, *Great Hostesses*, p. 167.
131. Masters, *Great Hostesses*, p. 163.
132. Harold Nicolson to Lady Colefax, 12 April 1929, in Colefax MSS, MS.Eng.3166, f.76 in the Bodleian Library, Oxford.
133. Michael Colefax, 'Sibyl Colefax. A Human Catalyst', f.25.
134. Michael Colefax, 'Sibyl Colefax, 1874–1950', f.2.

5 Domestic Affairs and Breaking the Mould

1. *Antiques Info*, May/June 2012 and Bevis Hillier, *Art Deco. A Design Handbook of the 20s and 30s* (London, 1985 edn), pp. 13 and 82.
2. Stanley Jackson, *The Savoy* (London, 1964), pp. 70, 77 and 113.
3. Philip Ziegler, *Diana Cooper* (Harmondsworth, 1985 edn), pp. 141–142.
4. Mark Pottle, ed., *Champion Redoubtable. The Diaries and Letters of Violet Bonham Carter 1914–45* (London, 1998), p. 173. Lord Oxford's cash problems led to some friends presenting him with a gift 'in the form of financial provision for his future'. See *The Times*, 30 July 1927. His daughter found this deeply humiliating. Patrick Balfour, *Society Racket. A Critical Survey of Modern Social Life* (London, 1933), p. 138.
5. Lady Troubridge, *The Book of Etiquette* (London, 1926), pp. 2–3.

6. Loelia, Duchess of Westminster, *Grace and Favour* (London, 1961), p. 94.

7. Samuel Mullins and Gareth Griffiths, *Cap and Apron. An Oral History of Domestic Service in the Shires, 1880–1950* (Leicester, 1986), p. 4.

8. Winterton Diary No. 23, entry for 30 November 1919. On the previous 17 February he noted that another servant, McGitheray, had given notice that morning, 'I think probably in consequence of a sharp word that I used to him yesterday, but I am really rather glad of it as he is unsuited for my work.'

9. Loelia, Duchess of Westminster, *Grace and Favour*, p. 94.

10. Mrs Lily Milgate, 'Memories of a Housemaid 1922–1930', manuscript at Market Harborough Museum, O.R.37, written in 1983.

11. Mullins and Griffiths, *Cap and Apron*, p. 46.

12. Loelia, Duchess of Westminster, *Grace and Favour*, p. 94.

13. Merlin Waterson ed., *The Country House Remembered. Recollections of Life Between the Wars* (London, Melbourne and Henley, 1985), pp. 197–198.

14. Rosina Harrison, *Gentlemen's Gentlemen. My Friends in Service* (London, 1976), pp. 31–32 and 81.

15. Georgina Howell, *Vogue. Six Decades of Fashion* (London, 1975), p. 66. 'Hutch' was Leslie Hutchinson, a leading black cabaret star of the 1920s who had many female admirers among the social elite.

16. Harrison, *Gentlemen's Gentlemen*, pp. 120–121.

17. Harrison, *Gentlemen's Gentlemen*, pp. 122–123.

18. Kirsty McLeod, *A Passion for Friendship. Sibyl Colefax and Her Circle* (London, 1991), pp. 79–80.

19. Hugo Vickers, *Gladys Duchess of Marlborough* (London, 1987 edn), pp. 183, 185, 196, 204 and 223–4.

20. Vickers, *Gladys Duchess of Marlborough*, p. 223.

21. Helen Hardinge, *Loyal to Three Kings. A Memoir of Alec Hardinge, Private Secretary to the Sovereign 1920–1943* (London, 1967), pp. 29 and 34.

22. Helen Hardinge to Lady Milner in Violet Milner MSS. at the Bodleian Library, MS.28, letter dated 11 September 1924.

23. Waterson, ed., *The Country House Remembered*, pp. 190–191.

24. Waterson, ed., *The Country House Remembered*, pp. 184–187.

25. Waterson, ed., *The Country House Remembered*, pp. 194–196.

26. Miss Irvine to Mrs E. Ford in Astor MSS. 1416/1/2/168, 21 June 1937, at MERL.

27. Miss Irvine to William Camm in Astor MSS. 1416/1/2/42, 10 September 1928.

28. Lady Astor to William Camm in Astor MSS. 1416/1/2/42, 15 November 1928.

29. Michael Astor, *Tribal Feeling* (London, 1963), p. 63.

30. Mary Soames, *Clementine Churchill* (London, 1979), p. 232.

31. Soames, *Clementine Churchill*, pp. 230–231.

32. Deborah Devonshire, *Wait for Me! Memoirs of the Youngest Mitford Sister* (London, 2010), pp. 27–28 and 63–64. Jessica Mitford, who was slightly older, remembered that when the family moved up to their Rutland Gate home in London, it resembled 'the evacuation of a small army', including the servants and 'mountains of suitcases'. Jessica Mitford, *Hons and Rebels* (London, 1960 edn), pp. 49–50.

33. Lesley Lewis, *The Private Life of a Country House (1912–1939)* (London, 1982 edn), pp. 55 and 130.

34. Waterson ed., *The Country House Remembered*, p. 208

35. Quoted in Pamela Horn, *My Ancestor was in Service* (London, 2009), p. 6.

36. Mrs Lily Milgate, 'Memories of a Housemaid 1922–1930', manuscript at Market Harborough Museum.

37. 'Recollections of a Kitchenmaid at Shugborough', R.87.005 at Shugborough Hall Oral History Transcripts Archive, Staffordshire County Council.

38. 'Recollections of an Under Stillroom Maid', R.87.008 at Shugborough Hall Oral History Transcripts Archive.

39. Pamela Sambrook, *The Country House Servant* (Stroud, 1999), pp. 78–81.

40. Information from an Exhibition 'From Parlourmaid to Peer: Life on Local Country Estates' at St. Barbe Museum and Art Gallery, Lymington, 2012, and from Sarah Newman at the Museum, to whom my thanks are due.
41. Harrison, *Gentlemen's Gentlemen*, p. 32.
42. Harrison, *Gentlemen's Gentlemen*, pp. 56–57 and 61.
43. Harrison, *Gentlemen's Gentlemen*, pp. 67–68 for Gordon Grimmett. Ernest King, *The Green Baize Door* (Bath, 1963), p. 42. King's decision to be employed by Mrs de Wichfeld was taken because he wished to earn higher pay: 'I wanted to break out into something entirely new to me, the world of the rich. Not the old rich but the new rich'.
44. Harrison, *Gentlemen's Gentlemen*, pp. 79–81.
45. Diary of Lady Jean Hamilton, Microfilm 20/1/5 at the Liddell Hart Centre for Military Archives, King's College Archives, London, entry for 5 April 1927.
46. Diary of Lady Jean Hamilton, Microfilm 20/1/5, entry for 21 May 1927.
47. Will of Lady Astor. Probate was granted on 19 August 1964. Mrs Hawkins, the long-serving London housekeeper received £300 per annum as her annuity.
48. *Daily Mail*, 30 July 1924.
49. John Scott, *The Upper Classes. Property and Privilege in Britain* (London and Basingstoke, 1982), p. 117.
50. Ross McKibbin, *Classes and Cultures. England 1918–1951* (Oxford, 2000 edn), pp. 16 and 21.
51. McKibbin, *Classes and Cultures*, p. 21.
52. McKibbin, *Classes and Cultures*, p. 21.
53. Quoted in McKibbin, *Classes and Cultures*, p. 34
54. Balfour, *Society Racket*, p. 78.
55. Michael Luke, *David Tennant and the Gargoyle Years* (London, 1991), pp. 19–21 and 30.
56. *Vogue*, 5 October 1927.
57. *Vogue*, 5 October 1927 and Balfour, *Society Racket*, p. 78.
58. Allyson Hayward, *Norah Lindsay. The Life and Art of a*

Garden Designer (London, 2007), p. 69. Balfour, *Society Racket*, p. 78.

59. Balfour, *Society Racket*, p. 79.

60. Balfour, *Society Racket*, p. 80. See advertisement for Lord Victor Paget's business in *Vogue*, 2 November 1927.

61. *Corsham Court Guide* (n.d. *c.* 2009, at the house), p. 30.

62. Daphne Fielding, *Mercury Presides* (London, 1954), p. 121.

63. See entry for Stephen Tennant in the *Oxford Dictionary of National Biography* (Oxford, 2004).

64. Charles F. G. Masterman, *England After War. A Study* (London, n.d. *c.* 1923), p. 38.

65. Barbara Cartland, *We Danced All Night* (London, 1994 edn), p. 55.

66. Balfour, *Society Racket*, pp. 148–149.

67. *Vogue*, early April 1927. Balfour, *Society Racket*, p. 148.

68. Janet Morgan, *Edwina Mountbatten. A Life of Her Own* (London, 1992 edn), pp. 192–193.

69. Balfour, *Society Racket*, p. 148.

70. Soames, *Clementine Churchill*, pp. 197–198.

71. Entry in *Oxford Dictionary of National Biography* (Oxford, 2004), p. 393. Cartland, *We Danced All Night*, p. 49.

72. Selina Hastings, *Nancy Mitford* (London, 2002 edn), pp. 69–71. Jonathan Guinness with Catherine Guinness, *The House of Mitford* (London, 2004 edn), pp. 297 and 299, Harold Acton, *Nancy Mitford* (London, 2010 edn), p. 41.

73. Hastings, *Nancy Mitford*, pp. 69–71. Acton, *Nancy Mitford*, p. 41.

74. Guinness with Guinness, *The House of Mitford*, p. 299.

75. Beverley Nichols, *All I Could Never Be. Some Recollections* (London, 1949), pp. 29–30.

76. *Vogue*, 28 December 1927.

77. *Vogue*, early February and early April 1927.

78. Balfour, *Society Racket*, p. 149.

79. *Vogue*, 19 October 1927, showing Nancy Beaton modelling a Lanvin gown, and Cartland, *We Danced All Night*, p. 49.

80. Balfour, *Society Racket*. Lillie Langtry, the Victorian and Edwardian actress and favourite of the Prince of Wales, had benefited by endorsing Pears soap for more than thirty years.

81. *Ibid.*

82. Balfour, *Society Racket*, p. 80 and *Vogue*, early January 1927.

83. Soames, *Clementine Churchill*, p. 244.

84. Brenda Dean Paul, *My First Life* (London, n.d. *c.* 1935), pp. 13, 54 and 57. Entry in the *Oxford Dictionary of National Biography* (Oxford, 2004) for Brenda Dean Paul.

85. *Oxford Dictionary of National Biography*, entry for Brenda Dean Paul. D. J. Taylor, *Bright Young People. The Lost Generation of London's Jazz Age* (New York, 2009 edn), p. 224.

86. Taylor, *Bright Young People*, p. 318.

87. Raymond A. Jones, *Arthur Ponsonby. The Politics of Life* (London, 1989), pp. 132, 159 and 183. Taylor, *Bright Young People*, pp. 100–101.

88. Richard B. Fisher, *Syrie Maugham* (London, 1978), p. 12. Cecil Beaton, *The Glass of Fashion* (London, 1954), pp. 204–5.

89. Beaton, *The Glass of Fashion*, p. 208.

90. *Vogue*, early July 1927.

91. Fisher, *Syrie Maugham*, p. 18. Entry for Syrie Maugham in the *Oxford Dictionary of National Biography* (Oxford, 2004).

92. Brian Masters, *Great Hostesses* (London, 1982), pp. 174–175. Kirsty McLeod, *A Passion for Friendship. Sibyl Colefax and her Circle* (London, 1991), pp. 140–141 and 158. Entry in the *Oxford Dictionary of National Biography* (Oxford, 2004). Nigel Nicolson ed., *A Reflection of the Other Person. The Letters of Virginia Woolf, Vol. IV, 1929–1931* (London, 1978), p. 254.

93. The entry in the *Oxford Dictionary of National Biography*

suggests that the 1929 Wall Street stock market crash meant a loss of investments estimated at £50,000.

94. Lady Colefax to Bernard Berenson, n.d. in Colefax MSS., MS.Eng.c.3176, f.49 in the Bodleian Library, Oxford.

95. Lady Colefax to Bernard Berenson, 17 November 1930 in Colefax MSS., MS.Eng.c.3176, f.76.

96. Nicolson ed., *A Reflection of the Other Person*, p. 243. Virginia Woolf to her sister, Vanessa Bell, 2 November 1930.

97. Masters, *Great Hostesses*, p. 175 and entry in the *Oxford Dictionary of National Biography*.

98. Hayward, *Norah Lindsay*, pp. 77 and 79.

99. Norah Lindsay to Lady Astor MSS. 1416/1/2/38 for 1927. Hayward, *Norah Lindsay*, pp. 126 and 129–130.

100. See list in Hayward, *Norah Lindsay*, pp. 256–260. In addition there were four cases in which owners were advised by Norah but no fee was paid, sometimes because she had had lengthy stays with them.

101. Hayward, *Norah Lindsay*, p. 8.

102. Hayward, *Norah Lindsay*, pp. 236 and 274.

103. C. L. Mowat, *Britain Between the Wars. 1918–1940* (London, 1983 edn), pp. 310 and 312.

104. Cartland, *We Danced All Night*, pp. 274–276.

105. Mowat, *Britain Between the Wars*, p. 313.

106. *The Bystander*, 26 May 1926.

107. *The Tatler*, 12–16 May 1926.

108. Cartland, *We Danced All Night*, p. 274.

109. Mary S. Lovell, *The Mitford Girls. The Biography of an Extraordinary Family* (London, 2010 edn), p. 55.

110. Morgan, *Edwina Mountbatten*, pp. 193–195.

111. Cartland, *We Danced All Night*, pp. 276 and 285.

112. *The Bystander*, 26 May 1926.

113. Mowat, *Britain Between the Wars*, p. 334.

114. Mowat, *Britain Between the Wars*, p. 329.

115. Morgan, *Edwina Mountbatten*, p. 195.

116. *The Bystander*, 9 June 1926.

117. Diary No. 33 of Earl Winterton at the Bodleian Library, Oxford, entry for 15 July 1926.

118. Cartland, *We Danced All Night*, pp. 285 and 289.

6 The 'Bright Young People' and the End of an Era

1. Carolyn Hall, *The Twenties in Vogue* (London, 1983), p. 8. For the view that 'youth monopolized the centre of the stage' see Patrick Balfour, *Society Racket. A Critical Survey of Modern Social Life* (London, 1933), p. 274.

2. Humphrey Carpenter, *The Brideshead Generation. Evelyn Waugh and his Friends* (London and Boston, 1990 edn), p. 146.

3. Balfour, *Society Racket*, p. 159.

4. Brenda Dean Paul, *My First Life. A Biography* (London, n.d., *c.* 1935), p. 96.

5. Quoted in Barbara Cartland, *We Danced all Night* (London, 1994 edn), p. 183.

6. 'Introduction' to Evelyn Waugh, *Vile Bodies* (London, 2000 edn), x-xiv and Hugo Vickers, *Cecil Beaton* (London, 1986 edn), pp. 96–101.

7. Raymond A. Jones, *Arthur Ponsonby. The Politics of Life* (London, 1989), p. 160.

8. Mary S. Lovell, *The Mitford Girls. The Biography of an Extraordinary Family* (London, 2010 edn), p. 71.

9. Douglas Goldring, *The Nineteen Twenties. A General Survey and Some Personal Memories* (London, 1945), p. 225. D. J. Taylor, *Bright Young People. The Lost Generation of London's Jazz Age* (New York, 2007), p. 8.

10. Carpenter, *The Brideshead Generation*, p. 81, quoting Alan Pryce-Jones.

11. Debates arising from a proposed new Criminal Law Amendment Act. *Hansard*, 5th Series, Vol. 145, 1799–1804, 4 August 1921, and Vol. 146, 1603–1610, 17 August 1921

and *Hansard (House of Lords)*, Vol. 46, 567–578, 15 August 1921.

12. Mitchell A. Leaska and John Phillips ed., *Violet to Vita. The Letters of Violet Trefusis to Vita Sackville-West* (London, 1989), pp. 20–31 and 51. Nigel Nicolson, *Portrait of a Marriage* (London, 1990 edn), pp. 3, 99–126.

13. Quentin Bell, *Virginia Woolf. A Biography*, Vol. II, *Mrs. Woolf 1912–1941* (London, 1972), p. 119. See also Anne Olivier Bell ed., *The Diary of Virginia Woolf*, Vol. II, *1920–1924* (London, 1978), p. 235, entry for 19 February 1923 and Anne Olivier Bell ed., *The Diary of Virginia Woolf*, Vol. III, *1925–1930* (London, 1980), pp. 197, 199 and 332, entries for 27 September and 27 October 1928 and 11 November 1930.

14. Michael Bloch, *James Lees-Milne. The Life* (London, 2009), p. 60.

15. Ross McKibbin, *Classes and Cultures. England 1918–1951* (Oxford, 2000 edn), pp. 324–325. See also entry for Radclyffe Hall in C. S. Nicholls ed., *Dictionary of National Biography: Missing Persons* (Oxford, 1993), p. 544.

16. Diary of Lady Hamilton, Microfilm 20/1/6 1928–1936, entry for 16 October 1928 in Liddell Hart Centre for Military Archives, King's College, London, Archives.

17. McKibbin, *Classes and Cultures*, p. 324.

18. Balfour, *Society Racket*, p. 164. Cartland, *We Danced All Night*, pp. 184 and 186.

19. Cartland, *We Danced All Night*, pp. 189–190.

20. Loelia, Duchess of Westminster, *Grace and Favour* (London, 1961), pp. 119–120.

21. Loelia, Duchess of Westminster, *Grace and Favour*, p. 120.

22. Cartland, *We Danced All Night*, p. 188.

23. Loelia, Duchess of Westminster, *Grace and Favour*, p. 122.

24. Loelia, Duchess of Westminster, *Grace and Favour*, pp. 121–122.

25. Cartland, *We Danced All Night*, pp. 188–189.

26. Carpenter, *The Brideshead Generation*, p. 166.
27. Balfour, *Society Racket*, p. 222.
28. Hall, *The Twenties in Vogue*, pp. 8–10.
29. Dean Paul, *My First Life*, p. 101.
30. Dean Paul, *My First Life*, p. 102.
31. *The Daily Mail*, 13 July 1928.
32. *The Daily Mail*, 14 July 1928.
33. Quoted in Taylor, *Bright Young People*, p. 5.
34. Cartland, *We Danced All Night*, p. 193.
35. Cartland, *We Danced All Night*, p. 193. Balfour, *Society Racket*, p. 171.
36. Cartland, *We Danced All Night*, pp. 193–194.
37. Cartland, *We Danced All Night*, p. 194.
38. *The Bystander*, 31 July 1929. Andrew Barrow, *Gossip. A History of High Society from 1920 to 1970* (London, 1978), p. 46. Taylor, *Bright Young People*, p. 143.
39. Marie Jaqueline Lancaster ed., *Brian Howard. Portrait of a Failure* (London, 1968), p. 267.
40. Lancaster, ed., *Brian Howard*, p. 283.
41. Taylor, *Bright Young People*, pp. 161–162. Jones, *Arthur Ponsonby*, pp. 182–183, 196 and 231. Elizabeth died, an alcoholic, at the end of July 1940, before her fortieth birthday. Taylor, *Bright Young People*, pp. 271–272.
42. Balfour, *Society Racket*, pp. 161, 166 and 172.
43. Loelia, Duchess of Westminster, *Grace and Favour*, p. 122.
44. Lancaster, ed., *Brian Howard*, p. 266. Allanah had gone to the party with Brian Howard, who was himself drinking heavily at this time.
45. Cecil Beaton, *The Glass of Fashion* (London, 1954), pp. 152–153.
46. Loelia, Duchess of Westminster, *Grace and Favour*, p. 124.
47. Cartland, *We Danced All Night*, p. 190. Dean Paul, *My First Life*, p. 102. Brenda Dean Paul claimed that the party had cost David Tennant nearly £3,000 and the menu was taken from the 'original Royal cookery book of Louis XVI'.

Balfour, *Society Racket*, p. 170. Taylor, *Bright Young People*, p. 195.

48. Cartland, *We Danced All Night*, pp. 185–186. Lancaster, ed., *Brian Howard*, pp. 272–274

49. Jonathan Guinness with Catherine Guinness, *The House of Mitford* (London, 2004 edn), p. 318.

50. Guinness with Guinness, *The House of Mitford*, p. 318.

51. E. T. Williams and C. S. Nicholls, eds, *Dictionary of National Biography 1961–1970* (Oxford, 1981), p. 499, entry for Clarence C. Hatry. *Daily Sketch*, 27 and 28 September 1929. Balfour, *Society Racket*, p. 69.

52. *Daily Sketch*, 27 September 1929.

53. Mary Soames, *Clementine Churchill* (London, 1979), p. 216.

54. Beverley Nichols, *All I Could Never Be. Some Recollections* (London, 1949), p. 165.

55. Ernest King, *The Green Baize Door* (Bath, 1963), p. 51. Daphne Fielding, *Emerald and Nancy. Lady Cunard and Her Daughter* (London, 1968), pp. 112 and 114–115.

56. See will of Lady Cunard at the Probate Office, London.

57. King, *The Green Baize Door*, p. 51.

58. Lovell, *The Mitford Girls*, p. 113.

59. Janet Morgan, *Edwina Mountbatten. A Life of Her Own* (London, 1992 edn), pp. 222–223 and 250–251.

60. Quoted in Cartland, *We Danced All Night*, p. 289.

61. *The Bystander*, 15 June 1932.

62. Taylor, *Bright Young People*, pp. 252–253. Morgan, *Edwina Mountbatten*, p. 221. Alec Waugh, *A Year to Remember. A Reminiscence of 1931* (London, 1975), p. 151.

63. Taylor, *Bright Young People*, p. 253.

64. *The Bystander*, 17 July 1929.

65. *The People*, 10 July 1932.

66. Balfour, *Society Racket*, pp. 60 and 65–66. Balfour himself was short of cash in the early 1930s and according to Alec Waugh spent the winter of 1931 at an inexpensive hotel in

Devon, where he could continue to write and was visited by his friends. He could not afford to live in London at that time. Waugh, *A Year to Remember*, p. 157.

67. Quoted in Taylor, *Bright Young People*, p. 252.

Index

313

Also available from Amberley Publishing

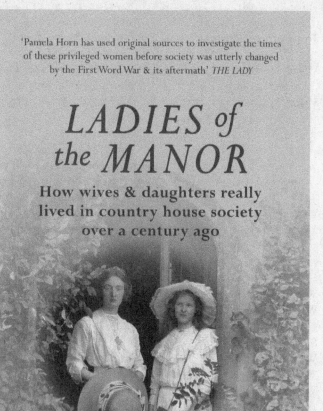

'Pamela Horn has used original sources to investigate the times of these privileged women before society was utterly changed by the First Word War & its aftermath' THE LADY

LADIES of the MANOR

How wives & daughters really lived in country house society over a century ago

PAMELA HORN